20-35mm

the photoshop®
elements 5
book
for digital photographers

Scott Kelby

**The Photoshop
Elements 5 Book for
Digital Photographers Team**

CREATIVE DIRECTOR
Felix Nelson

TECHNICAL EDITORS
**Cindy Snyder
Kim Doty**

TRAFFIC DIRECTOR
Kim Gabriel

PRODUCTION MANAGER
Dave Damstra

COVER DESIGNED BY
Jessica Maldonado

COVER PHOTOS
COURTESY OF
**iStockphoto.com
Scott Kelby**

Published by
New Riders

Copyright ©2007 by Scott Kelby

First edition: November 2006

Composed in Cronos, Helvetica, and Apple Garamond Light by Kelby Publishing

Trademarks
All terms mentioned in this book that are known to be trademarks or service marks have been appropriately capitalized. New Riders cannot attest to the accuracy of this information. Use of a term in the book should not be regarded as affecting the validity of any trademark or service mark.

Photoshop is a registered trademark of Adobe Systems, Inc.
Windows is a registered trademark of Microsoft Corporation.

Warning and Disclaimer
This book is designed to provide information about Photoshop Elements for digital photographers. Every effort has been made to make this book as complete and as accurate as possible, but no warranty of fitness is implied.

The information is provided on an as-is basis. The author and New Riders shall have neither liability nor responsibility to any person or entity with respect to any loss or damages arising from the information contained in this book or from the use of the discs or programs that may accompany it.

ISBN 0-321-47673-5

9 8 7 6 5 4 3

Printed and bound in the United States of America

www.newriders.com
www.scottkelbybooks.com

For my wonderful wife Kalebra,
my amazing little boy Jordan,
and my precious baby daughter Kira.
It's amazing just how much joy and
love these three people bring into my life.

ACKNOWLEDGMENTS

First, I want to thank my amazing wife Kalebra. As I'm writing this, she's sitting beside me on the couch watching *Grey's Anatomy*, but I have to say that just looking at her makes my heart skip a beat, and again reminds me how much I adore her, how genuinely beautiful she is, and how I couldn't live without her. She's the type of woman love songs are written for, and I am, without a doubt, the luckiest man alive to have her as my wife.

Secondly, I want to thank my 9-year-old son Jordan, who spent many afternoons with his adorable little head resting on my lap as I wrote this book. God has blessed our family with so many wonderful gifts, and I can see them all reflected in his eyes. I'm so proud of him, so thrilled to be his dad, and I dearly love watching him grow to be such a wonderful little guy, with such a tender and loving heart. (You're the greatest, little buddy.)

I also want to thank my big brother Jeffrey for being such a positive influence in my life, for always taking the high road, for always knowing the right thing to say, and just the right time to say it, and for having so much of our dad in you. I'm honored to have you as my brother and my friend.

I want to thank my beautiful daughter Kira, who is the best-natured, happiest little baby girl in the whole wide world. You're only eight months old, but you're already reflecting your mom's sweet nature, her beautiful smile, and her loving heart. You're too young to know what an amazing mother you have, but before long, just like your brother, you'll realize that your mom is someone very special, and that thanks to her you're in for a really fun, exciting, hug-filled, and adventure-filled life.

My heartfelt thanks go to the entire team at KW Media Group, who every day redefine what teamwork and dedication are all about. They are truly a special group of people, who come together to do some really amazing things (on really scary deadlines) and they do it with class, poise, and a can-do attitude that is truly inspiring. I'm so proud to be working with you all.

Thanks to my layout and production crew. In particular, I want to thank my friend and Creative Director Felix Nelson for his limitless talent, creativity, input, cover design, overall layout, and just for his flat-out great ideas. To my perennially positive tech editor Kim Doty, along with tech editor Cindy Snyder, for putting every technique through rigorous testing and for catching all sorts of little things that would have driven me crazy. To Kim Gabriel for keeping us all on track and organized, so we could face those really scary deadlines. To Dave Damstra and his amazing crew for giving the book such a tight, clean layout.

Thanks to my compadre Dave Moser, whose tireless dedication to creating a quality product makes every project we do better than the last. Thanks to Jean A. Kendra for her support, and for keeping a lot of plates in the air while I'm writing these books. A special thanks to my Executive Assistant Kathy Siler for all her hard work and dedication, and for finally convincing me to become a closet Redskins fan (which is easy this year when they're kicking butt, and my Bucs are in the basement).

Thanks to my Publisher Nancy Ruenzel, and the incredibly dedicated team at Peachpit Publishing Group. You are very special people doing very special things, and it's a real honor to get to work with people who really just want to make great books. Also many thanks to Ted "Are you done yet?" Waitt, and to marketing maverick Scott Cowlin.

I owe a special debt of gratitude to my friends Kevin Ames and Jim DiVitale for taking the time to share their ideas, techniques, concepts, and vision for a Photoshop Elements book for digital photographers that would really make a difference. Extra special thanks to Kevin for spending hours with me sharing some of his retouching techniques, as well.

I want to thank all the photographers, retouchers, and Photoshop experts who've taught me so much over the years, including Jack Davis, Deke McClelland, Ben Willmore, Julieanne Kost, Moose Peterson, Vincent Versace, Doug Gornick, Bill Fortney, Manual Obordo, Dan Margulis, Eddie Tapp, David Ziser, Peter Bauer, Joe Glyda, and Russell Preston Brown.

Also thanks to Dave Cross and Matt Kloskowski for sharing some of their Elements tips and techniques with me, and for being excellent sounding boards for new Elements ideas. You guys are the best!

Thanks to my friends at Adobe Systems: Terry White, Kevin Connor, Addy Roff, Cari Gushiken, Deb Whitman, John Nack, Marc Pawliger, Dave Story, Yoko Nakagawa, George Jardine, Julieanne, and Russell. Gone but not forgotten: Barbara Rice, Jill Nakashima, Bryan Lamkin, and Karen Gauthier.

Also an extra special thanks to Elements product manager Mark Dahm for taking my frantic late-night calls, and going above and beyond to help make this book a reality—and to the whole Elements team at Adobe, including Sharon Doherty, for making Elements 5 one kick-butt image editing app.

Thanks to my mentors whose wisdom and whip-cracking have helped me immeasurably, including John Graden, Jack Lee, Dave Gales, Judy Farmer, and Douglas Poole.

Also, my personal thanks to Patrick Lor at iStockphoto.com for enabling me to use some of their wonderful photography in this book.

Most importantly, I want to thank God, and His son Jesus Christ, for leading me to the woman of my dreams, for blessing us with such a special little boy and an amazing little girl, for allowing me to make a living doing something I truly love, for always being there when I need Him, for blessing me with a wonderful, fulfilling, and happy life, and such a warm, loving family to share it with.

ABOUT THE AUTHOR

Scott Kelby

Scott is Editor and Publisher of *Photoshop User* magazine, Editor and Publisher of *Layers* magazine (the how-to magazine for everything Adobe), and is Executive Editor of the *Photoshop Elements Techniques* newsletter.

Scott is President and co-founder of the National Association of Photoshop Professionals (NAPP) and is President of the software training, education, and publishing firm KW Media Group.

Scott is a photographer, designer, and award-winning author of more than 37 books, including *Photoshop Elements Down & Dirty Tricks, The Digital Photography Book, Photoshop Classic Effects,* and is Series Editor for the *Killer Tips* books series from New Riders. His books are translated into dozens of different languages, including Russian, Chinese, French, German, Spanish, Korean, Greek, Turkish, Japanese, Dutch, and Taiwanese, among others. For the past two years straight Scott was awarded the distinction of being the world's No. 1 best-selling author of all computer and technology books, across all categories.

Scott is Training Director for the Adobe Photoshop Seminar Tour and Conference Technical Chair for the Photoshop World Conference & Expo. He's featured in a series of Adobe Photoshop training DVDs and has been training Adobe Photoshop users since 1993.

For more information on Scott, visit scottkelby.com.

The Mask

Selection Techniques

Head Games

Retouching Portraits

I had no intentions of writing this book

(Actually, I mean the book that led to this book. Here's the story.) So here it was, about four weeks before I would be flying up to New York City to teach a one-day seminar to more than 1,200 professional Photoshop junkies. (Okay, it was more like 1,160 pros, 42 people who just wanted a paid day off from work, and one total freak who kept asking me if I'd ever been in prison. I told him unequivocally, "Not as far as you know.")

Anyway, the seminar was just four weeks away, and there was one session that I still didn't have an outline for. It was called "Correcting Photos from Digital Cameras" (which is dramatically better than my original working title for the class, "Die, Traditional Camera User, Die!").

I knew what I needed to cover in the session, because for the past 10 years I've trained thousands of traditional photographers on how to use Photoshop. Most of them either have now gone digital or are in the process of going digital, and all these digital photographers generally seem to have the same type of Photoshop questions, which I'm actually thankful for, because now I can give them the answers. If they constantly asked different questions, I'd get stumped from time to time, and then I'd have to resort to Plan B (providing answers that sound good, but are in reality just wild-ass guesses).

So I knew what I had to cover, but I wanted to do some research first, to see if other people in the industry were addressing these questions the same way I was, or did they have a different take on them, different techniques or ideas? So I went out and bought every single book I could find about digital photography and Photoshop. I spent nearly $1.2 million. Okay, it wasn't quite that much, but let's just say for the next few months I would have to cut out some luxuries such as running water, trash collection, heat, etc.

I started reading through all these books, and the first thing I thought I'd look up was how they dealt with digital noise (high ISO noise, Blue channel noise, color aliasing, etc.), but as I went through them, I was amazed to find out that not one single book addressed it. Not a one. Honestly, I was shocked. I get asked this question many times at every single seminar, yet not one of these books even mentioned it. So then I started looking for how they work with 16-bit photos. Nothing. Well, one book mentioned it, but they basically said "it's not for you—it's for high-end pros with $15,000 cameras." I just couldn't believe it—I was stunned. So I kept up my search for more topics I'd been asked about again and again, with the same results.

Well, I went ahead with my New York session as planned, and by all accounts it was a big hit. I had photographer after photographer coming up to tell me, "Thank you so much—those are exactly the things I was hoping to learn." That's when I realized that there's a book missing—a book for people who already know how to shoot—they even know what they want to do in Photoshop, they just need somebody to show them how to do it. Somebody to show them how to deal with the special challenges (and amazing opportunities) of using digital photos with Photoshop. I was so excited, because I knew in my heart I could write that book.

So now I had intentions

The day after the seminar I flew home and immediately called my editor at New Riders and I said, "I know what I want my next book to be—a Photoshop book for digital photographers." There was a long uncomfortable pause, and then he politely said, "Really, a digital photography book, huh?" It was clear he wasn't nearly as excited about this concept as I was (and that's being kind). He finally said, "Ya know, there are already plenty of digital photography books out there," and I agreed with him, because I just about went broke buying them all. So now I had to convince my editor that not only was this a good idea, but that it was such a good idea that he should put our other book projects on hold so I could write this book, of which there are (as he put it), "already plenty of digital photography books out there."

continued

Here's what I told my editor what would be different about my digital photography book:

(1) It's not a digital photography book; it's a Photoshop book. There'd be no discussion of film (gasp!), f-stops, lenses, or how to frame a photo. If they don't already know how to shoot, this book just won't be for them. (*Note:* Editors hate it when you start listing the people the book won't be appropriate for. They want to hear, "It's perfect for everybody! From grandma right up to White House press photographers," but sadly, this book just isn't.)

(2) I would skip the "Here's What a Digital Camera Is" section and the "Here's Which Printer to Buy" section, because they were in all those other books that I bought. Instead, I'd start the book at the moment the photo comes into Photoshop from the camera.

(3) It would work the way digital photographers really work—in the order they work—starting with sorting and categorizing photos from the shoot, dealing with common digital photography problems, color correcting the photos, selecting areas to work on, retouching critical areas, adding photographic special effects, sharpening their photos, and then preparing the photo to be output to a print.

(4) It wouldn't be another Photoshop book that focuses on explaining every aspect of every dialog. No sirree—instead, this book would do something different—it would show them how to do it! This is what makes it different. It would show photographers step-by-step how to do all those things they keep asking at my seminars, sending me email about, and posting questions about in our forums—it would "show them how to do it!"

For example, I told my editor that about every Photoshop book out there includes info on the Unsharp Mask filter. They all talk about what the Amount, Radius, and Threshold sliders do, and how those settings affect the pixels. They all do that. But you know what they generally don't do? They don't give you any actual settings to use! Usually, not even a starting point. Some provide "numerical ranges to work within," but basically they explain how the filter works, and then leave it up to you to develop your own settings. I told him I wouldn't do that. I would flat-out give them some great Unsharp Mask filter settings—the same settings used by many professionals, even though I know some highfalutin' Photoshop expert might take issue with them. I would come out and say, "Hey, use this setting when sharpening people. Use this setting to correct slightly out-of-focus photos. Use this setting on landscapes, etc." I give students in my live seminars these settings, why shouldn't I share them in my book? He agreed. I also told him that sharpening is much more than just using the Unsharp Mask filter, and it's much more important to photographers than the three or four pages every other book dedicates to it. I wanted to do an entire chapter showing all the different sharpening techniques, step-by-step, giving different solutions for different sharpening challenges.

He was starting to come on board with the idea. What he didn't want was the same thing I didn't want—another digital photography book that rehashes what every other digital photography and Photoshop book has already done. Well, he went with the idea, and thanks to him, you're holding the fourth Elements version of the book that I am so genuinely excited to be able to bring you. But the way the book was developed beyond that took it further than I had planned.

How the book was developed

When my Editor gave me the final approval (it was more like, "Okay, but this better be good or we'll both be greeting people by saying, 'Would you like to try one of our Extra Value Meals today?'"), I sat down with two of the industry's top digital photographers—commercial product photographer Jim DiVitale and fashion photographer Kevin Ames—to get their input on the book. These two guys are amazing—they both split their time between shooting for some of the world's largest corporations, and teaching other professional digital photographers how to pull off Photoshop miracles at events such as Photoshop World, PPA/PEI's Digital Conference, and a host of other events around the world. We spent hours hammering out which techniques would have to be included in the book, and I can't tell you how helpful and insightful their input was, and this book is far better than it would have been thanks to their contributions.

New and improved (with the same great taste!)

When we first released *The Photoshop Book for Digital Photographers*, it became a huge hit overnight, and became not only the best-selling Photoshop book, not only the best-selling digital photography book, but one of the top selling of all computer books on Amazon.com, and it's ranked as high as No. 12 of ALL books on Amazon.com. Pretty freaky!

In short—the concept worked, and that's why I knew I had to do a special version of the book for Photoshop Elements users because Elements was designed from the beginning as a tool for digital photography. Best of all, I learned a lot from writing that original book, and I've learned a lot of new techniques since I wrote it; and you're getting the benefit of both in this fourth version of the book created just for Elements users.

This version has a secret weapon

Although Elements does offer some cool digital photography features that Photoshop CS2 doesn't even offer, obviously there are plenty of features that Photoshop CS2 has that Photoshop Elements 5 still doesn't have (things like layer masking, Channel Mixer, etc.). But here's the cool part: the single thing that I'm most proud of in this Elements book is that I've been able to figure out workarounds, cheats, and some fairly ingenious ways to replicate some of those Photoshop features from right within Elements. In some cases, it may take a few more steps to get there than it does in Photoshop CS2, but son-of-a-gun, the result looks pretty darn close, and you'll be the only one who'll know the effect was created in Elements, not in Photoshop CS2. This will test how good you are at keeping secrets.

So what's not in this book?

There are some things I intentionally didn't put in this book. Like punctuation marks (kidding). No, seriously, I tried not to put things in this book that are already in every other Photoshop Elements book out there. For example, I don't have a chapter on the Layers palette, or a chapter on the painting tools, or a chapter showing how each Elements filter looks when it's applied to the same photograph. However, this Elements 5 version of the book does contain something no previous version has included (besides covering all the most important new features of Elements 5, of course), and that is a special chapter on how to set up Elements' color management and printing so when you print, your prints match what you saw onscreen.

Is this book for you?

I can't tell you that for sure, so let's take a simple yet amazingly accurate test that will determine without a doubt if this book is for you.

Please answer the following questions:

(1) Do you now, or will you soon have a digital camera?

(2) Do you now, or will you soon have Photoshop Elements?

(3) Do you now, or will you soon have about 40 bucks (the retail price of this book)?

Scoring: If you answered "Yes" to question 3, then yes, this book is for you. If you answered yes to questions 1 or 2, that certainly is a good indicator, too.

continued

Is this book for Windows users, Mac users, or both?

It's really just for Windows users, because at this point in time, the Mac version of Elements is stuck back on version 4 and doesn't even have all the features of the version 4 for Windows, let alone version 5. In fact, it has some totally different features. It's a long story, but the reality is, I felt that if I tried to cover two very different versions of the same product in one single book it would be somewhat of a train wreck for everybody. So, rather than making a half-butt book that covers both versions (I didn't want to use the word "butt" by the way), I made a kick-butt book for the Windows version, which makes up the vast, vast majority of all Elements users (in fact, I believe there are only six to eight Mac users of Elements, but apparently they're a very vocal group. I totally respect that. In fact, I dig it. But I can't totally trash this book because of it, so this book is really designed for Windows users of Elements 5. Hey, I'm glad you heard it from me first).

How should you use this book?

You can treat this as a "jump-in-anywhere" book because I didn't write it as a "build-on-what-you-learned-in-Chapter-1" type of book. For example, if you just bought this book, and you want to learn how to whiten someone's teeth for a portrait you're retouching, you can just turn to Chapter 7, find that technique, and you'll be able to follow along and do it immediately. That's because I spell everything out. Don't let that throw you if you've been using Elements since version 1; I had to do it because although some of the people who will buy this book are talented traditional photographers, since they're just now "going digital," they may not know anything about Elements. I didn't want to leave them out, or make it hard for them, so I really spell things out like: "Go under the Image menu, under Adjust Color, and choose Levels" rather than just writing "Open Levels." However, I did put the chapters in an order that follows a typical correction, editing, and retouching process; so you might find it useful to start with Chapter 1 and move your way through the book in sequence.

The important thing is that wherever you start, have fun with it, and even more importantly, tell your friends about it so I can recoup the millions I spent on all those digital photography books. Also, although the official name of the software is Adobe Photoshop Elements 5.0, just to keep things short and simple I usually refer to it as just "Elements 5" in the book.

Wait, one more thing! You can download the photos used in the book!

That's right—you can follow right along using downloadable versions of my own photography that's used here in the book, but when I couldn't come up with the ideal shot to illustrate a technique, I was lucky enough to be able to call upon the stock photography community over at iStockphoto.com. So, nearly all of the photos used in this book are available for you to download from the book's companion website at **www.scottkelbybooks.com/elements5**. Of course, the whole idea is that you'd use these techniques on your own photos, but if you want to practice on these, I won't tell anybody. Okay, now turn the page and get to work!

Organized Chaos
managing photos using the organizer

"Organized Chaos" is the perfect name for this chapter because not only is it a song title (by the band Benediction), it's also apparently a marketing directive put forth by a super-secret department at Adobe who, from what I gather, is charged with giving features and functions within Elements multiple names. Now, I must point out that this department is not as active in Elements 5, as they were back in Elements 4. Back then, they actually had two different names for what is now just called the Organizer. That's right, Elements 4 had buttons named "Photo Browser" and "Photo Organizer," but regardless of which one you clicked on it opened the Organizer. This led to untold hours of fun for new users of the product, and probably some sort of cash bonus for that department at Adobe. However, those lucrative bonuses are pretty much over in Elements 5 because now the Organizer is just called "The Organizer." However, if you're wondering if the hard-working people in that super-secret department are going to have to get part-time jobs to make up for the gap in their income, you only have to look as far as the Elements 5 Organizer's Window menu, where you'll find a menu command for Photo Browser, which tacitly lets you know their Porsche payments will be made on time. Whew! That was a close one.

Importing Your Photos

In Elements 5, Adobe has not only made the process of getting your photos from your digital camera into the Elements Organizer much easier, they also added some automation to make the task faster, so you can get back to shooting right away. Here's how to import your photos and take advantage of this new automation.

Step One:

When you attach a memory card reader to your computer (or attach your camera directly through a USB cable), the Photoshop Elements 5 Photo Downloader's standard dialog appears onscreen (shown here). By the way, it will also download photos from your mobile phone. The first thing it does is it searches the card for photos, and then it tells you how many photos it has found, and how much memory (hard disk space) those photos represent.

Step Two:

The Import Settings section is where you decide how the photos are imported. You get to choose where (on your hard disk) they'll be saved to, and you can choose to create subfolders with photos sorted by a custom name, today's date, when they were shot, and a host of attributes you can choose from the Create Subfolder(s) pop-up menu (as shown here).

Step Three:

If you want to rename the files as they're imported, you can do that in the next field down. You can use the built-in naming conventions, but I recommend choosing Custom Name from the pop-up menu, so you can enter a name that makes sense to you. You can choose to have the date the photo was shot before your custom name, but that's up to you. If you choose Custom Name, it reveals a text field under the Rename Files pop-up menu where you can simply type in the name that you want (you get a preview of how your new name will look). By the way, it automatically appends a three-digit number starting with 001 after your photo to keep each photo from having the exact same name.

Step Four:

The last option in this dialog is the Delete Options. Basically, it's this: do you want the photos deleted off your memory card after they're imported, or do you want to leave the originals on the card? What's the right choice? There is no right choice—it's up to you. If you have only one memory card, and that card is full and you want to keep shooting, well…the decision is pretty much made for you. You'll need to delete the photos so you can keep shooting. If you've got other back-up cards, you might want to leave the originals on the card until you can make a secure backup of your photos, then erase the card later. Again, the choice is up to you. Now, about that "Automatic Download" button….

Continued

Step Five:

The Automatic Download feature is designed to let you skip this whole Photo Downloader dialog, and when you plug in a memory card reader, or camera, it just goes and downloads your photos using your default preferences, with no input from you (well, except it asks if you want to erase the original photos on the card or not). Now, where are these default preferences set? (I knew you were going to ask that.) They're set in the Organizer's Preferences. To get to these, you go under the Organizer's Edit menu, under Preferences, and choose Camera or Card Reader. This brings up the Preferences dialog you see here.

Step Six:

In this Preferences dialog is where you decide what happens when you turn on the Automatic Download checkbox in the Photo Downloader. You get to choose a default location to save all your photos (like your My Pictures folder), and whether you want the Photo Downloader to automatically fix any photos that it detects have red eye. You can also choose to have it automatically suggest photo stacks (it groups photos it thinks belong together). You can have it ignore the Photo Downloader window (just turn off the Auto Launch Adobe Photo Downloader on Device Connect checkbox), and you can have settings for specific cameras or card readers (in case you want separate settings for your mobile phone, or a particular camera). At the bottom, you've got some other options (when to begin the downloading, if you're going to have subfolders, and your delete options). Click OK when the preferences are set the way you want them.

SCOTT KELBY

Step Seven:

Okay, back to the Photo Downloader. Now, at this point, all the photos on the card will be imported, but if you want to import just a few selected photos, then you'll need to click on the Advanced Dialog button at the bottom-left corner of the dialog (as shown here). That brings up a dialog that displays thumbnails of all the photos on the card. By default, every photo has a checkbox turned on below it, indicating that every photo will be imported. If you just want some of these photos imported, then you'll need to click the UnCheck All button at the bottom left of your thumbnails. This turns off all the photos' checkboxes, which enables you to then go and turn on the checkbox below only the photos you actually want imported.

Step Eight:

When you look at the right side of the advanced Photo Downloader dialog, you'll see some familiar Save Options (the subfolder choice, renaming files), and in the Advanced Options section, you'll see some of the choices from the Preferences dialog, including the ability to automatically fix red eyes, suggest photo stacks, and delete options. Another nice feature is the ability to embed metadata (like your name and your copyright info) directly into the digital file, just like your camera embeds information into your digital camera images. So, just type in your name and your copyright info, and these are embedded into each photo automatically as they're imported. This is a good thing. When you click Get Photos, your photos are imported (well, at least the photos with a checkmark under them). If you want to ignore these advanced features and just use the Standard dialog, click on the Standard Dialog button.

Backing Up Your Photos (on Disc or Online)

If you're concerned about having your hard disk crash one day, and losing your entire catalog of photos—you should be. It happens every single day. It's a harsh fact of computer life, and it's not really *will* your hard drive crash. It's a matter of *when*. One way to protect your irreplaceable photos is to either back your entire catalog up to disc and/or use an online backup, so your photos are protected in an off-site location. So even if your hard drive dies or your computer is lost, stolen, damaged in a fire, flood, or hurricane, you can retrieve your images.

Step One:
To back up your catalog to disc (I recommend backing up to DVD rather than CD if you have a lot of photos [and a DVD writer, of course]), you simply go under the Organizer's File menu and choose Backup Catalog (as shown here).

Step Two:
This brings up a dialog where you decide whether to do a Full Backup (you choose this the first time you back up your catalog), or an Incremental Backup (which is what you'll choose after your first backup, as it only backs up the files that have changed since your last backup, which is a big timesaver). In this case, since this is your first time, choose Full Backup (as shown here), then click the Next button.

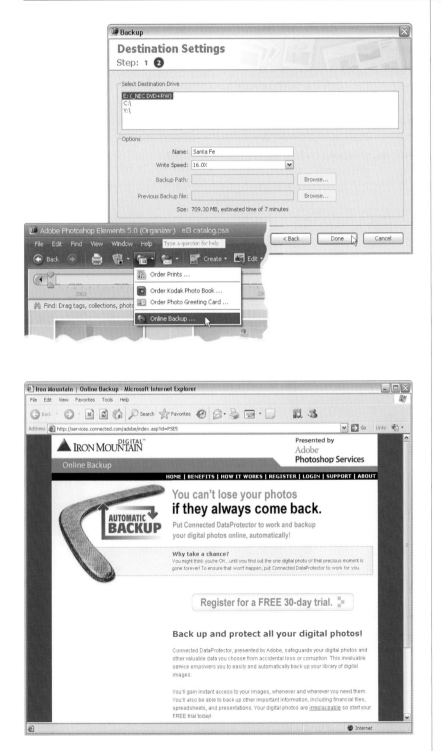

Step Three:

When you click Next, the Destination Settings screen appears, which is basically where you tell Elements to back up your stuff to. If it's a DVD or CD, just insert a blank DVD or CD into your DVD/CD drive and choose that drive from the list. Give your disc a name and click the Done button, and it does its thing. Now, that's the standard ol' backup, which is very necessary but doesn't help a lick if the place where you store your backup disc is damaged by fire, storm, flood, hurricane, tornado, a plague of locusts, etc., and that's why you might want to consider the second option—backing up to an offsite location. Luckily, Elements has a direct link to Iron Mountain, a company that offers secure offsite storage of your images for a fee. This works a bit differently, because instead of choosing Backup Catalog, you click on the Order Online button at the top of the Organizer (the one that looks like a globe with a postcard in front of it), and choose Online Backup from its pop-up menu.

Step Four:

When you choose Online Backup, you're taken directly to Iron Mountain's Adobe Photoshop Services website (shown here), where they offer you a free 30-day trial (at least they did when I wrote this book). The process is pretty simple: once you register, you download their free Connected DataProtector software, it finds all your digital photos (or you point it to a folder of your images), it uploads them to Iron Mountain for you, and keeps them in your personal storage account. It's all automated from that point on— every day it looks for new photos on your drive, and if it finds them, it backs them up online automatically. Your images are easily retrieved if something unfortunate should happen.

Creating a Contact Sheet for Your CD

All right, your CD of "digital negatives" is burned and it's time to get to work, but before you go any further, you can save yourself a lot of time and frustration down the road if you create a CD-jewel-case-sized contact sheet now. That way, when you pick up the CD, you'll see exactly what's on the disc before you even insert it into your computer. Luckily, if you have Adobe Acrobat, the process of creating this contact sheet is automated, but if not, you'll need to make a few decisions on how you want your contact sheet to look by "eyeing" it.

Step One:
First, open the photos you want to appear on your contact sheet in the Elements Editor, then go under the File menu and choose Print Multiple Photos (or press the keyboard shortcut Control-Alt-P). (*Note:* If you're already working in the Organizer, you can create a contact sheet from the currently open collection by going under the Organizer's File menu and choosing Print.)

Step Two:
Choosing Print Multiple Photos first brings up the Elements Organizer, and immediately after, the Print Photos dialog will appear. Along the left side of the dialog, you will see your image thumbnails. (*Note*: If you open the dialog from the Editor, Elements will place them in the reverse of the order in which you opened them. So, make sure you open them in reverse order, or open the dialog from the Organizer.) Then, there are three categories on the right side of the dialog. Under the Select Type of Print category, choose Contact Sheet from the pop-up menu.

SCOTT KELBY

Step Three:
Now that you've told Elements that you want to print a contact sheet (and the preview window shows how your selected photos would look as a contact sheet on a letter-sized page, which is its default size), your next step should be to specify the size you need your contact sheet to be (in this case, one that will fit in the front of a CD jewel case). To do that, start by choosing Adobe PDF in the Select Printer pop-up menu. Then, click on the blue-and-white icon that appears to the immediate right of the Select Printer pop-up menu at the top right of the dialog. *Note:* If you don't have Adobe Acrobat, this option will not appear, in which case, skip to the Alternate Step that starts after Step Seven.

Step Four:
This brings up a dialog with options for your printer (since we're printing to an Adobe PDF driver rather than printing the file out to a regular printer, you'll see the options for a PDF). Since Adobe didn't include a standard size for CD jewel cases, you're going to create one by clicking the Add button to the right of the Adobe PDF Page Size pop-up menu, which brings up the dialog shown here.

Continued

Step Five:

First, give your new paper size a name (something like "CD Jewel Case") in the Paper Names field. Then in the Paper Size section, enter 4.5 for Width and 4.5 for Height, click the Inch radio button in the Unit section (if it's not already selected), and then click the Add/Modify button to save your custom size in the Adobe PDF Page Size pop-up menu's list of presets.

Step Six:

When you click Add/Modify, it returns you to the Adobe PDF Document Properties dialog. Click on the Adobe PDF Page Size pop-up menu, and you'll see that your new custom size (CD Jewel Case) now appears in the list. Click on it to select it as your contact sheet size.

Step Seven:

When you click OK, the contact sheet preview will now display how your contact sheet thumbnail photos will appear on your CD jewel case. (*Note:* The name CD Jewel Case will appear below the preview.) If you have more than one page's worth of photos open, you'll have more than one page of thumbnails (instead of seeing page 1 of 1, it'll say something like 1 of 2, or 1 of 3, and so on). To see any additional pages, click on the right-facing arrow button below the preview.

Alternate Step:

If you don't have Acrobat, there is a hokey workaround (sorry, but until Adobe adds a CD jewel case option to this dialog, which had been there in previous versions of Elements, we're stuck with a hokey workaround). Simply choose a higher amount in the Columns pop-up menu in section 3. Try 7–8 columns, and then "eye" your contact sheet using the preview in the dialog. You're trying to create a block of thumbnails that will print no larger than 4.5x4.5", so you can then cut your sheet to this size after printing. With that set, move on to Step Eight.

Continued

Step Eight:

On the right side of the dialog, you can decide if you want to have Elements print the file's name below each thumbnail on your contact sheet. I strongly recommend turning this feature on because one day you may have to go back to this CD looking for a photo. The thumbnail will let you see if the photo you're looking for is on this CD (so you've narrowed your search a bit), but if there's no name below the image, you'll have to manually search through every photo on the CD to locate the exact one you saw on the cover. Believe me, it's one of those things that will keep you from ripping your hair out by the roots, one by one. Now you can click Print and your contact sheet is created in PDF format and opened in Elements. So, just go the File menu, select Print, and print your contact sheet to your printer.

Step Nine (or so you think…):

This is more like a tip than a step, but a number of photographers add a second contact sheet to make it even easier to track down the exact image they're looking for. It's based on the premise that in every roll (digital or otherwise) there are usually one or two key shots—two really good "keepers"—that will normally be the ones you'll go searching for. So what they do is make an additional contact sheet that either becomes the front cover of the jewel case (with the regular contact sheet behind it in the case) or vice versa. This additional contact sheet includes a description of the shots, to make finding the right image even easier.

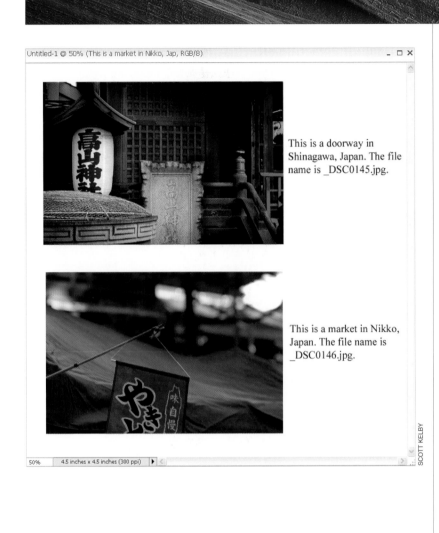

Untitled-1 @ 50% (This is a market in Nikko, Jap, RGB/8) – □ ×

This is a doorway in Shinagawa, Japan. The file name is _DSC0145.jpg.

This is a market in Nikko, Japan. The file name is _DSC0146.jpg.

50%   4.5 inches x 4.5 inches (300 ppi)

SCOTT KELBY

Step Ten:
Here's the final result with a two-photo contact sheet for the cover of the CD jewel case, after a regular contact sheet with multiple images was printed and slid into the CD jewel case behind it. To create this contact sheet, open one or two images in the Editor and create a new document that's 4.5x4.5". Press V to get the Move tool, drag-and-drop your open images onto your new document, and then press Control-T and then Control-0 (zero) to bring up Free Transform. Resize your images on the page, and then press the letter T to switch to the Type tool and enter descriptive text next to your contact sheet thumbnail(s). Now print your new contact sheet.

Dealing with the Welcome Screen

I know, the name "Dealing with the Welcome Screen" makes the Welcome Screen sound like something obtrusive, but really it's not. At least, not at first. In fact, at first it's welcome (like the way I worked that in there?), but after you've seen it a few hundred times, if you're like most folks you'll probably want it to go away. But before you make it go away for good, there are a few things you might want to decide first. And they are…

The First Time:

The Welcome Screen that appears when you launch the program is designed to help first-time users figure out what they want. If you're holding this book, my guess is you already know what you want, so click the Edit and Enhance Photos option near the top center of the Welcome Screen, which takes you right into the Elements Editor (which, if you've used previous versions of Elements, you know simply as Photoshop Elements).

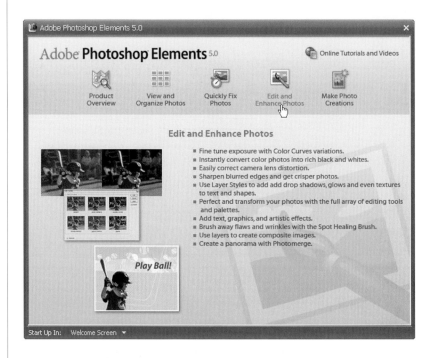

Future Uses:

You can use this Welcome Screen to decide what happens when you launch Elements 5 later. For example, by default it wants to show you this Welcome Screen each time you launch Elements. You may want that the first few times, but once the novelty wears off, you'll want to go straight to the Editor. So, you just need to change one thing: At the bottom left-hand corner of the Welcome Screen, where it says "Start Up In" you'll see the words "Welcome Screen." Click on Welcome Screen and choose Editor from the pop-up menu that appears. Now when you start up Elements, you'll get the Editor.

Start with Sorting:
If you'd prefer to skip the Welcome Screen and instead go right into sorting your images rather than editing them, you can go to the built-in Organizer (which used to be the standalone product Photoshop Album) by choosing Organizer from the Start Up In pop-up menu.

Welcome Back Welcome Screen:
Okay, what if you've chosen to start up in the Editor or Organizer, and then at some later date you think you'd like to get that Welcome Screen back again? It's easy—just go under the Window menu (in either the Editor or Organizer) and choose Welcome, and the screen will reappear. However, once you close it, it won't reappear at startup unless you change the Start Up In pop-up menu in the bottom-left corner to Welcome Screen.

Other Options:
One last thing—just to save you some time: If you have the Welcome Screen open, there are two buttons that actually take you to the Editor—they just take you to different parts. Quickly Fix Photos opens the Editor in the Quick Fix mode, and Edit and Enhance Photos just launches regular ol' Elements 5 (the Editor).

Importing Photos from Your Scanner

Because this is a book for digital photographers, I imagine most of your photos will come from a digital camera (if so, see "Importing Your Photos"), but if you've been a photographer for a while now, you probably have some traditional prints lying around that you'd like to scan in, so here we'll look at importing scanned images into the Organizer.

Step One:

To scan images and have them appear in your Organizer, click the Organize button in the Elements Editor's task bar (above the Options Bar) to launch the Organizer. Then in the Organizer's task bar (above the Timeline), click on the Get Photos button (it looks like a digital camera icon with photos behind it) and choose From Scanner. By the way, once the Organizer is open, you can also use the shortcut Control-U to import photos from your scanner.

Step Two:

Once the Get Photos from Scanner dialog is open, choose your scanner from the Scanner pop-up menu. Choose a high Quality setting (I generally choose the highest quality unless the photo is for an email to my insurance company for a claim—then I'm not as concerned). Then click OK to bring in the scanned photo. See, pretty straightforward stuff.

This feature in Elements is a huge timesaver because it lets you choose a folder that is "watched" by the Organizer. When you drag photos into this folder, they will automatically be added to your Organizer. Here's how to set it up:

Automating the Importing of Photos by Using Watched Folders

Step One:
Go under the Organizer's File menu and choose Watch Folders.

Step Two:
When the Watch Folders dialog appears, make sure the Watch Folders and Their Sub-Folders for New Files checkbox is turned on. In the Folders to Watch section, click the Add button, and then in the resulting dialog, navigate to any folders you want the Organizer to "watch" for the addition of new photos. Select the folder you want to watch, and then click OK. Continue to click the Add button and select more folders to watch. When you've selected all your folders, they will appear in the Folders to Watch section of the Watch Folders dialog, where you have the choice of having the Organizer alert you when new photos are found in the watched folders (meaning you can choose to add them) or you can have them added automatically, which is what this feature is really all about. But if you're fussy about what gets added when (i.e., you're a control freak), at least you get an option.

Changing the Size of Your Photo Thumbnails

Thumbnails of your photos are displayed in the Organizer's Photo Browser, and luckily you have great control over what size they're displayed at.

Step One:

The size of your thumbnails is controlled by a slider at the bottom-right corner of the Photo Browser window. Drag the slider to the right to make them bigger—to the left to make them smaller. To jump to the largest possible view, just click on the Single Photo View icon to the immediate right of the slider. To jump to the smallest size, click on the Small Thumbnail Size icon to the left of the slider. To jump up one size at a time, hold the Control key and press the Plus Sign (+) key. To go down in size, press Control-Minus Sign (−).

Step Two:

Another shortcut to jump to the largest view is to just double-click on your thumbnail. At this large view, you can enter a caption directly below the photo by clicking on the placeholder text (which reads "Click here to add caption") and typing in your caption.

How about this for a view? Elements lets you see a full-screen preview of a selected thumbnail—all without leaving the Organizer. It's like an onscreen slide show of your thumbnails. Here's how it works:

Seeing Full-Screen Previews

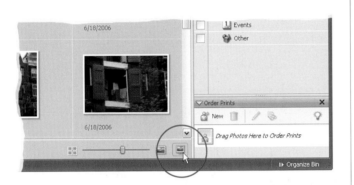

Step One:
To see a full-screen preview of your currently selected photo(s), click on the Full Screen View icon (it looks like a tiny monitor) in the far right-hand corner of the Photo Browser window (or just press F11).

Step Two:
This brings up the Full Screen View Options dialog with a number of presentation choices that you normally get for a slide show. Basically, that's what you'll use this Full Screen View feature for, but if you only select one photo, it shows just that one photo at full screen. So when this dialog appears, click OK and your photo will be displayed full screen. If you want to return to the Photo Browser, press the Escape key on your keyboard. By the way, once your photo(s) appears full screen, there's a floating palette at the top of the screen where you can control your viewing options—click the Play button to start it and click the Pause button to stop it. In case you want to create an actual slide show of those photos you're viewing, you can click on the Action Menu button in the middle of the palette and choose Create Slide Show from the pop-up menu.

Sorting Photos by Date

When photos are imported into the Organizer, the Organizer automatically sorts them by date. How does it know on which dates the photos were taken? The time and date are embedded into the photo by your digital camera at the moment the photo was taken (this info is called EXIF data). The Organizer reads this info and then sorts your photos automatically by date, but finding the photos by date takes a little doing on your part.

Step One:
By default, the newest photos are displayed first, so basically, the last photo you shot will be the first photo in the Organizer. Also, by default, the exact date each photograph was taken is shown directly below each photo's thumbnail. (*Note:* If you don't want this extra detail about each photo to be visible, just deselect the Details checkbox at the bottom-left side of the Photo Browser window.)

Step Two:
If you'd prefer to see your photos in reverse order (the oldest photos up top), then choose Date (Oldest First) from the pop-up menu in the bottom-left corner of the Photo Browser window. There you have it!

I know, I know—this is a book for "digital" photographers, but you know, and I know, that you've got a scanner. At some point you're going to scan some photos (then they'll become "digital images"), and then you'll want these images to be automatically organized in your catalog. All the scanned photos will have their "creation" date as the day you scanned them, unless you add your own date. This way, you can set the approximate date to when they were shot so they'll appear in your catalog when they were taken, rather than when they were imported.

Adding Scanned Photos? Enter the Right Time and Date

Step One:
First, get the photos from your scanner (see the "Importing Photos from Your Scanner" tutorial earlier in this chapter). Select all the photos you want to set the date for by Control-clicking each image (or Shift-clicking the first and last images if they are contiguous) in the Photo Browser window. Then, go under the Organizer's Edit menu and choose Adjust Date and Time (or press Control-J).

Step Two:
This brings up a dialog asking how you want to handle the date and time for these photos. For this example, select Change to a Specified Date and Time and click OK.

Step Three:
This brings up the Set Date and Time dialog, where you can use the pop-up menus to set your selected photos' date and time. Now these photos will appear sorted by the date you entered, rather than the date you imported them.

Finding Photos Fast by Their Month and Year

The method that the Organizer uses to help you find the photos you're looking for is month and year. It figures you might not know exactly when you took a group of photos, but let's say, for example, you're trying to find the photos from your last vacation. If you know you went sometime last summer—even if you can't remember whether it was May, June, or July—you can get mighty close mighty fast using the Month/Year Timeline. Here's how it works:

Step One:
We're going to assume you're trying to find vacation photos (as outlined above). You see those bars along the Timeline that look like the little bar charts from Microsoft Excel? Well, the higher the bar, the more photos that appear in that month. So click on any month in 2005 and only the photos taken in that month will appear in the Photo Browser window. As you slide your cursor to the left (or right), you'll see each month's name appear. When you get to July, only photos taken in July 2005 will appear. Take a quick look and see if any of those photos are your vacation photos. If they're not in July, scroll back on the Timeline to May, and only those photos will be visible.

SCOTT KELBY

Tagging Your Photos (Tags Are Keywords)

Although finding your photos by month and year is fairly handy, the real power of the Organizer appears when you assign tags (keywords) to your photos. This simple step makes finding the exact photos you want very fast and very easy. The first step is to decide whether you can use the pre-made tags that Adobe puts there for you or whether you need to create your own. In this situation, you're going to create your own custom tags.

Step One:
Start by clicking on the Tags button on the right side of the Organizer. Adobe's default set of tags will appear in a vertical list. (By the way, if you don't see the Tags and Collections buttons on the right side of the Organizer, click on the words "Organize Bin" at the bottom-right corner of the Organizer window.)

Step Two:
You'll start by creating your own custom category (in this case, we're going to create a category of all travel shots taken for a magazine client). Click on the New pop-up menu that appears just below the Tags button itself and choose New Category. This brings up the Create Category dialog. Type in "Travel Shots." Now choose an icon from the Category Icon list and then click OK. (The icon choices are all pretty lame, but at least we can use the globe icon.)

Continued

Step Three:

To create your own custom tag, click on the New pop-up menu again and choose New Tag. This brings up the Create Tag dialog. Choose Travel Shots from the Category pop-up menu (if it's not already chosen), then in the Name field, type in a name for your new tag (here I entered "Disney's Epcot Center"). If you want to add additional notes about the photo shoot, you can add them in the Note field, or you can choose a photo as an icon by clicking the Edit Icon button. Now click OK to create your tag.

Step Four:

Now you'll assign this tag to all the photos from this shoot. In the Photo Browser window, scroll to the photos from that shoot. We'll start by tagging just one photo, so click on your new tag that appears at the bottom of your Tags list and drag-and-drop that tag onto any one of the photos. That photo is now "tagged." If you have the photo's Details visible (if not, turn on the Details checkbox at the bottom-left corner of the Photo Browser window), you'll see a small tag icon appear below the photo's thumbnail (in this case, the globe icon).

SCOTT KELBY

Step Five:

So at this point, we've only tagged one photo from this shoot. Drag-and-drop that same tag onto five more photos from the shoot so a total of six photos are tagged. Now, in the list of Tags on the right side of the Organizer, click in the small box in the column to the left of your new tag (a tiny binoculars icon will appear in that box), and instantly, only the photos with that tag will appear in the Photo Browser window. To see all your photos again, click on the Back to All Photos button that appears at the top left of the Photo Browser window.

Tagging Multiple Photos

Okay, you've learned how to create your own custom category, then a custom tag so you can sort one shoot from the other, but you're dragging-and-dropping that tag onto one photo at a time (which takes too much time for an entire shoot). There are faster ways than this one-tag-at-a-time method. For example...

Step One:

To tag all the photos from your shoot at the same time, try this: First, click on any untagged photo from the shoot. Then hold the Control key and click on other photos from that particular shoot. As you click on them, they'll become selected (you'll see a thin blue box around each selected photo). Or, if all the photos are contiguous, click on the first image in the series, press-and-hold the Shift key, and then click on the last image in the series to select them all.

SCOTT KELBY

Step Two:

Now drag-and-drop your newly-created tag onto any one of those selected photos, and all of the selected photos will have that tag. If you want to see just the photos from that shoot, you can click in the box to the left of that tag and only photos with that tag will appear. By the way, if you decide you want to remove a tag from a photo, just Right-click on the photo and from the contextual menu that appears, choose Remove Tag. If you have more than one tag applied, you can choose which tag you want removed.

Okay, what if you want to assign a tag to a photo, but you also want to assign other tags (perhaps a "Client Work" tag and a "Make Prints" tag), as well? Here's how:

Assigning Multiple Tags to One Photo

Step One:
To assign multiple tags at once, first, of course, you have to create the tags you need, so go ahead and create two new tags by clicking on the New pop-up menu just below the Tags button—naming one "Client Work" and another "Make Prints." Now you have three tags you can assign. To assign all three tags at once, just hold the Control key, then in the Tags list, click on each tag you want to assign (Disney's Epcot Center, Client Work, and Make Prints).

Step Two:
Now click-and-drag those selected tags, and as you drag, you'll see you're dragging three tag icons as one group. Drop them onto a photo, and all three tags will be applied at once. If you want to apply the tags to more than one photo at a time, first hold the Control key and click on all the photos you want to have all three tags. Then, go to the Tags list, hold the Control key again, and click on all the tags you want to apply. Drag those tags onto any one of the selected photos, and all the tags will be applied at once. Cool.

Tagging Images of People (Face Tagging)

You're either going to think this is the coolest, most advanced technology in all of Elements 5, or you're going to think it's creepy and very Big Brother-ish (from the book by George Orwell, not the TV show). Either way, it's here to help you tag people easier because the Organizer can now automatically find photos of people for you—as it has some sort of weird science, facial-recognition software built in (that at one point was developed for the CIA, which is all the more reason it belongs in Elements).

Step One:

Okay, let's say you went on a family vacation, and you want to quickly find all the photos that have your daughter in them, without having to search through the hundreds of images you imported. Well, first go ahead and open the Organizer, because that's where our hunt will take place. Now select the group of photos you want to search through (you can do a Control-A to Select All, click on a collection, or just Control-click on as many images as you want to sort through).

Step Two:

Go under the Find menu, and at the bottom of the menu choose Find Faces for Tagging. This brings up the Face Tagging dialog. Within just a few moments (depending on how many photos you have), it will sort through your selected images and separate out the images that contain a human face.

©ISTOCKPHOTO AND JESSICA MALDONADO

Step Three:
Once these images appear in the Face Tagging dialog, you can Control-click on the photos of your family, and then drag-and-drop the appropriate tag from the Tags palette onto any one of the selected photos. They'll all be assigned that tag.

Step Four:
If you only want to see faces that haven't already been tagged, ensure the checkbox for Show Already Tagged Faces is off at the top of the Face Tagging dialog. When you're done, click Done to return to the main Organizer window.

TIP: As cool as this Face Tagging technology is, it doesn't stop there. Let's say you have a photo of a tall building, and you want to find all the similar photos that have a tall building. Just click on one of your building photos, then go under the Find menu and choose By Visual Similarity with Selected Photo(s). It will look for photos that have similar attributes (such as a building, similar colors, or orientation) to what you've already chosen. Pretty *CSI Las Vegas*, dontchathink?

Combining (Merging) Tags

It's easy to go "tag crazy," and if that happens (and you've got dozens of different tags applied to your photos), you may want to simplify by merging some of your tags together. For example, if you shot the Olympics, and you have tags for the 100-meter dash, 400-meter dash, 600-meter dash, and a half dozen more dashes, you may want to combine all those separate tags into just one tag. Here's how:

Step One:
To combine (merge) multiple tags into just one convenient tag, start by holding the Control key and clicking on all the tags that you want to combine in the Tags list on the right side of the Organizer. Then Right-click on any of your selected tags, and from the contextual menu that appears, choose Merge Tags.

Step Two:
This brings up a dialog that asks you which of the selected tags will be the surviving tag (in other words, which tag will remain after the rest are merged into this one). Choose the tag that will remain from the list of tags, then click OK. The tags will be merged into that one. Every photo that had any one of those selected tags will now have the one combined tag.

Sharing Your Tags (or Collections) with Others

Let's say you went to the Super Bowl with a group of photographers, and they're using Elements 5, too. If you've created a nice set of tags for identifying images, you can now export these tags and share them with the other photographers from that trip. That way, they can import them and start assigning tags to their Super Bowl photos without having to create tags of their own.

Step One:
To export your tags to share with others, start by going to the Tags palette (on the right side of the Organizer), then click on the New pop-up menu and choose Save Tags to File.

Step Two:
When the dialog appears, you can choose to Export All Tags, or better yet, click on the Export Specified Tags radio button, and then you can choose which tags you want to export from the pop-up menu. Choose the tags you want to export, and click OK. A standard Windows Save dialog will appear, so you can choose where you want your file saved. Name your file, click Save, and now you can email your exported tags to a friend.

Step Three:
Once your friends receive your tags, tell them they can import your tags by going to the Tags palette, clicking on the New pop-up menu, and choosing From File. Now they just locate the file on their hard drive and click Open. The new tags will appear in their Tags palette.

Collections: It's How You Put Photos in Order One by One

Once you've tagged all your photos, you may want to create a collection of just the best photos (the ones you'll show to your clients). You do that by creating a "collection." An advantage of collections is that once photos are in a collection, you can put the photos in the order you want them to appear (you can't do that with tags). This is especially important when you start creating your own slide shows and albums.

Step One:

To create a collection, click on the Collections button on the top-right side of the Organizer (it's just to the right of the Tags button when you have the Organize Bin open). You create a new collection by clicking on the New pop-up menu, then choosing New Collection. When the Create Collection dialog appears, enter a name for your collection, and then click OK.

Step Two:

Now that your collection has been created, you can either (a) drag the Collection icon onto the photos you want in your collection, or (b) Control-click photos to select them and then drag-and-drop them onto your Collection icon in the Collections palette. Either way, the photos will be added to your collection. To see just the photos in your collection, click on the box in the column to the left of your collection and tiny binoculars will appear. Now, to put the photos in the order you want, just click on any photo and drag it into position. The Organizer automatically numbers the photos for you in each thumbnail's top-left corner, so it's easy to see what's going on as you drag. To return to all of your images, click the Back to All Photos button in the top-left corner of the Photo Browser window.

SCOTT KELBY

By default, a tag or collection uses the first photo you add to that tag or collection as its icon. Unfortunately, these icons are so small that you probably can't tell what the icon represents. That's why you'll probably want to choose your own photo icons instead.

Choosing Your Own Icons for Tags and Collections

Step One:
It's easier to choose icons once you've created a tag or collection, meaning you've tagged a few photos or added some photos to a collection. Once you've done that, click on your tag or collection, then click on the Pencil icon (it's in the bar right under the Tags and Collections buttons). This brings up the Edit Tag (or Collection) dialog. In this dialog, click on the Edit Icon button to launch the dialog you see here.

Step Two:
You'll see the first photo in your collection in the preview window (this is why it's best to edit the icon *after* you've added tags or collections to the photos). If you don't want to use this first photo, click the arrow buttons under the bottom-right corner of the preview window to scroll through your photos. Once you find the photo you want to use, click on the little cropping border (in the preview window) to isolate part of the photo. This gives you a better close-up photo that's easier to see as an icon. Then click OK in the open dialogs and that cropped image becomes your icon.

Deleting Tags (or Collections)

If you've created a tag or a collection, and then later decide that you don't want that tag or collection, you can delete it in just three clicks.

Step One:
To delete a tag or collection, start by clicking on the tag or collection you want to delete in the Tags or Collections palette on the right side of the Organizer.

Step Two:
Once you've selected the tag or collection you want to delete, just click the Trash icon at the top of the Tags (or Collections) palette (it's found to the immediate right of the New pop-up menu). If you're deleting a tag, when you click on the Trash icon, it brings up a warning dialog letting you know that deleting the tag will remove it from all your photos. If you want to remove that tag, click OK. If you've got a collection selected when you click the Trash icon, it asks if you want to delete the collection. Click OK and it's gone. However, it does not delete these photos from your main catalog—it just deletes that collection.

Seeing Your Photo's Metadata (EXIF Info)

When you take a photo with a digital camera, a host of information about that photo is embedded into the photo by the camera itself. It contains just about everything, including the make and model of the camera that took the photo, the exact time the photo was taken, what the f-stop setting was, what the focal length of the lens was, and whether or not the flash fired when you took the shot. You can view all this info (called Exchangeable Image File [EXIF] data—also known as metadata) from right within the Organizer. Here's how:

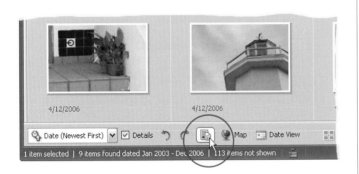

Step One:
To view a photo's EXIF data, first click on the photo in the Photo Browser, and then click the Show or Hide Properties button at the bottom-left side of the Photo Browser window to show the Properties palette.

Step Two:
When the Properties palette appears in the bottom-right corner of the Organize Bin, click the Metadata button at the top of the palette (it's the fourth button from the left). This shows an abbreviated version of the photo's EXIF data (basically, the make, model, ISO, exposure, f-stop, focal length of the lens, and the status of the flash). Of course, the camera embeds much more info than this. To see the full EXIF data, under the View section at the bottom of the palette, just select Complete and you'll get more information on this file than you'd probably ever want to know. One thing that isn't displayed in the Brief view that you probably might want to know is the date and time the photo was taken, and to see that you will have to open the Complete view.

Adding Your Own Info to Photos

Although your digital camera automatically embeds information into your photos, you can also add your own info from right within the Organizer. This includes simple things like a photo caption (that can appear onscreen when you display your photos in a slide show), or you can add notes to your photos for your personal use, either of which can be used to help you search for photos later.

Step One:
First, click on the photo in the Photo Browser window you want to add your own info to and click the Show or Hide Properties button at the bottom left of the Organizer, or you can also use the keyboard shortcut by pressing Alt-Enter.

Step Two:
This brings up the Properties palette along the bottom-right corner of the Organizer. At the top of the palette are four buttons for the four different sections of your photo's properties. By default, the General section is selected. In the General section, the first field is for adding captions (I know, that's pretty self-explanatory), and then the photo's file name appears below that. It's the third field down—Notes—where you add your own personal notes about the photo.

Step Three:
If you want to see other info about your photo (for example, which tags have been added to your photos; the date when you imported the photo or when you last printed, emailed, or posted the photo on the Web; or the info embedded into the photo by your digital camera), just click on the various buttons at the top of the palette.

Finding Photos

Finding a group of photos is fairly easy using the Organizer, especially if you've tagged your images, but finding an individual photo takes a bit of work. It's not hard; it just takes some effort because you essentially have to narrow the amount of photos down to a small group (like the month or day you shot the photos). Then you scroll through the photos in that group until you find the individual photo you want. It sounds complicated, but it's really quite easy. Here are the most popular searching methods:

From the Timeline:

The Timeline, which is a horizontal bar across the top of the Photo Browser, shows you all the photos in your catalog. Months and years are represented along the Timeline. The years are visible below the Timeline; the small light blue bars above the Timeline are individual months. If there is no bar visible, there are no photos stored in that month. A short blue bar means just a few photos were taken that month—a tall bar means lots of photos. If you hover your cursor over a blue bar, the month it represents will appear. To see the photos taken in that month, click on the bar and only those photos will be displayed in the Photo Browser window. Once you've clicked on a month, you can click-and-drag the locator bar to the right or left to display different months.

Using Tags:

If there's a particular shot you're looking for, and you've tagged all your shots with a particular tag, then just click on the Tags button and click on the empty box in the column to the left of that tag. Now only shots with that tag will appear in the Photo Browser window.

Continued

By Date Ranges:

Let's say you're looking to find a particular photo you shot on vacation. If you can remember approximately when you went on vacation, you can display photos taken within a certain date range (for example, all the photos taken between June 1 and June 30, 2005). Here's how: Go under the Organizer's Find menu and choose Set Date Range. This brings up a dialog where you can enter start and end dates. Click OK and only photos taken within that time frame will be visible. Scroll through those images to see if you can find your photo.

By Caption or Note:

If you've added personal notes within tags or you've added captions to individual photos, you can search those fields to help you narrow your search. Just go under the Organizer's Find menu and choose By Caption or Note. Then in the resulting dialog, enter the word that you think may appear in the photo's caption or note, and click OK. Only photos that have that word in a caption or note will appear in the Photo Browser window.

By History:

The Organizer keeps track of when you imported each photo and when you last shared it (via email, print, webpage, etc.); so if you can remember any of those dates, you're in luck. Just go under the Organizer's Find menu, under By History, and choose which attribute you want to search under in the submenu. A dialog with a list of names and dates will appear. Click on a date and name, click OK, and only photos that fit that criterion will appear in the Photo Browser window.

Finding Photos Using the Date View

Okay, I have to admit, this particular feature is probably going to be your least-used Organizer feature because it seems so…I dunno…cheesy (for lack of a better word). When you use it, you see a huge calendar, and if photos were created on a particular day in the currently visible month, you'll see a small thumbnail of one of those images on that date. Personally, when I see this view, I feel like I've just left a professional-looking application and entered a "consumer" application, so I avoid it like the plague, but just in case you dig it (hey, it's possible), here's how it works:

Step One:
To enter the Date View in the Organizer, click the Date View button at the bottom of the Photo Browser window.

Step Two:
This brings up the Date View calendar window with the Month view showing by default (if you're not in Month view, click the Month button along the bottom center of the window). If you see a photo on a date, it means there are photos that were taken (or you scanned or imported) on that day. To see a photo, click on it within the calendar and a larger version will appear at the top right of the Date View window. To see the rest of the photos on this day, click the Next Item on Selected Day button found directly under this preview window. Each time you click this button, the window displays a preview of the next photo taken on that day.

Step Three:
If you find the photo you're looking for (I'm assuming that if you're searching around in the Date View, you're looking for a particular photo) and you want to edit that photo, Right-click on the photo's preview and choose Go to Full Edit (or just press Control-I). The Elements Editor will launch with your photo open and ready to edit.

Step Four:
Return to the Organizer and click the Date View button again. While we're here, I want to show you a couple of the other features. Although the Month view is shown by default, there are buttons at the bottom center of the Date View window for viewing the entire year (where days that have photos appear as solid-color blocks) or an individual day (where all the photos from that day appear in a slide-show-like window as shown here).

Step Five:
While in the Date View, you can add a Daily Note, which is a note that doesn't apply to the current photo—it applies to every photo taken on that calendar day. If you change to the Day view (by clicking the Day button at the bottom of the Date View window), fields for adding a Caption and a Daily Note to the currently displayed photo will appear along the right side of the window. Now when you're in Day view, you can not only see your caption for your photo, but you can also see the Daily Note for each photo taken on that calendar day.

Seeing an Instant Slide Show

If you want to see a quick slide show of a collection or currently selected photos in the Organizer, it's pretty much just a two-click process. Later in this book, I show you how to create rich, fully featured slide shows using an entirely different feature of Elements 5, but for now we'll just look at how to create a quickie slide show with minimum time and effort.

Step One:
First, open the Organizer. Now press-and-hold the Control key and click on each photo you want to appear in your slide show (if the photos are contiguous, you can click on the first photo, hold the Shift key, click on the last photo, and all the photos in between will be selected). Once the photos you want are selected, click on the Full Screen View icon (it looks like a little monitor) at the bottom right of the Photo Browser window.

SCOTT KELBY

Step Two:
This brings up the Full Screen View Options dialog, which contains presentation options for your slide show. You can choose music that will play during your slide show from the Background Music pop-up menu. You can also choose how long each photo will appear onscreen. By default, it assumes you want any captions included, but you can turn that off by clicking the Include Captions checkbox, and you can also have your slide show loop when it reaches the end by turning on the Repeat Slide Show checkbox. Now click OK to begin your slide show.

Step Three:

Once you click OK, you'll enter Full Screen View mode, where you'll see a floating slide show control palette on the top-left side of your screen. Your slide show won't actually start advancing until you click the Play button (or press the Spacebar, or the shortcut F5). To stop your slide show from advancing (to pause it), click the Pause button in the control palette (the Play button toggles to the Pause button while the slides are in motion), and then to resume the slide show, just click Play/ Pause one more time.

Step Four:

Besides the standard Previous, Play/Pause, Next, and Exit buttons that appear in the control palette, you'll also see other controls on the right. These extra controls are for comparing still images and are not for use during your slide show. To hide these other controls, click on the tiny left-facing arrow on the far-right side of the control palette and it will collapse down to just display the slide show controls.

Step Five:

To quit your slide show and return to the Photo Browser, press the Escape key on your keyboard or click the Exit (X) button on the control palette.

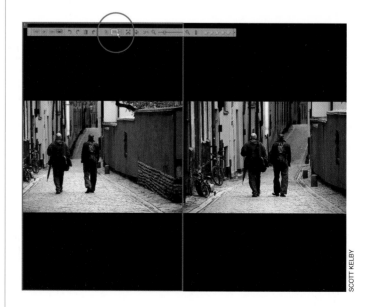

Comparing Photos

Let's say you've just shot some city life photos, and now you're looking at 14 shots of people and city streets. The Organizer has a great feature that lets you compare two images onscreen (either side by side or one above the other) to help you narrow down your choice to the best possible photo.

Step One:
First, open the Organizer. To compare (or review) photos side by side, hold the Control key and click on all the photos you want to compare. Then click the Full Screen View icon at the bottom right of the Photo Browser window (or just press the F11 key on your keyboard). This brings up the Full Screen View Options dialog, which presents options for a slide show. You can ignore those slide show options and just click OK to enter Full Screen View mode, which can be used to compare images.

Step Two:
The photo you selected first will appear in Full Screen View mode, and you'll see a floating control palette at the top-left side of your screen. Click on the Side by Side View button (it looks like two boxes), which puts the first and second photos you selected side by side onscreen. The first photo (on the left) has the number 1 in its upper left-hand corner, and the second photo (the one being compared) is noted as number 2 when clicked on.

SCOTT KELBY

Step Three:
Now visually compare these two photos. You'll want the one that looks best to remain onscreen so you can compare other selected photos against it, right? To do that, click on the "bad" photo, and a blue highlight will appear around that photo, indicating that this is the one that will change. In this example, I thought the second photo looked better, so I clicked on photo number 1 (the one on the left).

Step Four:
Now go to the control palette, click on the Next Photo button, and the first photo will be replaced with your next photo in that series. Again, review which of these two looks the best, then click on the photo that looks worst (that way, you can replace it with another photo you want to compare). Click the Next Photo button to compare the next photo (and so on). To back up and review a previous photo, click the Previous Photo button in the control palette.

Step Five:
Besides this side-by-side mode, there's also an option that lets you see your photos stacked one on top of the other (which you might like for comparing photos in landscape orientation). To change to that mode, click on the down-facing arrow to the immediate right of the Side by Side View button, and from the pop-up menu that appears, choose Above and Below. Cycle through the images as you did before—just repeat Steps Three and Four until you find the photo you like best. When you're finished, press the Escape key on your keyboard or click the Exit (X) button in the control palette.

Comparing Photos by Zooming and Panning

This isn't exactly an Organizer technique, but there's also a way to compare photos in the Elements Editor. This is a cool feature that Elements borrows from Photoshop—the ability to view multiple images at once (for comparison purposes)—but more importantly, to be able to view each one at the same magnification (even when changing zoom magnifications). You can scroll around (pan) to inspect images and have all the images pan at the same location and rate. This is one you need to try to really appreciate.

Step One:
Open the multiple photos you want to compare in the Editor. (In this instance, we'll compare four photos, so open four photos, which will appear in the Photo Bin at the bottom of the Editor window. The power of this feature will be more apparent if you open four similar images, like four portraits of the same person at one sitting, etc.)

Step Two:
Go under the Window menu, under Images, and choose Tile. This will put all your photos in their own separate windows, and then it will tile these four open windows across your screen so you can see all four photos at once.

Step Three:

Now that your photos are tiled, return to the Window menu, under Images, and choose Match Zoom. Now, press-and-hold the Shift key, press Z to switch to the Magnifying Glass tool (okay, it's called the Zoom tool, but its icon looks like a magnifying glass), and click-and-drag a selection around a person or object in one of the active image windows. You'll notice that all four photos jump to the same zoom. *Note:* If the Resize Windows To Fit feature is selected in the Zoom tool's Options Bar, this won't work properly.

Step Four:

Now go under the Window menu, under Images, and choose Match Location. Press H to switch to the Hand tool (it's right under the Zoom tool in the Toolbox), press-and-hold the Shift key, then click within your image and drag to pan around your photo. If you don't hold the Shift key first, it will just pan around the front-most active window. By holding Shift, all the windows pan at the same time and speed, enabling you to compare particular areas of your photos at the same time.

Reducing Clutter by Stacking Your Photos

This is one of my favorite features because it lets you reduce "photo clutter" and makes things more organized when working in the Photo Browser window. It's called "stacking," and it lets you stack similar photos together, leaving just one photo to represent a stack of photos. So, if you took 120 shots and you've already sorted the best of the bunch into a collection, you don't have to have 120 shots cluttering up your catalog. Instead, you can have just one representative photo, and underneath it are the 119 others.

Step One:

With the Organizer open, press-and-hold the Control key on your keyboard and click on all the photos you want to add to your stack (or if the images are contiguous, simply click the first image in the series, press-and-hold the Shift key, and click on the last image in the series). Once they're all selected, go under the Organizer's Edit menu, under Stack, and choose Stack Selected Photos in the submenu.

Step Two:

No dialog appears, it just happens—in this case, your three other photos now are stacked behind the first photo you selected (think of it as four layers, and on each layer is a photo, stacked one on top of another). You'll know a photo thumbnail contains a stack because a Stack icon (which looks like a little blue stack of paper) will appear in the upper-right corner of your photo. You'll also see a right-facing arrow to the right of the image thumbnail.

SCOTT KELBY

Step Three:
Once your photos are stacked, you can view these photos at any time by clicking on the photo with the Stack icon, and then going under the Edit menu, under Stack, and choosing Expand Photos in Stack, or just click on the right-facing arrow to the right of the image thumbnail. This is like doing a "Find," where all the photos in your stack will appear in the Photo Browser window within a gray shaded area so you can see them without unstacking them. Then, to collapse the stack, just click on the left-facing arrow that appears to the right of the last image thumbnail in the stack.

Step Four:
If you do want to unstack the photos, select the photo with the Stack icon in the Photo Browser window, then go under the Edit menu, under Stack, and choose Unstack Photos. If you decide you don't want to keep any of the photos in your stack, select the photo with the Stack icon in the Photo Browser window, go back under the Edit menu, under Stack, and choose Flatten Stack. It's like flattening your layers—all that's left is that first photo. However, when you choose to flatten, you will have the choice of deleting the photos from your hard disk or not.

Putting Your Photos on the Map!

If this isn't cool, I don't know what is. Imagine being able to send friends or relatives to an online customized version of Yahoo! Maps, and when they click on a map pin, they see your photos, and the exact location where they were taken on the map. Seriously, is that cool or what? A totally interactive online map you create and link to your own photos at the spot where they were taken. Now, come on, if it doesn't sound that cool, then you've got to try it once and you'll be totally hooked.

Step One:
You start by going to the Organizer and switching it into Map mode by clicking on the Map icon at the bottom of the Organizer (as shown here). This splits the screen, and shows your photos on the right side, and a Yahoo! map of North America on the left side. (By the way, since this whole Yahoo! Maps thing is Internet-based, I guess it goes without saying that you need to have an Internet connection, right? Right.)

Step Two:
Now let's create a custom tag for the photos you want to appear on a certain city on the map. For example, let's say that you've got a number of photos taken from your vacation in Miami, Florida. You'd start by creating a new tag (in the Organizer portion of the screen) and then link that tag to a particular city on the map (don't worry, it's easier than it sounds). Start by clicking on the Tags button in the Organize Bin on the right side of the Organizer. Then click the New button and choose New Tag from the pop-up menu. When the Create Tag dialog appears, name this tag Miami (as shown here), but don't click OK yet.

Step Three:
Now click on the Place on Map button, which brings up a dialog asking you to enter the location where the photos where taken (in this case, I just typed in Miami, FL), then click the Find button (as shown here).

Step Four:
This brings up the Look Up Address dialog, where it queries its database to find a match on the map. Luckily, Miami's a pretty popular place, so in less than a second it popped up with "Miami, FL, US." If that's the city you're looking for (and we are), click OK. However, you can get a lot more exact than just this. I typed in my exact home address, and it pinpointed it exactly on the map, so don't be afraid to get really precise if you know the exact address of where the photos were taken. In fact, let's go ahead and enter the exact address of the Marseilles Hotel (a very cool art deco hotel in the heart of South Beach). Its address is 1741 Collins Ave., Miami Beach, FL. So click on the Place on Map button again, but this time enter that new address, and then click the Find button. It will find it right away, so once it appears (in about two seconds), just click OK, and you'll notice that the map on the left side of the window zooms into that exaction location on Collins Avenue in Miami Beach. Pretty slick. But we're not done yet. Change the name of your tag to Miami Beach, and then click OK. When you do this, you'll see a red pin appear, marking the exact location you entered on the map.

Continued

Step Five:

Now, in the Organizer, select the photos you want to tag with your Miami Beach tag (hold the Control key and click on each photo you want selected), then click directly on the tag in your list of tags, and drag-and-drop that tag onto one of your selected photos. (By the way, if you previously tagged images with a tag that contains an exact address, you can simply click-and-drag the photos with that tag to a spot on the map.)

Step Six:

Want to make sure this process really worked? Then move your cursor over the red pin on the map, and click once. A mini slide show viewer will appear, and you can click on the tiny thumbnails below the main photo to see individual photos, but that's not the cool feature. Go ahead and click on the main photo, and you jump straight into an instant full-screen slide show of the photos you tagged with that tag, and are pinned at that map location (see, I told you this was cool). To leave the slide show and return to the Organizer, just press the Escape key on your keyboard. Seeing the photos on your own computer is one thing, but now let's get these up on the Web so other people can see them. That's when it gets really fun.

Step Seven:

To share these map photos (and the map itself), you simply click once on the Share button located just below the bottom-right corner of the map. You'll get a dialog that lets you know that if you share the map, it means you agree to Yahoo! Maps API's terms of service. Go ahead and click Share. This brings up the Photo Galleries Wizard (yup, this is the same Wizard you use to create websites, and the reason you're using this is because your Yahoo! map will be Flash-based, just like Elements 5's other interactive Web galleries). On the left side of this dialog, you'll enter your gallery title, a text caption (if you like), and then some descriptive text in the About This Gallery text field. Below that, enter your name and email address.

Step Eight:

To see a preview of your finished Map, click the Preview in Browser button, and it launches your Web browser and displays your interactive map. If you click on the red pin, it shows the photos attached to that pin, just as it did in the Organizer. If you click on one of the photos, it starts the Flash-based slide show. To return to the map, click the small Map icon at the bottom of the window. To return to Elements 5, close your Web browser. To put your final map on the Web, go to the Save and Share section at the bottom of the Photo Galleries Wizard, and choose where you want to save this (to your website, the free Photoshop Showcase website, or even to CD) from the Share To pop-up menu, then click the Share button at the bottom of the dialog to complete the process. Now you can point friends and family to your new interactive map-based online photo gallery. Cool!

Raw Hide
mastering camera raw

This book has an entire chapter devoted to Camera Raw. So why a whole chapter? Three reasons: (1) Camera Raw is that important, and has so many features in Elements 5, I felt I needed to cover them all; (2) I needed the extra pages to get my page count up; (3) I really didn't need the page count, but you can't be sure of that. Now, is this chapter for everybody? No. It's really only for people who shoot in RAW format (you'll know if your digital camera can shoot RAW, because the salesman who sold you the camera would've been totally naked at the time of your purchase). Okay, I'm going to get serious for just a moment (and only for a moment, so don't get excited—especially with that naked salesman around). Camera Raw isn't for everybody. For example, if you're a seasoned pro who gets the exposure dead-on every time and never has white balance issues, go ahead and shoot in a high-quality JPEG format. But for everyone else, RAW lets us fix all sorts of things after the fact, in Photoshop Elements, and because it's all happening within the data from the camera, we can tweak the exposure, white balance, and a dozen other settings to create a new, perfectly balanced "original" from our digital negative. This is very powerful stuff. Now, back to the crazy crap. See the title for this chapter, "Raw Hide"? You're thinking it's that old western TV show, right? Well, I'm thinkin' it's the theme song from that old western TV show. Come on, sing with me: "Head 'em up, move 'em out, Rawwwww Hidddeeee!" (Note to editors: Insert whip sound effect here.)

Editing Your RAW Images in Camera Raw

The RAW format is about the hottest thing happening in digital photography. There are two reasons why: (1) unmatched quality, and (2) you become the processing lab, creating your own custom originals from your digital negative (the RAW file itself, which remains unchanged). Think of it this way: With traditional film, someone at a lab processes your prints from a negative. Well, with RAW, you are the person processing the photo—with control over white balance, exposure, and more—all before your file opens in Elements 5. Oh yeah, there's another benefit—it's easier (nobody tells you that one).

Step One:

If you have a digital camera that is capable of shooting in RAW format, you may want to start shooting in RAW so you can start taking advantage of all the things we mentioned at the top of this page (if you don't shoot in RAW, you won't have access to the Camera Raw processing dialog or any of the RAW features. By the way, we call the act of editing and correcting your images in the Camera Raw dialog "processing" the image. Why processing? Because it sounds cool).

Once you've set your camera to shoot in RAW, you can open these RAW photos in one of two places:

(1) By going under Elements' File menu and choosing Open. Navigate your way to the file, click the Open button, and your file will open in the Camera Raw processing dialog (shown here).

(2) You can open RAW images from the Organizer by clicking on the thumbnail for the RAW photo and pressing Control-I on your keyboard (the shortcut to switch to Full Edit mode). Either way you do it, Elements opens the RAW photo in the Camera Raw processing dialog.

SCOTT KELBY

Step Two:
Your RAW photo is displayed in the large preview area on the left side of the dialog. There are only three tools: the Zoom tool (Z) (for zooming in/out of the preview), the Hand tool (H) (for panning around when you're zoomed in), and the White Balance tool (I) (which looks like the Eyedropper tool used for sampling colors or reading tones). The two circular arrow icons to the right of these tools are used to rotate photos.

Step Three:
To take advantage of that large preview area, here are some quick preview short-cuts: The Zoom tool works just like the one in the Elements Editor. If you double-click on it (in the top-left corner above the preview), it zooms your image to a 100% view. When you're zoomed in tight, press-and-hold the Spacebar on your keyboard to get the Hand tool, then just click-and-drag in the preview area to move around the image (as shown here). To quickly fit your entire photo in the preview area, double-click on the Hand tool above the preview or press Control-0 (zero). You can press Control–+ (Plus key) to zoom in and Control–– (Minus key) to zoom out. Also, you can rotate a photo left or right by pressing the L or R key, respectively.

Continued

Step Four:

You do your photo processing in the right column of the Camera Raw dialog. There are two tabs with different sets of controls under each, but all the basic essential adjustments are found under the Adjust tab (make sure it's visible by clicking on its tab). We'll start by adjusting the white balance setting. When you open a photo in Camera Raw, Elements looks at the white balance setting that was used when the photo was taken. It will display that setting in the White Balance pop-up menu (the menu will show the words "As Shot" by default). If the white balance looks good to you, you can leave it set as-is, but if the white balance wasn't set correctly in your camera (or if you just want to see if you can come up with a setting that looks better), you can apply a preset option by choosing one from the White Balance pop-up menu.

Step Five:

Besides using these preset white balance settings, you can create your own custom white balance using the Temperature and Tint sliders. To make your white balance more blue, drag the Temperature slider to the left. To add more yellow, drag it to the right. The Tint slider basically does the same thing, just with different colors: dragging to the left brings more green into your photo and dragging to the right brings in more red. By using these two sliders, you can pretty much create whatever white balance situation you prefer (this is totally a personal preference thing).

Step Six:

There's another way to set your white balance: use the White Balance tool (found at the top of the Camera Raw dialog—it looks like the regular Eyedropper tool). You just press the letter I to get the tool, then click it once in a neutral area of your photo (you don't want to click in a perfectly white area with no detail; you want an area that's off-white or light gray with some detail).

TIP: To help you find this neutral color in your images, I've included a black-and-white swatch card for you in the back of this book (it's perforated so you can tear it out). Just put this card into your RAW shot, take the shot, and when you open the RAW file in Camera Raw, you can then click the White Balance tool on the neutral gray swatch on the swatch card. When you're done, just crop the card out of the image. (See the chapter on color correction for more information on how to use this handy card.)

Step Seven:

Now, let's move on to your tonal adjustments (which are located just below the White Balance section). The top slider (and probably the most widely used slider in all of Camera Raw) is for adjusting the exposure of your photo. (You can increase the exposure up to four f-stops and decrease it up to two f-stops. So, an Exposure slider setting of +1.50 would be an increase of a stop and a half.) One way to make this adjustment is to "eye" it: just drag the slider, then look at the preview to see how your image looks. But there are some other features to help you make more informed exposure decisions.

Continued

Step Eight:

By default, when you open a RAW image, Camera Raw tries to automatically set the Exposure, Shadows, Brightness, and Contrast settings for you. Sometimes Auto settings do a surprisingly good job of adjusting your RAW images, so it's worth seeing how your image is affected by these Auto corrections (just turn off the Preview checkbox that appears above the preview area to see what your image looks like without these Auto corrections, press Control-U to toggle them on/off, or just click on any of the Auto checkboxes to turn them off).

Step Nine (Exposure):

If you want to set the exposure manually, you can still get some help. The method I use to set the exposure is to have Camera Raw tell me how far I can go (either increasing or decreasing the Exposure setting), so I get the best possible exposure, without clipping off any highlights or shadows. To do this, press-and-hold the Alt key and drag the Exposure slider (moving any slider automatically turns off the Auto checkbox for that slider). When you do this, the screen will turn black. If anything shows up in white (or red, green, or blue), that's a warning that the highlights are clipping (basically, that means there will be no detail in that area, which may actually be okay—clipping areas like a bright reflection on a car's bumper or the center of the sun isn't a problem). So, as long as important areas aren't clipped off, I keep clicking-and-dragging to the right (with Alt held down) until some real clipping starts to appear.

Step Ten (Shadows):

Now that your Exposure is set (and you protected your highlights from clipping), what about the shadows? Well, there's a slider for that too—it's called (surprisingly enough) the Shadows slider, and sliding it to the right increases the shadows in your photo. Again, there's an Auto checkbox (and you should give that a try), but you can also use the Alt-drag trick on the Shadows slider. This time, the preview will show shadow areas (with no detail) in pure black (meaning these areas are getting clipped—white areas are not clipped). If you see other colors (like red, green, or blue), they're getting clipped a bit too, but not as significantly as the overall shadows (so I'm not as concerned about a little bit of clipping in color). If there's significant clipping, drag to the left to reduce the amount of shadows. If not, drag to the right until you start getting some clipping.

TIP: Adobe added a very helpful feature to keep you from clipping either your highlights or shadows. At the top of the Camera Raw dialog, there are two checkboxes: one for Highlights, one for Shadows. When you turn them on, anytime highlight areas start getting clipped (regardless of which slider you're using), the clipped areas will appear in solid red, while clipped shadow areas will appear in blue, giving you an instant visual warning exactly where clipping is occurring. Not bad, eh?

Continued

Step Eleven (Brightness):

The next adjustment slider is Brightness. Since you've already adjusted the highlights (with Exposure) and shadows (with the Shadows slider), the Brightness slider adjusts everything else (I always relate this slider to the midtones slider in the Levels dialog, so that might help in understanding how this slider differs from Exposure or Shadows). There is an Auto checkbox for Brightness, but I'm not too crazy about this particular Auto setting, as it seems (to me anyway) to give the photo a flat look, but hey—that's just me. Turn Auto on/off to see if you agree—or just drag the slider to the right (above 50) to lighten the midtones or to the left (below 50) to darken them.

Step Twelve (Contrast):

The Contrast slider does pretty much what you'd expect it to—adds or reduces contrast (depending on which way you drag it). If you drag to the right, it increases the contrast in the image (so you can imagine you'll probably be dragging right most of the time), or if you want to reduce the contrast in your image (making it look flat), drag to the left. There's also an Auto checkbox here, but to me it never seems to add enough contrast, so I usually wind up adjusting this one myself while looking at the preview (and the histogram) as a guide.

Step Thirteen (Saturation):

The Saturation slider makes the colors in your RAW photo either more saturated and colorful (by dragging to the right) or less saturated and flat (by dragging to the left). This is my least-used slider in Camera Raw, as I normally wait until I'm in Elements, because I view adding saturation as a special effect, and not generally something I do when I'm just trying to create a nicely exposed, well-balanced image. In fact, I only adjust this setting if some of the other changes I made in Camera Raw make my colors look flat. Otherwise, I ignore that slider, but that's just me; if you want more saturated photos, go for it (I won't tell anybody). By the way, there's no Auto checkbox for Saturation. I call that an act of mercy.

TIP: I'm sure you've noticed that the Auto checkboxes are "on" by default, but what if you want to see your images without them on at all (of course you could turn off the Preview checkbox or press Control-U)? If you really want to turn them off for good, though, here's what you do: Open a RAW file, turn off all the Auto checkboxes by pressing Control-U, and then go to the Settings flyout menu (it's the right-facing arrow to the right of the Settings pop-up menu) and choose Save New Camera Raw Defaults. Now when you open a RAW image, all the Auto checkboxes will be off by default.

Noise Reduction in Camera Raw

While you're processing your image, if you notice that your image has digital noise (those annoying red-and-green spots or splotchy patches of color), you can reduce that noise—especially the color part—from right within Camera Raw.

Step One:

Open a RAW image in Camera Raw that has a digital noise issue, press Z to get the Zoom tool, and zoom in tight so the noise is easily visible. There are two types of noise you can deal with in Camera Raw: (1) high ISO noise, which often happens when you're shooting in low-light situations, especially when using a high ISO setting (hence the name); and (2) color noise, which can happen even in normal situations (this noise is more prevalent in some cameras than others).

Step Two:

Click on the Detail tab along the right side of the dialog. To decrease the amount of color noise, drag the Color Noise Reduction slider to the right. As you can see, it does a pretty fair job of removing the color noise, though it does tend to desaturate the overall color just a bit. That's why it's good to zoom out to see the preview so you don't wash out the photo. If the problem is mostly in shadow areas (high ISO noise), you can use the Luminance Smoothing slider in the same way—drag to the right to reduce the noise—but use this carefully, because it can tend to make your photo look a bit soft.

Sharpening within Camera Raw

Although Camera Raw enables you to sharpen your image at this early stage in the correction process, you have to decide if this is something you really want to do. I've heard arguments for sharpening at this stage, but many more against it, so like most corrections, it'll come down to your own personal preference. If you do decide to sharpen now (or if you want to turn off the sharpening that's on by default), here's how:

Step One:
When you open an image in Camera Raw, by default it applies a small amount of sharpening to your photo. You can see how much by clicking on the Detail tab (along the right side of the dialog) and looking at the Sharpness slider. To add additional sharpness, drag the slider to the right (if you do this, first set your zoom to 100% in the pop-up menu at the bottom left of the preview window so you can see the effect of sharpening).

Step Two:
Now that you know how to apply more sharpness (I hate to tell you this), I recommend setting the Sharpness slider at 0% (essentially turning it off). I recommend this for two reasons: first, because there's just one slider, you basically have to take whatever it gives you. Second, I feel sharpening should be done right before you save the file, not when you're initially creating it, so it does the minimum amount of damage to the image. If you agree (hey, it's up to you), set the Sharpness slider to 0%, then go to Camera Raw's flyout menu (it's to the right of the Settings pop-up menu) and choose Save New Camera Raw Defaults. Now when you open RAW photos, no sharpness will be applied, unless you use the slider to add it.

Bracketing with Camera Raw

If you forgot to bracket in the camera itself, you can use Camera Raw to create multiple exposures, and then open those images in Elements 5, where you can composite them together to create an image that one exposure alone couldn't capture. Here's how it's done:

Step One:
Using the Organizer, press Control-I to open the RAW image to which you want to apply a bracketing technique. In this example, the sky's exposure looks pretty decent, but the subject (the rocks) is almost totally in the shadows. So, using Camera Raw (and the default Auto settings), create the first photo that has the proper exposure for the sky. So even though the rocks are dark as long as the sky looks good to you, click Open to create the first version of your bracketed photo in the Elements Editor.

Step Two:
In the Editor, go under the File menu and choose Duplicate to make a copy of this image. Click on the original photo and close this original image (without saving it). By doing this, we can reopen the RAW file in the next step and create a second version of this image that exposes the foreground, taking the rocks out of the shadows.

Step Three:
Now, go back to the Organizer, click on the thumbnail for that same RAW photo, then press Control-I to open the RAW file again. Once the photo is open in Camera Raw, drag the Exposure slider to the right until the rocks are properly exposed. This will totally blow out the sky, but just ignore that and focus on getting a good exposure for the rocks, our subject. When it looks good to you, click the Open button to create this exposed version of the photo in the Elements Editor.

Step Four:
Now you should have both versions of the image open in the Elements Editor: the brighter one exposed for the high-lights (to bring out the rocks) and the darker one exposed for the shadows (to bring out the sky). Arrange the windows so you can see both onscreen at the same time. Press V to get the Move tool, and with the shadow image active, press-and-hold the Shift key and drag-and-drop the darker version on top of the lighter version. The key to this part is holding down the Shift key while you drag between documents, which perfectly aligns the dark copy (that now appears on its own layer in the Layers palette) with the lighter version on the Background layer. (This exact alignment of one identical photo over another is referred to as being "pin registered.") You can now close the shadow document without saving, as both versions of the image are contained within the lighter version.

Continued

Step Five:

Go to the Layers palette, hold down the Control key, and click the Create a New Layer icon at the top of the Layers palette. This creates a new blank layer directly beneath the photo exposed for the sky. Now, in the Layers palette, click on the photo exposed for the sky (it should be the top layer), and then press Control-G. This groups your image with the blank layer, covering it so you now only see the version of the photo that's exposed for the rocks (which is on the Background layer).

Step Six:

It's time to "reveal" the sky on the darker version of the photo. Here's how: First, in the Layers palette, click on the blank layer between the two image layers. Then press the letter B to get the Brush tool, and click on the down-facing arrow next to the Brush thumbnail in the Options Bar. Choose a medium-size, soft-edged brush from the Brush Picker that appears. Now, press the letter D to set your Foreground color to black, and start painting over the areas of the photo that you want to be darker (in this case, the sky). As you paint, the sky is revealed. (*Note:* If you make a mistake, press E to switch to the Eraser tool and begin erasing.)

Step Seven:

Keep going until you've painted the entire sky area in, so you have an image that your digital camera couldn't possibly have captured, because in a situation like this it's going to either expose for the ground or the sky, but not both. (*Note:* If you need to create a transition between the darker sky and lighter ground—like the hills in the distance here—lower the Brush tool's Opacity in the Options Bar.) If you want this "best of both worlds," where the sky and the subject/ground are perfectly exposed, you'll have to pull it off here in Photoshop Elements, but that's not a bad thing. In fact, it totally rocks (sorry, I mean "that's fascinating"). By taking these few extra steps, you'll wind up with an image like the one shown below—one where the subject and background are perfectly exposed—it's the best of two photos combined.

Before   *After*

Saving RAW Files in Adobe's Digital Negative (DNG) Format

At this point in time, there's a concern with the RAW file format because there's not a single, universal format for RAW images—every digital camera manufacturer has its own. That may not seem like a problem, but what happens if one of these camera companies stops developing or supporting a format and switches to something else? Seriously, what if a few years from now there was no easy way to open your saved RAW files? Adobe recognized this problem and created the Digital Negative (DNG) format for long-term archival storage of RAW images.

Step One:

As of the writing of this book, only a few major camera manufacturers have built in the ability to save RAW files in Adobe's DNG format (although we believe it's only a matter of time before they all do); so if your camera doesn't support DNG files yet—no sweat—you can save your RAW file to Adobe DNG format from right within the Camera Raw dialog. Just open your image in Camera Raw and hit the Save button. This brings up the Save Options dialog, which saves your RAW file to DNG by default.

Step Two:

At the bottom of this dialog, you have some additional DNG options: You can choose to embed the original RAW file into your DNG (making the file larger, but your original is embedded for safe-keeping in case you ever need to extract it—and if you have the hard disk [or CD] space—go for it!). There's a compression option (and it's "lossless," meaning you don't lose quality like you do with JPEG compression). You can also choose to include a JPEG preview with your DNG file. That's it—click Save and you've got a DNG archival-quality file that can be opened by Photoshop Elements (or the free DNG utility from Adobe).

Many high-end pro photographers want to work in 16-bit depth as much as possible because it maintains more tonal quality than 8-bit. Although Elements 5 supports opening RAW images and working in 16-bit depth, what you can do is very limited. In fact, you're basically limited to tonal adjustments because features such as layers, most filters, and a host of other cool features are not available at all when working in 16-bit—you have to convert to 8-bit to get Elements' full feature set back. Is 16-bit really that much better? It's a matter of constant debate among photographers.

Working with 16-Bit Images

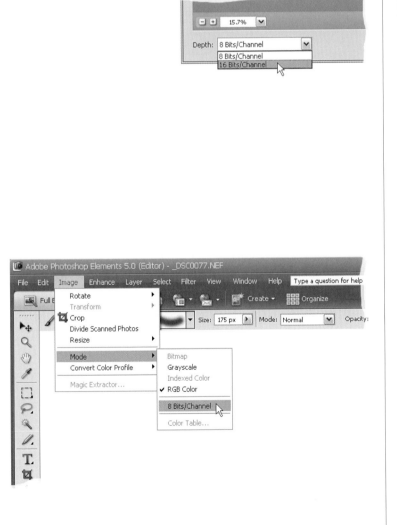

Step One:
You have to start by opening an image in a "high-bit" format (like RAW) to be able to create a real 16-bit image (go to File, choose Open, and navigate to your RAW file). Opening a regular 8-bit JPEG image and then converting it to 16-bit depth won't add quality that wasn't there in the first place. You have to start with a RAW image, then you can decide whether you want to continue working in 16-bit or process the file as a regular 8-bit image. Choose your bit-depth setting from the Depth pop-up menu in the bottom-left corner of the Camera Raw dialog.

Step Two:
If you choose to process the image as a 16-bit image and click Open in the Camera Raw dialog, take a quick look under the Elements Editor's Filter menu and you'll see how few filters are available to you. Pretty much all of Elements will feel this same way—almost everything's grayed out (you can't access it). However, after you've made your tonal adjustments in 16-bit mode, you can convert to 8-bit mode by going under the Image menu, under Mode, and choosing 8 Bits/Channel.

Black & White Conversions in Camera Raw

One of the easiest ways to make great black-and-white photos (from your color images) is to do your conversion completely within Camera Raw. You're basically just three sliders away from a stunning black-and-white photo, and then all you have left to do is finish off the image by opening it in Photoshop Elements 5, and adding some sharpening. Here's how it's done:

Step One:
Start by opening a RAW photo you want to convert to black and white. You can use the Auto settings or adjust the Exposure and Brightness sliders to get a more balanced looking photo overall, but leave the rest of the sliders alone for now.

Step Two:
The first step in converting to black and white is to remove the color from the photo. Go to the Saturation slider and drag it all the way to the left (as shown here). Although this removes all the color, it usually makes for a pretty flat-looking (read as: lame) black-and-white photo, so in the next two steps we'll add back in the missing contrast and depth that we want from our black-and-white prints.

Step Three:

Now, go to the Shadows slider and drag it to the right until you get very rich looking shadows. One of the characteristics of great black-and-white prints is that they have deep rich blacks, and bright crisp whites, so don't be shy when you're dragging this slider to the right.

Step Four:

The final step is to add extra contrast by (you guessed it) dragging the Contrast slider to the right until the photo gets real contrasty (as shown here). Now, that's pretty much it, but if you feel the photo needs some tweaking, here's what to check: first check the Exposure slider and make sure you've brightened the highlights enough. If you're afraid you might blow out the highlights by dragging too far to the right, then turn on the Highlights checkbox at the top of the dialog. As you drag to the right, if you start to see areas turning red, you've dragged too far. The other thing you might try is going through each of the White Balance settings (in the White Balance pop-up menu) to see how they affect your black-and-white photo. You'll be amazed at how this little change can pay off (make sure you try Fluorescent and Tungsten— they often look great in black-and-white).

Super Size Me
resizing and cropping

If a chapter on resizing and cropping doesn't sound exciting, really, what does? It's sad, but a good portion of our lives is spent doing just that—resizing and cropping. Why is that? It's because nothing, and I mean nothing, is ever the right size. Think about it. If everything were already the right size, there'd be no opportunity to "Super Size" it. You'd go to McDonald's, order an Extra Value Meal, and instead of hearing, "Would you care to Super Size your order?" there would just be a long uncomfortable pause. And frankly, I'm uncomfortable enough at the McDonald's drive-thru, what with all the cropping and resizing I'm constantly doing. Anyway, although having a chapter on cropping and resizing isn't the kind of thing that sells books (though I hear books on crop circles do fairly well), both are impor-

tant and necessary, especially if you ever plan on cropping or resizing things in Elements. Actually, you'll be happy to learn that I "Super Sized" the chapter with other cool techniques that honestly are probably a bit too cool to wind up in a chapter called "Resizing and Cropping," but it's the only place they'd fit. But don't let the extra techniques throw you; if this chapter seems too long to you, flip to the end of the chapter, rip out a few pages, and you have effectively cropped the chapter down to size. (And by ripping the pages out yourself, you have transformed what was originally a mere book into an "interactive experience," which thereby enhances the value of the book, making you feel like a pretty darn smart shopper.) See, it almost makes you want to read it now, doesn't it?

Cropping Photos

After you've sorted your images in the Organizer, one of the first editing tasks you'll probably undertake is cropping a photo. There are a number of different ways to crop a photo in Elements. We'll start with the basic garden-variety options, and then we'll look at some ways to make the task faster and easier.

Step One:
Open the image you want to crop in the Elements Editor, and then press the letter C to get the Crop tool (you could always select the tool directly from the Toolbox, but I only recommend doing so if you're charging by the hour).

Step Two:
Click within your photo and drag out a cropping border. The area to be cropped away will appear dimmed (shaded). You don't have to worry about getting your cropping border right when you first drag it out, because you can edit it by dragging the control handles that appear in each corner and at the center of each side.

TIP: If you don't like seeing your photo with the cropped-away areas appearing shaded (as in the previous step), you can toggle this shading feature off/on by pressing the Forward Slash key (/) on your keyboard. When you press the Forward Slash key, the border remains in place but the shading is turned off.

Step Three:
While you have the cropping border in place, you can rotate the entire border. Just move your cursor outside the border, and your cursor will change into a double-headed arrow. Just click-and-drag, and the cropping border will rotate in the direction that you drag. (This is a great way to save time if you have a crooked image, because it lets you crop and rotate at the same time.)

Continued

Step Four:

Once you have the cropping border where you want it, click on the green checkmark icon at the bottom-right corner of your cropping border, or just press the Enter key on your keyboard. To cancel your crop, click the red international symbol for "No Way!" at the bottom-right corner of the cropping border, or press the Escape key on your keyboard.

Before

After

The "rule of thirds" is a trick that photographers sometimes use to create more interesting compositions. Basically, you visually divide the image you see in your camera's viewfinder into thirds, and then you position your horizon so it goes along either the top imaginary horizontal line or the bottom one. Then, you position the subject (or focal point) at the center intersections of those lines. But if you didn't use the rule in the viewfinder—no sweat! Here's how to crop your image using the rule of thirds to create more appealing compositions in Elements 5:

Cropping Using the "Rule of Thirds"

SCOTT KELBY

Step One:
Open the photo to which you want to apply the rule-of-thirds cropping technique (the shot here is poorly composed, with the egret smack dab in the center of the image—it just screams "snapshot!"). Since this is a cropping technique, you realize that the dimensions of your photo are going to get smaller, right? Good. So create a new document that is somewhat smaller than the photo you want, but using the same resolution and color mode (this is very important, otherwise your image won't fit properly in this new document). In the example here, my original photo is about 12x8", so the new document I created is only 9x7"; that way, there's room to play with my cropping (you'll see how in just a moment).

Step Two:
While your new document is active, go under the Edit menu, under Preferences, and choose Grid. In the resulting dialog, enter 33.33 in the Gridline Every field, and then choose Percent from the pop-up menu on the right. In the Subdivisions field, change the default setting of 4 to just 1, and then click OK. You won't see anything in your document yet.

Continued

Step Three:

Go under the View menu and choose Grid. When you do this, the nonprinting grid you created in the previous step (the one divided into horizontal and vertical thirds) will appear in your image area as a visual representation of the rule-of-thirds grid, which you'll use for visual composition cropping.

Step Four:

Return to your image document, press V to switch to the Move tool, and click-and-drag your image onto your blank document. Here's where you create a better composition: Using the Move tool, position your image's horizon along one of the horizontal grid lines (here I used the top line), and be sure your focal point (the egret in this case) falls on one of the intersecting points (the top-right intersection in this example). Because your image is larger than the new document, you have plenty of room to position your photo.

Step Five:

You can now crop away the sides of your image. Press the letter C to switch to the Crop tool and click-and-drag around your entire image. With your cropping border in place, press Enter to complete your crop. Now just hide the grid lines by returning to the View menu and deselecting Grid—then enjoy your new, cropped image.

Before

After

Auto-Cropping to Standard Sizes

If you're outputting photos for clients, chances are they're going to want them in standard sizes so they can easily find frames to fit. If that's the case, here's how to crop your photos to a predetermined size (like a 5x7", 8x10", etc.).

Step One:

Open an image in the Elements Editor that you want to crop to be a perfect 5x7" (or in this case, 7x5" because our image is horizontal). Press C to get the Crop tool, then go to the Options Bar, and from the Aspect Ratio pop-up menu, click on the words "No Restriction." When the list of preset crop sizes appears, click on 5x7 in.

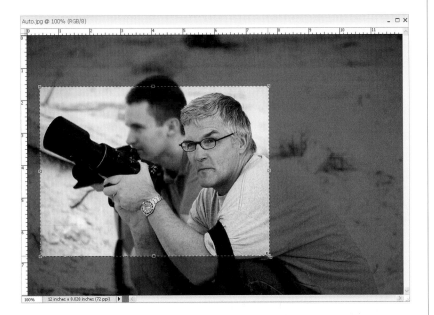

Step Two:
Now click-and-drag the Crop tool over the portion of the photo that you want to be 5x7" (or if your image is horizontal, Elements will automatically adjust your border to 7x5", as it did here). While dragging, you can press-and-hold the Spacebar to adjust the position of your border. Once it's set, press the Enter key and the area inside your cropping border will become 5x7".

Before

After

Cropping to an Exact Custom Size

Okay, now you know how to crop to Elements' built-in preset sizes, but how do you crop to a nonstandard size—a custom size that you determine? Here's how:

Step One:

Open the photo that you want to crop in the Elements Editor. (I want to crop this image to 8x6".) First, press C to get the Crop tool. In the Options Bar, you'll see fields for Width and Height. Enter the size you want for Width, followed by the unit of measure you want to use (e.g., enter "in" for inches, "px" for pixels, "cm" for centimeters, "mm" for millimeters, etc.). Next, press the Tab key to jump over to the Height field and enter your desired height, again followed by the unit of measure.

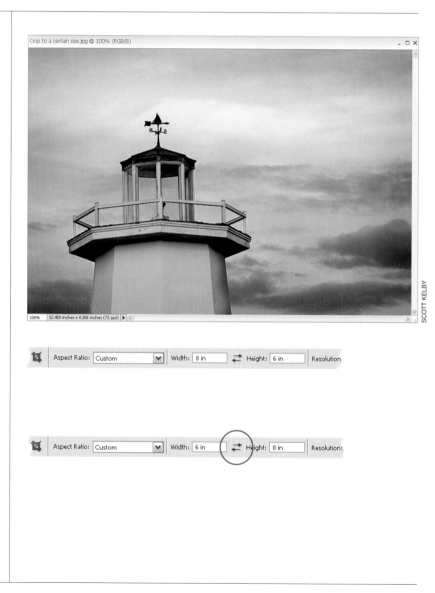

TIP: You can swap the figures in the Height and Width fields by clicking on the Swaps icon between the fields in the Options Bar.

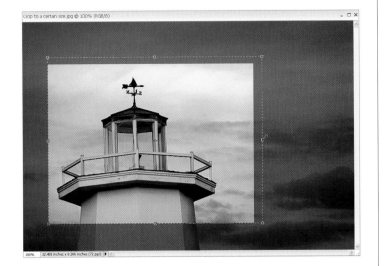

Step Two:
Once you've entered these figures in the Options Bar, click within your photo with the Crop tool and drag out a cropping border. You'll notice that as you drag, the border is constrained to an 8x6" aspect ratio; no matter how large of an area you select within your image, the area within that border will become your specified size. When you release your mouse button, you'll still have both side handles and corner handles visible, but the side handles will act like corner handles to keep your size constrained.

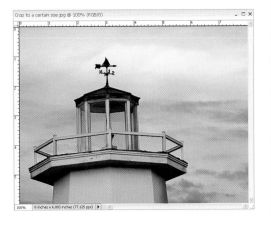

Step Three:
Once your cropping border is onscreen, you can resize it using the corner handles or you can reposition it by moving your cursor inside the border. Your cursor will change to a Move arrow, and you can now click-and-drag the border into place. You can also use the arrow keys on your keyboard for more precise control. When it looks right to you, press Enter to finalize your crop or click on the checkmark icon in the bottom-right corner of your cropping border. (I made the rulers visible [Control-Shift-R] so you could see that the image measures exactly 8x6".)

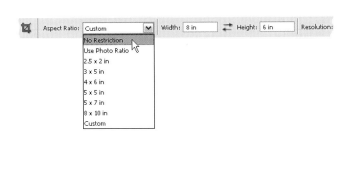

TIP: Once you've entered a Width and Height in the Options Bar, those dimensions will remain there. To clear the fields, just choose No Restriction from the Aspect Ratio pop-up menu. This will clear the Width and Height fields, and now you can use the Crop tool for freeform cropping (you can drag it in any direction—it's no longer constrained to your specified size).

Continued

COOLER TIP: If you already have a cropping border in place, you can change your dimensions without re-creating the border. All you have to do is enter the new sizes you want in the Width and Height fields in the Options Bar, and Elements 5 will resize your cropping border.

Before   *After*

Elements 5 has a cool feature that lets you crop your photo into a pre-designed shape (like putting a wedding photo into a heart shape), but even cooler are the edge effects you can create by cropping into one of the pre-designed edge effects that look like old Polaroid transfers. Here's how to put this feature to use to add visual interest to your own photos (of course, you can use the heart shape and do the whole wedding photo thing, but that's so "five-minutes-ago").

Cropping into a Shape

Step One:
In the Elements Editor, open the photo you want to crop into a pre-designed shape, and press the letter Q to get the Cookie Cutter tool.

Step Two:
Now, go up to the Options Bar and click on the down-facing arrow to the right of the word "Shape." This brings up the Custom Shape Picker, which contains the default set of 30 shapes. To load more shapes, click on the right-facing arrow at the top right of the Picker and a list of built-in shape sets will appear. From this list, choose Crop Shapes to load the edge-effect shapes, which automatically crop away areas outside your custom edges.

Continued

Step Three:

Once you find the custom edge shape you want to use from the Custom Shape Picker, just click-and-drag it over your image to the size you want it. When you release the mouse button, your photo is cropped to fit within the shape. *Note:* I like Crop Shape 10 (which is shown here) for something simple, and Crop Shape 21 for something a little wilder. The key thing here is to experiment and try different crop shapes to find your favorite.

Step Four:

You'll see a bounding box around the shape, which you can use to resize, rotate, or otherwise mess with your shape. To resize your shape, hold the Shift key to keep it proportional while you drag a corner point. To rotate the shape, move your cursor outside the bounding box until your cursor becomes a double-sided arrow, and then click-and-drag. As long as you see that bounding box, you can still edit the shape. When it looks good to you, press Enter and the parts of your photo outside that shape will be permanently cropped away.

TIP: If you want your image area tightly cropped, so it's the exact size of the shape you drag out, just turn on the Cookie Cutter's Crop checkbox (up in the Options Bar) *before* you drag out your shape. Then when you press Enter to lock in your final shape, Elements will tightly crop the entire image area to the size of your shape. *Note:* The checkerboard pattern you see around the photo is letting you know that the background around the shape is transparent. If you want a white background behind the shape, click on the Create a New Layer icon at the top of the Layers palette, and then drag your new layer below the Shape layer. Press D then X to set your Foreground to white, then press Alt-Backspace to fill this layer with white.

Before

After

Cropping without the Crop Tool

Sometimes it's quicker to crop your photo using some of Elements' other tools and features than it is to reach for the Crop tool every time you need a simple crop. This is the method I probably use the most for cropping images of all kinds (primarily when I'm not trying to make a perfect 5x7", 8x10", etc.—I'm basically just "eyeing" it).

Step One:
Start by opening a photo in the Elements Editor that you need to crop, and press M to get the Rectangular Marquee tool from the Toolbox. (I use this tool so much that I usually don't have to switch to it—maybe that's why I use this method all the time.) Drag out a selection around the area you want to keep (leaving all the other areas outside the selection that you want cropped away).

Step Two:
Choose Crop from the Image menu. When you choose Crop, the image is immediately cropped. There are no crop handles, no dialogs—bang—it just gets cropped—down and dirty, and that's why I like it. Just press Control-D to deselect.

TIP: One instance where you'll often use the Crop command from the Image menu is when you're creating collages. When you drag photos from other documents onto your main document and position them within your collage, any parts of the images that extend beyond the document borders are actually still there. So to keep your file size manageable, choose All from the Select menu or press Control-A, then choose Crop from the Image menu. This deletes all the excess layer data that extends beyond the image border and brings your file size back in line. To deselect, press Control-D.

Before   *After*

Using the Crop Tool to Add More Canvas Area

I know the heading for this technique doesn't make much sense—"Using the Crop Tool to Add More Canvas Area." How can the Crop tool (which is designed to crop photos to smaller sizes) actually make the canvas area (white space) around your photo larger? That's what I'm going to show you.

Step One:
In the Elements Editor, open the image to which you want to add additional blank canvas area. Press the letter D to set your Background color to its default white.

Step Two:
If you're in Maximize Mode, press Control-Minus to zoom out a bit (so your image doesn't take up your whole screen). If you're not in Maximize Mode, click-and-drag out the bottom corner of the document window to see the gray desktop area around your image. (To enter Maximize Mode, click the Maximize Mode icon in the top-right corner of the image window or go under the Window menu, under Images, and choose Maximize Mode.)

Step Three:
Press the letter C to switch to the Crop tool and drag out a cropping border to any random size (it doesn't matter how big or little it is at this point).

Step Four:
Now, grab any one of the side or corner points and drag outside the image area, out into the gray area that surrounds your image. The cropping border extending outside the image is the area that will be added as white canvas space, so position it where you want to add the blank canvas space.

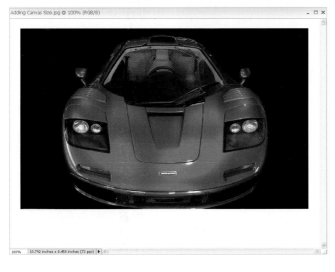

Step Five:
Now, just press the Enter key to finalize your crop, and when you do, the area outside your image will become white canvas area.

Auto-Cropping Gang-Scanned Photos

A lot of photographers scan photos using a technique called "gang scanning." That's a fancy name for scanning more than one picture at a time. Scanning three or four photos at once with your scanner saves time, but then you eventually have to separate these photos into individual documents. Here's how to have Elements 5 do that for you automatically.

Step One:
Place the photos you want to "gang scan" on the bed of your flatbed scanner, and scan the images into Elements using the Organizer (they'll appear in one Elements document). You can access the scanned images by clicking on the Get Photos button in the Organizer's task bar. Choose From Scanner from the pop-up menu, and in the dialog that appears, select where and at what quality you want to save your scanned document.

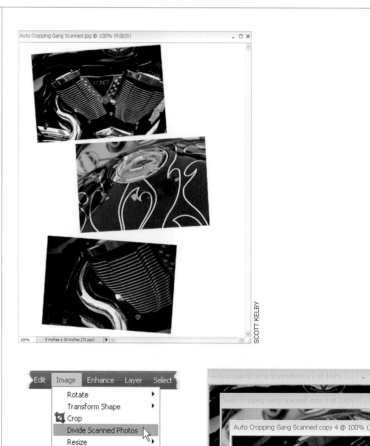

Step Two:
Once your images appear as one document in the Editor, go under the Image menu and choose Divide Scanned Photos. It will immediately find the edges of the scanned photos, straighten them if necessary, and then put each photo into its own separate document. Once it has "done its thing," you can close the original gang-scanned document, and you'll be left with just the individual documents.

In Elements 5 there's a simple way to straighten photos, but it's knowing how to set the options for the tool that makes your job dramatically easier. Here's how it's done:

Straightening Photos with the Straighten Tool

Step One:
Open the photo that needs straightening. The photo shown here looks like the sidewalk is sloping down to the left.

Step Two:
Choose the Straighten tool from the Toolbox (or just press the P key).

Continued

Step Three:

Take the Straighten tool and drag it along an edge in the photo that you think should be perfectly horizontal, like a horizon line (although in this case, we dragged out the tool along the edge of the sidewalk).

Step Four:

When you release the mouse button, the image is straightened, but as you can see here, the straightening created a problem of its own—the photo now has to be re-cropped because the edges are showing a white background (as the image was rotated until it was straight). That's where the options (which I mentioned in the intro to this technique) come in. You see, the default setting does just what you see here—it rotates the image and leaves it up to you to crop away the mess. However, you can have Elements do the work for you (as you'll see in the next step).

Step Five:
Once you click on the Straighten tool, go up to the Options Bar, and in the Canvas Options pop-up menu, choose Crop to Remove Background.

Step Six:
Now when you drag out the tool and release the mouse, not only is the photo straightened, but the annoying white background is automatically cropped away, giving you the clean result you see here.

TIP: In this example, we used the Straighten tool to straighten our image along a horizontal plane, but if you wanted to straighten the photo using a vertical object instead (like a column or light pole), just press-and-hold the Control key before you drag the Straighten tool, and that will do the trick.

Straightening Crooked Photos

If you hold your digital camera by hand for most of your shots rather than using a tripod, you can be sure that some of your photos are going to come out a bit crooked. Well, I have good news and bad news. First, the good news: Elements has a built-in function for straightening crooked images. Now, the bad news: It doesn't always work. That's why I included a pretty slick workaround for when the auto-straighten function doesn't work.

Automated Straightening

Step One (The Only One):
Open the photo that needs straightening. To use Elements' automated straightening (which works fairly well in many cases), simply go under the Image menu, under Rotate, and choose Straighten Image. If it can find a straight edge, it'll straighten your image (well, most of the time). *Note:* Oftentimes when the image is rotated, you'll see white canvas area around the image, so if you want to straighten and crop at the same time, choose (do I even have to say it?) Straighten and Crop Image from the Image menu, under Rotate. That does it (there is no Step Two).

Manual Straightening

Step One:
Open the photo that needs straightening. Go under the Window menu and choose Info to bring up the Info palette.

Step Two:
Next choose the Line tool from Elements' Toolbox. (It's in the Custom Shape tool's flyout menu just below the Gradient tool. You can press the letter U to cycle through the Custom Shape tools until you get the Line tool.)

Step Three:
Find a straight edge in your photo that is supposed to be horizontal (such as the horizon, a table, a window, etc.—anything that you think should be horizontal). Click-and-drag the Line tool along this straight edge in your photo, starting from the left and extending right, but don't let go of the mouse button (that's important).

Step Four:
While you're still holding down the mouse button, look over on the right side of the Info palette, and third from the top is the letter "A" representing "Angle." Look at the amount and remember that number. Now you can release the mouse button.

Continued

Step Five:

Using the Line tool in this fashion creates a Shape layer, so press Control-Z to undo this layer (it's no longer needed). Next, go under the Image menu, under Rotate, and choose Custom to bring up the Rotate Canvas dialog. Recall that angle you were supposed to remember? That goes in the Angle field in this dialog. You also have to click on the radio button for whether it should rotate to the Right or Left, then click OK and whammo! (whammo! being a technical term); your image is straightened. *Note:* If the rotation leaves white space near the image's corners, you can crop your image with the Crop tool (C). Click-and-drag the tool avoiding the white space and press Enter to finalize the crop.

Before

After

If you're more familiar with resizing scanned images, you'll find that resizing images from digital cameras is a bit different, primarily because scanners create high-resolution scans (usually 300 ppi or more), but the default setting for most digital cameras usually produces an image that is large in physical dimension, but lower in ppi (usually 72 ppi). The trick is to decrease the physical size of your digital camera image (and increase its resolution) without losing any quality in your photo. Here's the trick:

Resizing Digital Camera Photos

Step One:
Open the digital camera image that you want to resize. Press Control-Shift-R to make Elements' rulers visible. Check out the rulers to see the approximate dimensions of your image. As you can see from the rulers in the example here, this photo is around 12x8".

Step Two:
Go under the Image menu, under Resize, and choose Image Size to bring up the Image Size dialog. Under the Document Size section, the Resolution setting is 72 pixels/inch (ppi). A resolution of 72 ppi is considered "low resolution" and is ideal for photos that will only be viewed onscreen (such as Web graphics, slide shows, etc.). This res is too low to get high-quality results from a color inkjet printer, color laser printer, or for use on a printing press.

Continued

Step Three:

If we plan to output this photo to any printing device, it's pretty clear that we'll need to increase the resolution to get good results. I wish we could just type in the resolution we'd like it to be in the Resolution field (such as 200 or 300 ppi), but unfortunately, this "resampling" makes our low-res photo appear soft (blurry) and pixelated. That's why we need to turn off the Resample Image checkbox (it's on by default). That way, when we type in the setting that we need in the Resolution field, Elements automatically adjusts the Width and Height fields for the image in the exact same proportion. As your Width and Height decrease (with Resample Image turned off), your Resolution increases. Best of all, there's absolutely no loss of quality. Pretty cool!

Step Four:

Here I've turned off Resample Image, then I typed 150 in the Resolution field (for output to a color inkjet printer— I know, you probably think you need a lot more resolution, but you usually don't). At a resolution of only 150 ppi, I can actually print a photo that is about 6 inches wide by 4 inches high.

Step Five:
Here's the Image Size dialog for my source photo, and this time I've increased the Resolution setting to 212 ppi (for output to a printing press; again, you don't need nearly as much resolution as you'd think). As you can see, the Width and Height fields for my image have changed.

Step Six:
When you click OK, you won't see the image window change at all—it will appear at the exact same size onscreen. But now look at the rulers—you can see that your image's dimensions have changed. Resizing using this technique does three big things: (1) It gets your physical dimensions down to size (the photo now fits on an 8x10" sheet); (2) it increases the resolution enough so you can even output this image on a printing press; and (3) you haven't softened or pixelated the image in any way—the quality remains the same—all because you turned off Resample Image. *Note:* Do not turn off Resample Image for images that you scan on a scanner—they start as high-res images in the first place. Turning off Resample Image is only for photos taken with a digital camera.

Resizing and How to Reach Those Hidden Free Transform Handles

What happens if you drag a large photo onto a smaller photo in Elements? (This happens all the time, especially if you're collaging or combining two or more photos.) You have to resize the photo using Free Transform, right? Right. But here's the catch—when you bring up Free Transform, at least two (or, more likely, all four) of the handles that you need to resize the image are out of reach. You see the center point, but not the handles you need to reach to resize. Here's how to get around that hurdle quickly and easily.

Step One:

Open two photos in the Elements Editor. Use the Move tool (V) to drag-and-drop one photo on top of the other (if you're in Maximize Mode, drag one image onto the other image's thumbnail in the Photo Bin). To resize a photo on a layer, press Control-T to bring up the Free Transform command. Next, hold the Shift key (to constrain your proportions), grab one of the Free Transform corner points, and (a) drag inward to shrink the photo, or (b) drag outward to increase its size (not more than 20%, to keep from making the photo look soft and pixelated). But wait, there's a problem. The problem is—you can't even see the Free Transform handles in this image.

Step Two:

To instantly have full access to all of Free Transform's handles, just press Control-0 (zero), and Elements will instantly zoom out of your document window and surround your photo with gray desktop, making every handle well within reach. Try it once, and you'll use this trick again and again. *Note:* You must choose Free Transform first for this trick to work.

Making Your Photos Smaller (Downsizing)

There are a different set of rules we use for maintaining as much quality as possible when making an image smaller, and there are a couple of different ways to do just that (we'll cover the two main ones here). Luckily, maintaining image quality is much easier when sizing down than when scaling up (in fact, photos often look dramatically better—and sharper—when scaled down, especially if you follow these guidelines).

Downsizing photos where the resolution is already 300 ppi:
Although earlier we discussed how to change image size if your digital camera gives you 72-ppi images, with large physical dimensions (like 24x42" deep), what do you do if your camera gives you 300-ppi images at smaller physical dimensions (like a 10x6" at 300 ppi)? Basically, you turn on Resample Image (in the Image Size dialog under the Image menu, under Resize), then simply type the desired size (in this example, we want a 4x6" final image size), and click OK (don't change the Resolution setting, just click OK). The image will be scaled down to size, and the resolution will remain at 300 ppi. IMPORTANT: When you scale down using this method, it's likely that the image will soften a little bit, so after scaling you'll want to apply the Unsharp Mask filter to bring back any sharpness lost in the resizing (look at the sharpening chapter to see what settings to use).

Continued

Making one photo smaller without shrinking the whole document:

If you're working with more than one image in the same document, you'll resize a bit differently. To scale down a photo on a layer, first click on that photo's layer in the Layers palette, then press Control-T to bring up Free Transform. Pressing-and-holding the Shift key (to keep the photo proportional), grab a corner point and drag inward. When it looks good to you, press the Enter key. If the image looks softer after resizing it, apply the Unsharp Mask filter (again, see the sharpening chapter).

Resizing problems when dragging between documents:

This one gets a lot of people, because at first glance it just doesn't make sense. You have two documents, approximately the same size, side-by-side onscreen. But when you drag a 72-ppi photo (of my buddy Matt Kloskowski, in this case) onto a 300-ppi document (Untitled-1), the photo appears really small. Why is that? Simply put: resolution. Although the documents appear to be the same size, they're not. The tip-off that you're not really seeing them at the same size is found in the title bar of each photo. For instance, the photo of Matt is displayed at 100%, but the Untitled-1 document is displayed at only 25%. So, to get more predictable results, make sure both documents are at the same viewing size and resolution (check in the Image Size dialog under the Image menu, under Resize).

This is a resizing technique I learned from my friend (and world-famous nature photographer) Vincent Versace. His poster-sized prints (24x36") always look so sharp and crisp—but we're both shooting with the same 6-megapixel camera—so I had to ask him his secret. I figured he was using some scaling plug-in, but he said he does the whole thing when editing his images. My thanks to Vinny for sharing his simple, yet brilliant technique with me, so I could share it with you.

Rule-Breaking Resizing for Poster-Sized Prints

Step One:
Open the photo you want to resize, then go under the Image menu, under Resize, and choose Image Size, or use the keyboard shortcut Control-Alt-I.

Step Two:
Type in the dimensions you want as your final print size. My original width for my 6-megapixel image is just a hair over 10", so when I type 36" for the Width, the Height field will automatically adjust to around 24" (the Width and Height are linked proportionally by default—adjust one and the other adjusts in kind). Of course, not all images scale perfectly, so depending on how many megapixels your camera is, you may not be able to get exactly 24" (and in fact, you may not want to go that big, but if you do, you might need to enter more than 36" to make your Height reach 24", and then you can go back and crop your Width down to 36" [see the "Cropping to an Exact Custom Size" technique earlier in this chapter]).

Continued

Step Three:

Once your size is in place, you'll need to adjust your resolution upward, so go to the Resolution field and enter 360. Now, you know and I know that this goes against every tried-and-true rule of resolution, and breaks the "never-just-type-in-a-higher-number-with-the-Resample-Image-checkbox-turned-on" rule that we all live and die by, but stick with me on this one—you've got to try it to believe it. So, type it in, grit your teeth, but don't click OK yet.

Step Four:

Adobe introduced some new sampling algorithms for resizing images, and according to Vincent's research, the key to this resizing technique is to not use the sampling method Adobe recommends (which is Bicubic Smoother). Instead, choose Bicubic Sharper in the Resample Image pop-up menu, which actually provides better results—so much so that Vincent claims the printed results are not only just as good, but perhaps better than those produced by the expensive, fancy-schmancy upsizing plug-ins.

Step Five:

I've tried this technique numerous times, and I have to say—the results are pretty stunning. But don't take my word for it—click OK, print it out, and see for yourself. Here's the final image resized to 36x24" (you can see the size using the rulers by pressing Control-Shift-R).

Elements has a pretty slick little utility that lets you take a folder full of images and do any (or all) of the following automatically at one time: (1) rename them; (2) resize them; (3) change their resolution; (4) color correct and sharpen them; and (5) save them in the file format of your choice (JPEG, TIFF, etc.). If you find yourself processing a lot of images, this can save a ton of time. Better yet, since the whole process is automated, you can teach someone else to do the processing for you, like your spouse, your child, a neighbor's child, passersby, local officials, etc.

Automated Saving and Resizing

Step One:
In the Elements Editor, go under the File menu and choose Process Multiple Files.

Step Two:
When the Process Multiple Files dialog opens, the first thing you have to do is choose the folder of photos you want to process by clicking on the Source Browse button in the first section of the dialog. Then navigate to the folder you want and click OK. If you already have some photos open in Elements, you can choose Opened Files from the Process Files From pop-up menu (or you can choose Import to import files). Then, in the second field, you decide whether you want the new copies to be saved in the same folder (by clicking the Same as Source checkbox), or copied into a different folder (in which case, click on the Destination Browse button and choose that folder).

Continued

Step Three:

The second section is File Naming. If you want your files automatically renamed when they're processed, turn on the Rename Files checkbox, then in the fields directly below that checkbox, type the name you want these new files to have and choose how you want the numbering to appear after the name (a two-digit number, three-digit, etc.). Then, choose the number with which you want to start numbering images. You'll see a preview of how your file naming will appear just below the Document Name field.

Step Four:

In the Image Size section, you decide if you want to resize the images (by turning on the Resize Images checkbox), and you enter the width and height you want for your finished photos. You can also choose to change the resolution if you like. Then, if you want to change their file type (like from RAW to JPEG High Quality), you choose that in the bottom section—File Type. Just turn on the Convert Files To checkbox, and then choose your format from the pop-up menu. On the right side of the dialog, there is a list of Quick Fix cosmetic changes you can make to these photos as well, including Auto Levels (to adjust the overall color balance and contrast), Auto Contrast (this is kind of lame if you ask me), Auto Color (it's not bad), and Sharpen (it works well). Click OK and it does its thing, totally automated based on the choices you made in this dialog. How cool is that!

Color Me Badd
color correction for photographers

The subtitle for this chapter is "Color Correction for Photographers," which invites the question "How is color correction for photographers different from color correction for anybody else?" Actually, it's quite a bit different, because photographers generally work in RGB or black and white. And in reality, digital photographers mostly work in RGB because, although we can manage to build reusable spacecraft and have GPS satellites orbiting in space so golfers here on earth know how far it is from their golf cart to the green, for some reason creating a color inkjet printer that prints a decent black-and-white print is still apparently beyond our grasp. Don't get me started. Anyway, this chapter isn't entirely about black-and-white prints,

and now that I think about it, I'm sorry I brought it up in the first place. So forget I ever mentioned it, and let's talk about color correction. Why do we even need color correction? Honestly, it's a technology thing. Even with traditional film cameras, every photo needs some sort of color tweaking (either during processing or afterward in Elements), because if it didn't need some correction, we'd have about 30-something pages in this book that would be blank, and that would make my publisher pretty hopping mad. So, for the sake of sheer page count, let's all be glad that we don't live in an ideal world where every photo comes out perfect and 6-megapixel cameras are only 200 bucks and come with free 1-GB memory cards.

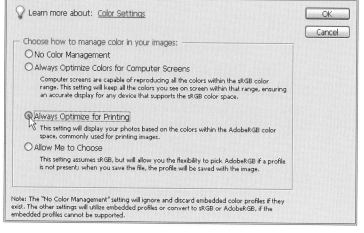

Before You Color Correct Anything, Do This First!

Before you color correct even a single photo, you need to consider a couple of settings that can affect the results you'll get. It's important to note that the changes you make will remain as your defaults until you change them again, and that (particularly with Color Settings) you may change your settings from time to time based on individual projects.

Step One:
From the Edit menu, choose Color Settings (or press Control-Shift-K).

Step Two:
In the Color Settings dialog, choose from the four options: No Color Management, Always Optimize Colors for Computer Screens, Always Optimize for Printing, or Allow Me to Choose. To a large degree, your choice will depend on your final output; but for photographers, I recommend using Always Optimize for Printing because it reproduces such a wide gamut of colors using the Adobe RGB profile (if your photos don't already have a profile assigned), and it's ideal if your photos will wind up in print. *Note:* For more on color management, see Chapter 14.

Step Three:

Now we're moving to a completely different area. Press the letter I to switch to the Eyedropper tool. In the Options Bar, the Sample Size setting for this tool (Point Sample) is fine for using the Eyedropper to steal a color from within a photo and making it your Foreground color. However, Point Sample doesn't work well when you're trying to read values in a particular area (such as flesh tones), because it gives you the reading from just one individual pixel, rather than an average reading of the surrounding area under your cursor.

Step Four:

For example, flesh tones are actually composed of dozens of different colored pixels (just zoom way in and you'll see what I mean); and if you're color correcting, you want a reading that's representative of the area under your Eyedropper, not just a single pixel within that area, which could hurt your correction decision-making. That's why you need to go to the Options Bar, under the Sample Size pop-up menu, and choose 3 by 3 Average. This changes the Eyedropper to give you a reading that's the average of 3 pixels across and 3 pixels down in the area that you're sampling. Once you've completed the changes on these two pages, it's safe to go ahead with the rest of the chapter and start correcting your photos.

Photo
Quick Fix

If you have a photo that has some serious problems (bad color, bad lighting, bad everything, etc.), and you have no experience with color correction or repairing other color or lighting nightmares, you'll love Elements 5's Quick Fix. It's where you go when you're not experienced at color correcting or fixing tonal problems, but you can see something's wrong with your photo and you want it fixed fast with the least amount of sweat. You'll eventually outgrow Quick Fix and want to use Levels and Unsharp Mask and all that cool stuff, but if you're new to Elements, Quick Fix can do a pretty decent job for ya.

Step One:
Open the photo that needs color correcting (in this example, our photo [shown below] needs the works—color correction, more contrast, and some sharpening). Then, click on the Quick Fix button at the top-left side of the task bar to enter the Quick Fix mode.

Step Two:
The Quick Fix window shows you side-by-side before-and-after versions of the photo you're about to correct (before on the top or left, after on the bottom or right). If you don't see this view, go to the View pop-up menu in the bottom left of the Quick Fix window and select Before and After (Portrait or Landscape). To the right of your side-by-side preview is a group of nested palettes offering tonal and lighting fixes you can perform on your photo. Start with the General Fixes palette at the top. The star of this palette is Smart Fix. Click the Auto button and Smart Fix will automatically analyze the photo and try to balance the overall tone (adjusting the shadows and highlights), fixing any obvious color casts while it's at it. In most cases this feature does a surprisingly good job. There's an Amount slider under Smart Fix that you can use to increase (or decrease) the effect of the Smart Fix.

TIP: By the way, you can also access the Auto Smart Fix command without entering Quick Fix mode by going under the Enhance menu and choosing Auto Smart Fix (or just press the keyboard shortcut Control-Alt-M). However, there are two advantages to applying the Smart Fix here in Quick Fix mode: (1) you get the Amount slider, which you don't get by just applying it from the menu or the shortcut; and (2) you get a side-by-side, before-and-after preview so you can see the results before you click OK. So if it turns out that you need additional fixes (or Smart Fix didn't work as well as you'd hoped), you're already in the right place.

Step Three:
If you apply Smart Fix and you're not happy with the results, don't try to stack more "fixes" on top of that—instead, click the Reset button that appears over the top-right corner of the After preview to reset the photo to how it looked when you first entered Quick Fix mode. If the color in your photo looks a little flat and needs more contrast, try the Auto button in the Levels category, found in the Lighting palette (the second palette down). I generally stay away from Auto Contrast, as Auto Levels seems to do a better job.

Continued

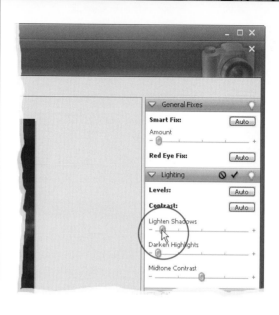

Step Four:
Besides Auto Contrast, there's another very powerful tool—the Lighten Shadows slider. Drag it to the right a bit, and watch how it opens up the dark shadow areas in your photo. Now, on to more Quick Fixing.

Step Five:
The next palette down, Color, has an Auto button that (surprisingly enough) tries to remove color casts and improve contrast like Smart Fix and Levels do, but it goes a step further by including a mid-tones correction that can help reduce color casts in the midtone areas of your photo. Hit the Reset button to remove any corrections that you've made up to this point, and then try the Auto button in the Color palette. See if the grays in the photo don't look grayer and less reddish. The sliders in the palette are mostly for creating special color effects (move the Hue slider and you'll see what I mean). You can pretty much ignore these sliders unless you want to get "freaky" with your photos.

Step Six:

After you've color corrected your photo (using the Auto buttons and the occasional slider), the final step is to sharpen your photo (by the way, to maintain the best quality, this should be the final step—the last thing you do in your correction process). Just click the Auto button in the Sharpen palette and watch the results. If the photo isn't sharp enough for you, drag the Amount slider to the right to increase the amount of sharpening, but be careful—oversharpening can ruin the photo by becoming too obvious, and it can introduce color shifts and "halos" around objects.

Step Seven:

There are a few other things you can do while you're here (think of this as a one-stop shop for quickly fixing images). Along the bottom of the window are icons you can click to rotate your photo (this photo doesn't need to be rotated, but hey, ya never know). In the General Fixes palette, there's an Auto Red Eye Fix if your photo needs it. If you don't like the results, try using the Red Eye Removal tool from the Toolbox on the left side of the window. Just click-and-drag over the problem area in your After preview for more red-eye control. Also, there are other tools: You know what the Zoom and Hand tools do (they zoom you in, and then move you around once you're zoomed in), but you can also crop your photo by using the Crop tool within the After preview, so go ahead and crop your photo down a bit.

Continued

Step Eight:

Okay, you've color corrected, fixed the contrast, sharpened your image, and even cropped it down to size. So how do you leave Quick Fix mode and return to regular Elements 5? Go to the left-hand corner of the task bar and click on the Full Edit button. That's basically the OK button—it applies all the changes to your photo and returns you to the normal editing mode.

Before

After

In previous versions of Elements, there were two ways to see a histogram. (A histogram is a graph showing the tonal range of your photo.) You could either view it when using Levels, or you could open a dialog that would display a histogram. But you could only view it in this dialog—it wasn't updated live as you made tonal adjustments. Starting in Elements 3, Adobe made the Histogram its own floating palette, so now you can have it open as you apply adjustments while in Full Edit mode. Plus, it shows you before-and-after readings before you click the OK button in a tonal adjustment dialog, such as the Adjust Smart Fix dialog.

Getting a Visual Readout (Histogram) of Your Corrections

Step One:
Open the photo that needs a tonal adjustment. Now, go under the Window menu and choose Histogram to open the Histogram palette. (By the way, this palette is only available in Elements 5's Full Edit mode—not in Quick Fix mode.)

Step Two:
Go under the Enhance menu and choose Auto Color Correction. Take a look in the floating Histogram palette and you'll see how the Auto Color Correction command affected the photo's histogram. *Note:* If you see a small symbol in the upper right-hand corner of the graph that looks like a tiny yellow yield sign with an exclamation point in it, that's a warning that the histogram you're seeing is not a new histogram—it's a previous histogram cached from memory. To see a fresh histogram, click directly on that warning symbol and a new reading will be generated based on your current adjustment.

Color Correcting Digital Camera Images

As far as digital technology has come, there's still one thing that digital cameras won't do—give you perfect color every time. In fact, if they gave us perfect color 50% of the time, that would be incredible, but unfortunately, every digital camera (and every scanner that captures traditional photos) sneaks some kind of color cast into your image. Generally, it's a red cast, but depending on the camera it could be blue. Either way, you can be pretty sure there's a cast. (Figure it this way—if there wasn't, the term "color correction" wouldn't be used.) Here's how to get your color in line:

Step One:
Open the digital camera photo you want to color correct. (The photo shown here doesn't look too bad, but as we go through the correction process, you'll see that, like most photos, it really needed a correction.)

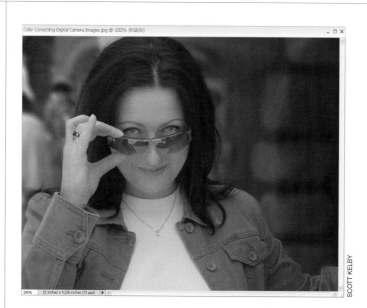

Step Two:
Go under the Enhance menu, under Adjust Lighting, and choose Levels (or press Control-L). The dialog may look intimidating at first, but the technique you're going to learn here requires no previous knowledge of Levels, and it's so easy, you'll be correcting photos using Levels immediately.

Step Three:

First, we need to set some preferences in the Levels dialog so we'll get the results we're after when we start correcting. We'll start by setting a target color for our shadow areas. To set this preference, in the Levels dialog, double-click on the black Eyedropper tool (it's on the lower right-hand side of the dialog, the first Eyedropper from the left). A Color Picker will appear asking you to "Select target shadow color." This is where we'll enter values that, when applied, will help remove any color casts your camera introduced in the shadow areas of your photo.

Step Four:

We're going to enter values in the R, G, and B (red, green, and blue) fields of this dialog.

For R, enter 10
For G, enter 10
For B, enter 10

TIP: To move from field to field, just press the Tab key.

Then click OK. Because these figures are evenly balanced (neutral), they help ensure that your shadow areas won't have too much of one color (which is exactly what causes a color cast—too much of one color).

Continued

Step Five:

Now we'll set a preference to make our highlight areas neutral. Double-click on the highlight Eyedropper (the third of the three Eyedroppers in the Levels dialog). The Color Picker will appear asking you to "Select target highlight color." Click in the R field, and then enter these values:

For R, enter 240
For G, enter 240
For B, enter 240

Then click OK to set those values as your highlight target.

Step Six:

Finally, set your midtone preference. You know the drill—double-click on the midtones Eyedropper (the middle of the three Eyedroppers) so you can "Select target midtone color." Enter these values in the R, G, and B fields (if they're not already there by default):

For R, enter 128
For G, enter 128
For B, enter 128

Then click OK to set those values as your midtone target.

Step Seven:

Okay, you've entered your preferences (target colors), so go ahead and click OK in the Levels dialog (without making any changes to your image). You'll get an alert dialog asking you if you want to "Save the new target colors as defaults?" Click Yes, and from that point on, you won't have to enter these values each time you correct a photo, because they'll already be entered for you—they're now the default settings.

Step Eight:

You're going to use these Eyedropper tools that reside in the Levels dialog to do most of your correction work. Your job is to determine where the shadow, mid-tone, and highlight areas are, and click the right Eyedropper in the right place (you'll learn how to do that in just a moment). So remember your job—find the shadow, midtone, and highlight areas and click the right Eyedropper in the right spot. Sounds easy, right? It is.

    You start by opening Levels and setting the shadows first, so you'll need to find an area in your photo that's supposed to be black. If you can't find something that's supposed to be the color black, then it gets a bit trickier—in the absence of something black, you have to determine which area in the image is the darkest. If you're not sure where the darkest part of the photo is, you can use the following trick to have Elements tell you exactly where it is.

Step Nine:

Go to the top of the Layers palette and click on the half-black/half-white circle icon to bring up the Create Adjustment Layer pop-up menu. When the menu appears, choose Threshold, which brings up a dialog with a histogram and a slider under it.

Continued

Step Ten:

When the Threshold dialog appears, drag the Threshold Level slider under the histogram all the way to the left. Your photo will turn completely white. Slowly drag the slider back to the right, and as you do, you'll start to see some of your photo reappear. The first area that appears is the darkest part of your image. That's it—that's Elements telling you exactly where the darkest part of the image is. Now that you know where your shadow area is, make a mental note of its location, but don't click OK yet. Now to find a white area in your image.

Step Eleven:

If you can't find an area in your image that you know is supposed to be white, you can use the same technique to find the highlight areas. With the Threshold dialog still open, drag the slider all the way to the right. Your photo will turn black. Slowly drag the slider back toward the left, and as you do, you'll start to see some of your photo reappear. The first area that appears is the lightest part of your image. Make a mental note of this area as well (yes, you have to remember two things, but you have to admit, it's easier than remembering two PIN numbers). You're now done with Threshold so just click Cancel because you don't actually need the adjustment layer anymore.

Step Twelve:

Press Control-L to bring up the Levels dialog. First, select the shadow Eyedropper (the one half filled with black) from the bottom right of the Levels dialog. Move your cursor outside the Levels dialog into your photo and click once in the area that Elements showed you was the darkest part of the photo (in Step Ten). When you click there, you'll see the shadow areas correct. (Basically, you just reassigned the shadow areas to your new neutral shadow color—the one you entered earlier as a preference in Step Four.) If you click in that spot and your photo now looks horrible, you either clicked in the wrong spot or what you thought was the shadow point actually wasn't. Undo the setting of your shadow point by clicking the Reset button in the dialog and try again. If that doesn't work, don't sweat it; just keep clicking in areas that look like the darkest part of your photo until it looks right.

Step Thirteen:

While still in the Levels dialog, click on the highlight Eyedropper (the one filled with white). Move your cursor over your photo and click once on the lightest part (the one you committed to memory in Step Eleven) to assign that as your highlight. You'll see the highlight colors correct.

Continued

Step Fourteen:

Now that the shadows and highlights are set, you'll need to set the midtones in the photo. It may not look as if you need to set them, because the photo may look properly corrected, but chances are there's a cast in the midtone areas. You may not recognize the cast until you've corrected it and it's gone, so it's worth giving it a shot to see the effect (which will often be surprisingly dramatic). Unfortunately, there's no Threshold adjustment layer trick that works well for finding the midtone areas, so you have to use some good old-fashioned guesswork (or try "Dave's Amazing Trick for Finding a Neutral Gray" in this chapter). Ideally, there's something in the photo that's gray, but not every photo has a "gray" area, so look for a neutral area (one that's obviously not a shadow, but not a highlight either). Click the middle (gray) Eyedropper in that area. If it's not right, click the Reset button and repeat Steps Twelve through Fourteen.

Step Fifteen:

There's one more important adjustment to make before you click OK in the Levels dialog and apply your correction. Under the Histogram (that's the black mountain-range-looking thing), click on the center slider (the Midtone Input Levels slider—that's why it's gray) and drag it to the left a bit to brighten the midtones of the image. This is a visual adjustment, so it's up to you to determine how much to adjust, but it should be subtle—just enough to bring out the midtone detail. When it looks right to you, click OK to apply your correction to the highlights, midtones, and shadows, removing any color casts and brightening the overall contrast.

Before   *After*

Dave's Amazing Trick for Finding a Neutral Gray

Finding a neutral midtone during color correcting has always been kind of tricky. Well, it was until Dave Cross, who works with me as Senior Developer of Education and Curriculum for the National Association of Photoshop Professionals (NAPP), came into my office one day to show me his amazing new trick for finding right where the midtones live in just about any image. When he showed me, I immediately blacked out. After I came to, I begged Dave to let me share his very slick trick in my book, and being the friendly Canadian he is, he obliged.

Step One:
Open any color photo and click on the Create a New Layer icon at the top of the Layers palette to create a new blank layer. Then, go under the Edit menu and choose Fill Layer. When the Fill Layer dialog appears, in the Contents section, under the Use pop-up menu, choose 50% Gray, and then click OK to fill your new layer with (you guessed it) 50% gray.

Step Two:
Now, go to the Layers palette and change the blend mode pop-up menu to Difference. Changing this layer's blend mode to Difference doesn't do much for the look of your photo (in fact, it rarely does), but just remember—it's only temporary.

Step Three:

Choose Threshold from the Create Adjustment Layer pop-up menu at the top of the Layers palette. When the dialog appears, drag the slider all the way to the left (your photo will turn completely white). Now, slowly drag the slider back to the right, and the first areas that appear in black are the neutral midtones. Make a mental note of where those gray areas are, and then click Cancel in the dialog, because you no longer need the adjustment layer. (In the example shown here, the neutral midtones are in the top of the bicycle seat.)

Step Four:

Now that you know where your midtone point is, go back to the Layers palette and drag the 50% gray layer onto the Trash icon (it already did its job, so you can get rid of it). You'll see your full-color photo again. Now, press Control-L to open Levels, get the midtones Eyedropper (it's the middle Eyedropper), and click directly on one of the neutral areas. That's it; you've found the neutral midtones and corrected any color within them. So, will this work every time? Almost. It works most of the time, but you will run across photos that just don't have a neutral midtone, so you'll have to either not correct the midtones or go back to what we used to do—guess.

Studio Portrait Correction Made Simple

If you're shooting in a studio—whether it's portraits or products—there's a technique you can use that makes the color-correction process so easy that you'll be able to train laboratory test rats to correct photos for you. In the back of this book, I've included a color swatch card (it's perforated so you can easily tear it out). After you get your studio lighting set the way you want it, and you're ready to start shooting, just put this swatch card into your shot (just once) and take the shot. What does this do for you? You'll see.

Step One:
When you're ready to start shooting and the lighting is set the way you want it, tear out the swatch card from the back of this book and place it within your shot (if you're shooting a portrait, have the subject hold the card for you), and then take the shot. After you've got one shot with the swatch card, you can remove it and continue with the rest of your shoot.

Step Two:
When you open the first photo taken in your studio session, you'll see the swatch card in the photo. By having a card that's pure white, neutral gray, and pure black in your photo, you no longer have to try to determine which area of your photo is supposed to be black (to set the shadows), which area is supposed to be gray (to set the midtones), or which area is supposed to be white (to set the highlights). They're right there in the card. *Note:* I've even included a Camera Raw White Balance swatch if you're working with RAW files. See "Editing Your RAW Images in Camera Raw" in Chapter 2 for more info.

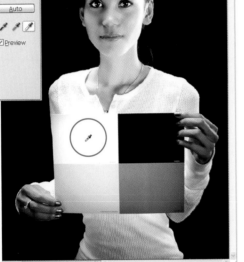

Step Three:
Press Control-L to bring up the Levels dialog. Click the black Eyedropper on the black panel of the card (to set shadows), the middle Eyedropper on the gray panel (for midtones), and the white Eyedropper on the white panel (sets the highlights), and the photo will nearly correct itself. No guessing, no Threshold adjustment layers, no using the Info palette to determine the darkest areas of the image—now you know exactly which part of that image should be black and which should be white.

Step Four:
Press C to get the Crop tool, crop the card out of the image, and you're set. Best of all, now that you have the Levels settings for the first image, you can correct the rest of the photos using the same settings: Just open the next photo and press Control-Alt-L to apply the exact settings to this photo that you did to the swatch card photo. Or, you can use the "Drag-and-Drop Instant Color Correction" method that appears in this chapter.

TIP: If you want to take this process a step further, many professionals use a ColorChecker color-swatch chart (from GretagMacbeth; www.gretagmacbeth.com), which also contains a host of other target colors. It's used exactly the same way: Just put the chart into your photo, take one shot, and then when you correct the photo, each color swatch will be in the photo, just begging to be clicked on.

Drag-and-Drop Instant Color Correction

This is a wonderful timesaving trick for quickly correcting an entire group of photos that have similar lighting. It's ideal for shots where the lighting conditions are controlled, but works equally well for outdoor shots, or really any situation where the lighting for your group of shots is fairly consistent. Once you try this, you'll use it again and again and again.

Step One:

First, here's a tip-within-a-tip: If you're opening a group of photos, you don't have to open them one by one. Just go under the File menu and choose Open. In the Open dialog, click on the first photo you want to open, then press-and-hold the Control key and click on any other photos you want to open. Then, when you click the Open button, Elements will open all the selected photos. (If all your photos are contiguous, hold the Shift key and click on the first and last photos in the list to select them all.) So now that you know that tip, go ahead and open at least three or four images, just to get you started.

Step Two:

At the top of the Layers palette, click on the Create Adjustment Layer pop-up menu and choose Levels. *Note:* An adjustment layer is a special layer that contains the tonal adjustment of your choice (such as Levels, Brightness/Contrast, etc.). There are a number of advantages to having this correction applied as a layer, as you'll soon see, but the main advantage is that you can edit or delete this tonal adjustment at any time while you're working, plus you can save this adjustment with your file as a layer.

Step Three:
When you choose this adjustment layer, you'll notice that the regular Levels dialog appears, just like always. Go ahead and make your corrections using Levels (see "Color Correcting Digital Camera Images" earlier in this chapter), and when your correction looks good, click OK. In the Layers palette, you'll see that a new Levels adjustment layer is created.

Step Four:
Because you applied this correction as an adjustment layer, you can treat this adjustment just like a regular layer, right? Right! And Elements lets you drag layers between open documents, right? Right again! So, go to the Layers palette, click on the Levels adjustment layer thumbnail, and drag-and-drop this layer right onto one of your other open photos. That photo will instantly have the same correction applied to it. This technique works because you're correcting photos that share similar lighting conditions. Need to correct 12 open photos? Just drag-and-drop it 12 times (making it the fastest correction in town!).

Continued

SCOTT KELBY

Step Five:

Okay, what if one of the "dragged corrections" doesn't look right? That's the beauty of these adjustment layers. Just double-click directly on the adjustment layer thumbnail for that photo, and the Levels dialog will reappear with the last settings you applied still in place. You can then adjust this individual photo separately from the rest. Try this "dragging-and-dropping-adjustment-layers" trick once, and you'll use it again and again to save time when correcting a digital roll that has similar lighting conditions.

So what do you do if you've used Levels to properly set the highlights, midtones, and shadows, but the flesh tones in your photo still look too red? You can try this quick trick for getting your flesh tones in line by removing the excess red. This one small adjustment can make a world of difference.

Adjusting Flesh Tones

Step One:
Open a photo that needs red removed from the flesh tones. If the whole image appears too red, skip this step and move on to Step Three. However, if just the flesh-tone areas appear too red, press L to switch to the Lasso tool and make a selection around all the flesh-tone areas in your photo. (Press-and-hold the Shift key to add other flesh-tone areas to the selection, such as arms, hands, legs, etc.)

©ISTOCKPHOTO/IRYNA KURHAN

Step Two:
Go under the Select menu and choose Feather. Enter a Feather Radius of about 3 pixels, then click OK. By adding this feather, you're softening the edges of your selection, preventing a hard, visible edge from appearing around your adjustments.

Continued

Step Three:

Go under the Enhance menu, under Adjust Color, and choose Adjust Hue/Saturation. When the dialog appears, click on the Edit pop-up menu and choose Reds so you're only adjusting the reds in your photo (or in your selected areas if you put a selection around the flesh tones).

Step Four:

The rest is easy—you're simply going to reduce the amount of saturation so the flesh tones appear more natural. Drag the Saturation slider to the left to reduce the amount of red. With the Preview checkbox turned on, you'll be able to see the effect of reducing the red as you lower the Saturation slider.

TIP: If you made a selection of the flesh-tone areas, you might find it easier to see what you're correcting if you hide the selection border from view by pressing Control-H while the Hue/Saturation dialog is open.

Step Five:
When the flesh tones look right, just click the OK button and you're set. But don't forget that your selection is still in place, so press Control-D to deselect.

Before

After

Warming Up (or Cooling Down) a Photo

Back in the day, when we needed to adjust our camera to a particular lighting situation (let's say the image would come out too blue or too warm because of the lighting), we would use color filters that would screw onto the end of our lens. Now we "warm up" or "cool down" a photo digitally using Elements 5's Photo Filter adjustment layer. Here's how:

Step One:
Open the photo that needs cooling down (or warming up). In the example shown here, the photo is too warm and has a yellowish tint, so we want to cool it down and make it look more natural. Go to the Layers palette and choose Photo Filter from the Create Adjustment Layer pop-up menu at the top of the palette (its icon looks like a half-black/half-white circle).

Step Two:
When the Photo Filter dialog appears, choose Cooling Filter (82) (or choose a Warming Filter if your image is too cool) from the Filter pop-up menu (this approximates the effect of a traditional screw-on lens filter). If the effect isn't cool enough for you, drag the Density slider to the right to cool the photo some more. Then click OK.

Step Three:
Because this Photo Filter is an adjustment layer, you can edit where the cooling is applied, so press B to switch to the Brush tool, and in the Options Bar, click on the down-facing arrow next to the Brush thumbnail and choose a soft-edged brush in the Brush Picker. Then, press X to make black your Foreground color, and begin painting over any areas that you don't want to be cool (for example, if you wanted part of the chair on the right to stay warm, you'd paint over that area). The original color of the image will be revealed wherever you paint.

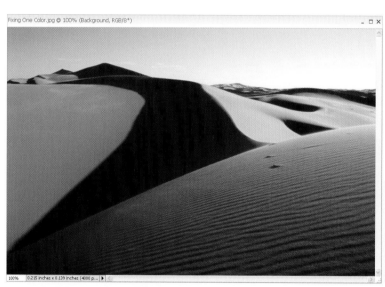

Color Correcting One Problem Area Fast!

This technique really comes in handy when shooting outdoor scenes because it lets you enhance the color in one particular area of the photo, while leaving the rest of the photo untouched. Real-estate photographers often use this trick because they want to present a house on a bright sunny day, but the weather doesn't always cooperate. With this technique, a blown-out sky shot at daybreak can become a beautiful blue sky in just seconds.

Step One:
Open the image that has an area of color you would like to enhance, such as the sky.

©ISTOCKPHOTO/TOMASZ RESIAK

Step Two:
Go to the top of the Layers palette and choose Hue/Saturation from the Create Adjustment Layer pop-up menu (it's the half-black/half-white circle icon). A new layer named "Hue/Saturation 1" will be added to your Layers palette and the Hue/Saturation dialog will appear.

Step Three:

From the Edit pop-up menu at the top of the Hue/Saturation dialog, choose the color that you want to enhance (Blues, Reds, etc.), then drag the Saturation slider to the right. You might also choose Cyans, Magentas, etc., from the Edit pop-up menu and do the same thing—drag the Saturation slider to the right, adding even more color. In the example here, I increased the saturation of the Blues to 60. When your image's area looks as enhanced as you'd like it, click OK.

Step Four:

Your area is now colorized, but so is everything else. That's okay; you can fix that easily enough. Press the letter X until your Foreground color is set to black, then press Alt-Backspace to fill the Hue/Saturation layer mask with black. Doing this removes all the color that you just added, but now you can selectively add (actually paint) the color back in where you want it.

Step Five:

Press the letter B to switch to the Brush tool. In the Options Bar, click the down-facing arrow to the right of the Brush thumbnail, and in the Brush Picker choose a large, soft-edged brush. Press X again to toggle your Foreground color to white, and begin painting over the areas where you want the color enhanced. As you paint, the version of your enhanced photo will appear. For well-defined areas, you may have to go to the Brush Picker again in the Options Bar to switch to a smaller, hard-edged brush.

Continued

TIP: If you make a mistake and paint over an area you shouldn't have—no problem—just press X again to toggle your Foreground color to black and paint over the mistake—it will disappear. Then, switch back to white and continue painting. When you're done, the colorized areas in your photo will look brighter.

Before

After

If you've ever converted a color photo to black and white, chances are you were disappointed with the results. That's because Elements simply throws away the color, leaving a fairly bland black-and-white photo in its wake. In the full version of Adobe Photoshop, there's a feature called Channel Mixer that lets you custom create a better black-and-white image. Unfortunately, that feature isn't in Elements 5, but I figured out a way to get similar control using a little workaround. Here's how:

Getting a Better Conversion from Color to Black and White

Step One:
Open the color photo you want to convert to black and white. Press D to set your Foreground and Background to the default black and white.

Step Two:
To really appreciate this technique, it wouldn't hurt if you went ahead and did a regular conversion to black and white, just so you can see how lame it is. Go under the Image menu, under Mode, and choose Grayscale. When the "Discard color information?" dialog appears, click OK, and behold the somewhat lame conversion. Now that we agree it looks pretty bland, press Control-Z to undo the conversion, so now you can try something better.

Continued

Step Three:

Go to the top of the Layers palette and choose Levels from the Create Adjustment Layer pop-up menu (it's the half-black/half-white circle icon). When the Levels dialog appears, don't make any changes, just click OK. This will add a layer to your Layers palette named "Levels 1."

Step Four:

Press X until your Foreground color is set to black, then go to the top of the Layers palette and choose Gradient Map from the Create Adjustment Layer pop-up menu. This brings up the Gradient Map dialog.

Step Five:

All you have to do here is click OK, and it gives you a black-and-white image. (And doing just this, this one little step alone, usually gives you a better black-and-white conversion than just choosing Grayscale from the Mode submenu. Freaky. I know.) Clicking OK will add another layer to the Layers palette (above your Levels 1 layer) named "Gradient Map 1."

Step Six:
In the Layers palette, double-click directly on the Levels thumbnail in the Levels 1 layer to bring up the Levels dialog again. In the Channel pop-up menu at the top of the dialog, you can choose to edit individual color channels (kind of like you would with Photoshop's Channel Mixer). Choose the Red color channel.

Step Seven:
You can now adjust the Red channel, and you'll see the adjustments live onscreen as you tweak your black-and-white photo. (It appears as a black-and-white photo because of the Gradient Map adjustment layer above the Levels 1 layer. Pretty sneaky, eh?) You can drag the shadow Input Levels slider to the right a bit to increase the shadows in the Red channel, but don't click OK.

Continued

Step Eight:
Now, switch to the Green channel in the Channel pop-up menu in the Levels dialog. You can make adjustments here as well. Try increasing the highlights in the Green channel by dragging the highlight Input Levels slider to the left. Don't click OK yet.

Step Nine:
Now, choose the Blue channel from the Channel pop-up menu in the Levels dialog. Try increasing the highlights quite a bit and the shadows just a little by dragging the Input Levels sliders. These adjustments are not standards or suggested settings for every photo; I just experimented by dragging the sliders, and when the photo looked better, I stopped dragging. When the black-and-white photo looks good to you (good contrast and good shadow and highlight details), click OK in the Levels dialog.

Step Ten:
To complete your conversion, go to the Layers palette, click on the More flyout menu, then choose Flatten Image to flatten the adjustment layers into the Background layer. Although your photo looks like a black-and-white photo, technically, it's still in RGB mode, so if you want a grayscale file, go under the Image menu, under Mode, and choose Grayscale.

Before (lame grayscale conversion)

After (awesome adjustment layers conversion)

Correcting Color and Contrast Using Color Curves

Users of the full professional version of Adobe Photoshop have had the benefit of using Curves since version 1, and it's the pros' choice for color correction without a doubt. There's only one problem—it's a bit hard for most folks to master. That's why you'll fall in love with the new Color Curves just introduced in Elements 5, because it makes using Curves so easy, it will actually make pro users of Photoshop jealous. Adobe has done a really brilliant job of giving us the power of Curves without the hassles and steep learning curve. Life is good.

Step One:
Open the photo you want to adjust with Color Curves (a typical situation might be a photo that lacks contrast or has an obvious color cast, but in reality most photos can benefit from a short trip to Color Curves, so don't just save it for really messed up photos). Then go under the Enhance menu, under Adjust Color, and choose Adjust Color Curves (as shown here).

Step Two:
When the Adjust Color Curves dialog first appears, it appears in "simple" mode (I don't know if that's its official name, but that's what I've been calling it, so simple mode it is). This simple mode lets you simply point-and-click on the version of your photo that looks better than the original photo you have opened (you can still see your original photo behind the Adjust Color Curves dialog) and it applies a color curve for you. Easy enough, right? You click on any thumbnail that looks better than your existing photo, and it applies that curves correction. (By the way, don't click on Solarize unless you've had a few glasses of Merlot first.) *Note:* You can only apply one curve at a time. If you want to apply more than one thumbnail adjustment, click OK, then reopen the Adjust Color Curves dialog and click on another thumbnail to add it.

SCOTT KELBY

Step Three:

So, you might get lucky—a few clicks on a couple of those thumbnails, and your photo looks great. However, to reveal the real power of these curves, you'll need to reveal the Advanced Options. You do that by clicking directly on the little right-facing arrow that appears to the left of the words "Advanced Options" at the bottom right of the dialog. Click on that, and four sliders (and the curve itself) appear. Now, as you drag the sliders, you'll see how the curve is affected. For example, drag the Adjust Highlights slider to the right, and you'll see the top-right curve point move upward. That's because the highlights are controlled by that upper-right point.

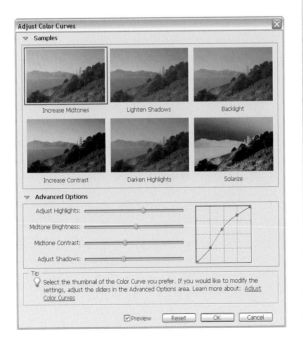

Step Four:

The center point represents the midtones in your photo. Try dragging the Midtone Brightness slider to the right, and look over at the curve. See how the center point moves upward? Now, drag the Midtone Contrast slider to the left, and watch how the contrast increases. Anytime you make the curve steeper, it adds contrast to your photo, but you don't want it to get too steep, or your photo will lose quality. Lastly, drag the Adjust Shadows slider to the left. Notice how the shadow point on the curve (the far-left point) moves downward, darkening the shadow area. These sliders make it easy to adjust the tone and contrast in your photo without having to manually move points on the curve (like you do in the pro version of Photoshop).

Continued

Step Five:

Now let's click the Reset button, and start over from scratch. Let's fix the problem photo we have here, using nothing but Adjust Color Curves. First, let's start at the top and see if any of the thumbnails look better than our current photo. To me, the Increase Contrast thumbnail looks better than the original photo, so go ahead and click on that. It makes a great starting point for our correction.

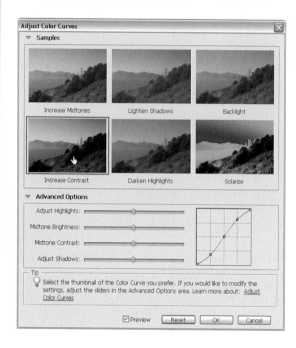

Step Six:

Okay, here's the problem (at least as I see it). Although we increased the contrast, and I think the photo certainly looks better than it did, it seems a little dark, and it looks like it's lacking highlights. So, drag the Adjust Highlights slider over to the right a little bit and see how that looks. Now, to me, that looks better (but hey, that's just me. There is no official government agency that determines whether your photo has enough highlights or not, so the choice is really up to you—the photographer). In fact, since it's up to you (or me, in this case), I think I might even drag it a little farther to the right, to really open up those highlights. In fact, I'll keep dragging until the white areas of my photo start to look blown out (lacking detail).

Step Seven:

Now, if it were me (and it is, by the way), I'd then drag the Midtone Contrast slider to the left a bit to add more contrast in the midtones. This tends to brighten the midtones. I won't do this for every photo, but for this photo, it seems to look better. That's the great thing about these sliders—you can drag one to the left, and if your photo looks better, then great. If it doesn't, drag it to the right and see how that looks. If it looks better when you drag it to the right, then great. If not, drag it back to the center and leave it alone. In this case, I dragged both ways, and I like the way the midtone contrast looked when I had the slider dragged to the left a bit, so that's where I'm leaving it.

Step Eight:

My final two tweaks are to drag the Midtone Brightness slider to the left, then the right, to see which one looks better. I like the way it looks when I dragged it to the right, so to the right it stays. I know this sounds like a really simplistic way to adjust your photos, but it's deeper than you think. If you drag a slider in either direction, and your photo looks better, than how could that be wrong? Lastly, let's drag the Adjust Shadows slider. Dragging just a little bit to the left seemed to make the shadow areas darker, while dragging it to the right made them looked washed out. So, needless to say, I left it a little to the left. If you look at the curve itself, you'll see the classic "S" shape (known as the "S" curve), which is pretty common in curves correction, as that shape adds contrast and helps to make colors rich and saturated. So, in short, don't be afraid to slide those sliders.

Continued

Before   *After*

The Big Fixx
digital camera image problems

Okay, did you catch that reference to the band The Fixx in the title? You did? Great. That means that you're at least in your mid-30s to early 40s. (I myself am only in my mid- to early 20s, but I listen to oldies stations just to keep in touch with baby boomers and other people who at one time or another tried to break-dance.) Well, The Fixx had a big hit in the early '80s (around the time I was born) called "One Thing Leads to Another" and that's a totally appropriate title for this chapter because one thing (using a digital camera) leads to another (having to deal with things like digital noise, color aliasing, and other nasties that pop up when you've finally kicked the film habit and gone totally digital). Admittedly, some of the problems we bring upon ourselves (like leaving the lens cap on; or forgetting to bring our camera to the shoot, where the shoot is, or who hired us; or we immersed our flash into a tub of Jell-O, you know—the standard stuff). And other things are problems caused by the hardware itself (the slave won't fire when it's submerged in Jell-O, you got some Camembert on the lens, etc.). Whatever the problem, and regardless of whose fault it is, problems are going to happen, and you're going to need to fix them in Elements. Some of the fixes are easy, like running the "Remove Camembert" filter, and then changing the blend mode to Fromage. Others will have you jumping through some major Elements hoops, but fear not, the problems you'll most likely run into are all covered here in a step-by-step format that will have you wiping cold, congealed water off your flash unit faster than you can say, "How can Scott possibly be in his mid-20s?"

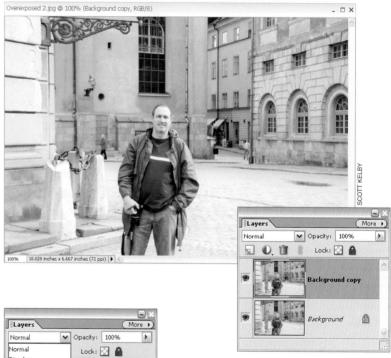

Fixing Overexposed Images

Overexposed photos, or photos where your flash was too close to the subject (which also creates an overexposed photo), can be pretty easily fixed—usually in just a few seconds—by using Elements' layer blend modes. I know, I know, you want to use Levels or Adjust Color Curves, but this is so much faster, and doesn't mess with the colors in your image as much.

Step One:
Open the photo that is suffering from overexposure or "flashaphobia," meaning the entire subject is washed out. Make a copy of the photo layer by dragging-and-dropping your Background layer onto the Create a New Layer icon at the top of the Layers palette. This will create a layer titled "Background copy."

Step Two:
Next, change the layer blend mode of the Background copy from Normal to Multiply in the pop-up menu at the top left of the Layers palette. This blend mode has a "multiplier" effect and brings back a lot of the original detail the flash "blew out."

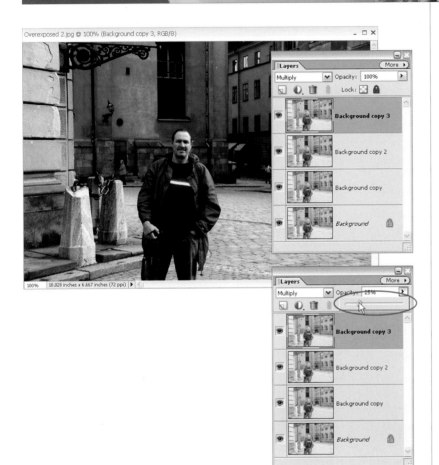

Step Three:
If the photo still looks washed out, you may need to make duplicates of the Background copy layer. Just press Control-J a few times to duplicate this layer. These additional copies of the Background copy layer will already be in Multiply mode.

TIP: Incidentally, because of the immutable laws of life, chances are that creating one layer with its blend mode set to Multiply won't be enough, but adding another layer (in Multiply mode) will be "too much." If that's the case, just go to the Layers palette and lower the Opacity setting of the top layer to 50% or less—this way, you can "dial in" just the right amount of flash.

Before

After

Removing Digital Noise

If you're shooting in a low-lighting situation or shooting with a high ISO, chances are you're going to get some amount of "digital noise" (also referred to as "color aliasing"). You generally can't remove all this noise, but you usually can reduce it—and Elements has a feature to help you do just that. However, remember this is one of those "the-cheaper-the-digital-camera-the-more-noise-it-creates" situations, so if you're shooting with an "el cheapo" digital camera, this is a technique you'll be using a lot.

Step One:
Open the photo that was taken in low lighting (or using a high ISO setting) and has visible digital noise. This noise will be most obvious when viewed at a magnification of 100% or higher. *Note:* If you view your photos at smaller sizes, you may not notice the noise until you make your prints.

Step Two:
Go under the Filter menu, under Noise, and choose Reduce Noise. The default settings really aren't too bad, but if you're having a lot of color aliasing (dots or splotchy areas of red, green, and blue), drag the Reduce Color Noise slider to the right (try 65% and see how that works).

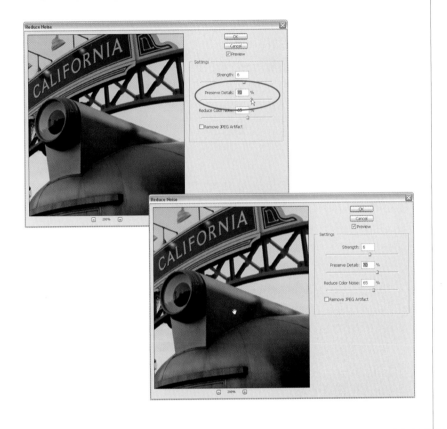

Step Three:

One thing to watch out for when using this filter is that although it can reduce noise, it can also make your photo a bit blurry, and the higher the Strength setting and the higher the amount of Reduce Color Noise, the blurrier your photo will become. If the noise is really bad, you may prefer a bit of blur to an incredibly noisy photo, so you'll have to make the call as to how much blurring is acceptable, but to soften the noise a bit, drag the Preserve Details slider to the right.

TIP: To see an instant before/after of the Reduce Noise filter's effect on your photo without clicking the OK button, click your cursor within the Reduce Noise's preview window. When you click-and-hold within that window, you'll see the before version without the filter (zoom in if you need to). When you release the mouse, you'll see how the photo will look if you click the OK button.

Before: Although it's difficult to see, look for the digital noise within the sign and around the palm fronds.

After: Noise removed using a slight blur from the Reduce Noise filter.

Focusing Light with Digital Dodging and Burning

If you've ever used Elements' Dodge and Burn tools, you already know how lame they are. That's why the pros choose this method instead—it gives them a level of control that the Dodge and Burn tools just don't offer, and best of all, it doesn't "bruise the pixels." (That's digital retoucher-speak for "it doesn't mess up your original image data while you're editing.")

Step One:
In this tutorial, we're going to dodge areas to add some highlights, then we're going to burn in the background a bit to darken some of those areas. Start by opening the photo you want to dodge and burn.

Step Two:
Go to the Layers palette, and from the More flyout menu choose New Layer (or just Alt-click on the Create a New Layer icon). This accesses the New Layer dialog, which is needed for this technique to work.

Step Three:
In the New Layer dialog, change the Mode to Overlay, then right below it, choose "Fill with Overlay-neutral color (50% gray)." This is normally grayed out, but when you switch to Overlay mode, this choice becomes available. Click the checkbox to make it active, then click OK.

Step Four:
This creates a new layer, filled with 50% gray, above your Background layer. (When you fill a layer with 50% gray and change the Mode to Overlay, Elements ignores the color. You'll see a gray thumbnail in the Layers palette, but the layer will appear transparent in your image window.)

Step Five:
Press B to switch to the Brush tool, and choose a medium, soft-edged brush in the Brush Picker (which opens when you click the Brush thumbnail in the Options Bar). While in the Options Bar, lower the Opacity to approximately 30%.

Continued

Step Six:

Press D then X to set your Foreground color to white. Begin painting over the areas that you want to highlight (dodge). As you paint, you'll see white strokes appear in the thumbnail of your gray transparent layer, and in the image window you'll see soft highlights.

Step Seven:

If your first stab at dodging isn't as intense as you'd like, just release the mouse button, click again, and paint over the same area. Since you're dodging at a low opacity, the highlights will "build up" as you paint over previous strokes. If the highlights appear too intense, just go to the Layers palette and lower the Opacity setting until they blend in.

Step Eight:

If there are areas you want to darken (burn) so they're less prominent (such as the background), just press D to switch your Foreground color to black and begin painting in those areas. Okay, ready for another dodging-and-burning method? Good, 'cause I've got a great one.

Alternate Technique:

Open the photo that you want to dodge and burn, then just click the Create a New Layer icon in the Layers palette and change the blend mode in the Layers palette to Soft Light. Now, set white as your Foreground color and you can dodge right on this layer using the Brush tool set to 30% Opacity. To burn, just as before—switch to black. The dodging and burning using this Soft Light layer appears a bit softer and milder than the previous technique, so you should definitely try both to see which one you prefer.

Before

After

Opening Up Shadow Areas That Are Too Dark

If you have a problem with your photo, there's a pretty good chance it's in the shadow areas. Either you shot the photo with the light source behind the subject, or the lighting in the room put part of the subject in the shadows, or...well...you just messed up (hey, it happens). Luckily, you can open up just the shadows by moving one simple slider. Of course, you have to know where to look.

Step One:
Open the photo that needs to have its shadow areas opened up to reveal detail that was "lost in the shadows."

Step Two:
Go under the Enhance menu, under Adjust Lighting, and choose Shadows/ Highlights. When the dialog appears, it already assumes you have a shadow problem (sadly, most people do but never admit it), so it automatically opens up the shadow areas in your document by 25% (you'll see that the Lighten Shadows slider is at 25% by default [0% is no lightening of the shad-ows]). If you want to open up the shad-ow areas even more, drag the Lighten Shadows slider to the right. If the shad-ows appear to be opened too much with the default 25% increase, drag the slider to the left to a setting below 25%. When the shadows look right, click OK. Your repair is complete.

Before   *After*

Fixing Areas That Are Too Bright

Although most of the lighting problems you'll encounter are in the shadow areas of your photos, you'll be surprised how many times there's an area that is too bright (perhaps an area that's lit with harsh, direct sunlight, or you exposed for the foreground but the background is now overexposed). Luckily, this is now an easy fix, too!

Step One:

Open the photo that has highlights that you want to tone down a bit. *Note:* If it's an individual area (like the sun shining directly on your subject's hair), you'll want to press the L key to switch to the Lasso tool and put a loose selection around that area. Then go under the Select menu and choose Feather. For low-res, 72-ppi images, enter 2 pixels and click OK. For high-res, 300-ppi images, try 8 pixels.

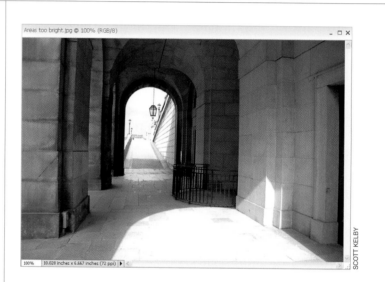

Step Two:

Now go under the Enhance menu, under Adjust Lighting, and choose Shadows/Highlights. When the dialog appears, drag the Lighten Shadows slider to 0% and drag the Darken Highlights slider to the right, and as you do, the highlights will decrease, bringing back detail and balancing the over-all tone of your (selected) highlights with the rest of your photo. Sometimes when you make adjustments to the highlights (or shadows), you can lose some of the contrast in the midtone areas (they can become muddy or flat looking, or they can become oversaturated). If that happens, drag the Midtone Contrast slider (at the bottom of the dialog) to the right to increase the amount of midtone contrast, or drag to the left to reduce it. Then click OK. *Note:* If you made a selection, you'll need to press Control-D to deselect when you're finished.

Before   *After*

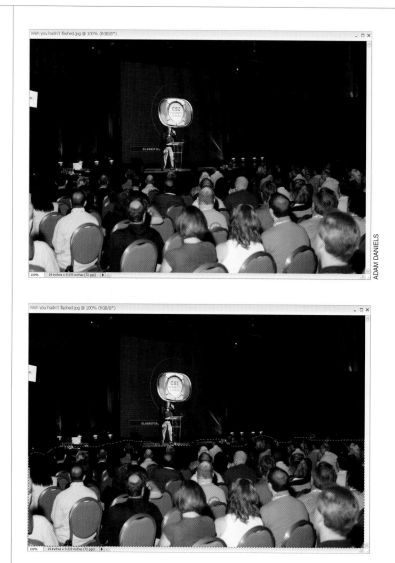

Fixing Photos Where You Wish You Hadn't Used the Flash

There's a natural tendency for some photographers to react to their immediate surroundings, rather than what they see through the lens. For example, at an indoor concert, there are often hundreds of lights illuminating the stage. However, some photographers think it's one light short—their flash—because where they're sitting, it's dark. When they look at their photos later, they see that the flash lit everyone in front of them (which wasn't the way it really looked—the crowd is usually in the dark), ruining an otherwise great shot. Here's a quick fix to make it look as if the flash never fired at all.

Step One:
Open a photo where shooting with the flash has ruined part of the image.

Step Two:
Press the letter L to get the Lasso tool, and draw a loose selection around the area where the flash affected the shot.

ADAM DANIELS

Feather Selection

Learn more about: Feather Selection

OK

Cancel

Feather Radius: 25 pixels

Levels

Learn more about: Levels

OK

Cancel

Channel: RGB

Reset

Input Levels: 0 1.00 255

Auto

☑ Preview

Output Levels: 0 60

Step Three:

In the next step, we're going to adjust the tonal range of this selected area, but we don't want that adjustment to appear obvious. We'll need to soften the edges of our selection quite a bit so our adjustment blends in smoothly with the rest of the photo. To do this, go under the Select menu and choose Feather. When the Feather Selection dialog appears, enter 25 pixels to soften the selection edge. (By the way, 25 pixels is just my guess for how much the selection might need. The rule of thumb is the higher the resolution of the image, the more feathering you'll need, so don't be afraid to use more than 25 if your edge is visible when you finish.) Click OK.

Step Four:

It will help you make a better adjustment if you hide the selection border (I call it "the marching ants") from view. We don't want to deselect—we want our selection to remain intact—but we don't want to see the annoying border, so press Control-H to hide the selection border. Now, press Control-L to bring up the Levels dialog. At the bottom of the dialog, drag the right Output Levels slider to the left to darken your selected area. Because you've hidden the selection border, it should be very easy to match the selected area to its surroundings when you drag this slider to the left.

Continued

Step Five:

When the photo looks about right, click OK to apply your Levels adjustment. Then, press Control-H to make your selection visible again (this trips up a lot of people who, since they don't see the selection anymore, forget it's there, and then nothing reacts as it should from that point on). So now press Control-D to deselect and view your repaired "flash-free" photo.

Before

After

Wouldn't it be great if Elements had a "Fill Flash" brush, so when you forgot to use your fill flash, you could just paint it in? Well, although it's not technically called the Fill Flash brush, you can use a brush to achieve the same effect. I predict you'll like this technique. Hey, it's just a prediction.

When You Forget to Use Fill Flash

Step One:
Open a photo where the subject of the image appears too dark. Make a copy of the Background layer by pressing Control-J. This will create a layer titled "Layer 1."

Step Two:
Go under the Enhance menu, under Adjust Lighting, and choose Levels. Drag the middle Input Levels slider (the gray one) to the left until your subject looks properly exposed. (*Note:* Don't worry about how the background looks—it will probably become completely blown out, but you'll fix that later—for now, just focus on making your subject look right.) If the midtones slider doesn't bring out the subject enough, you may have to increase the highlights as well, so drag the far-right Input Levels slider to the left to increase the highlights. When your subject looks properly exposed, click OK.

Continued

Step Three:

Hold the Control key and click on the Create a New Layer icon at the top of the Layers palette. This creates a new blank layer beneath your duplicate layer. In the Layers palette, click on the top layer (Layer 1), then press Control-G to group this photo layer with the blank layer beneath it. This removes the brightening of the photo from Step Two.

Step Four:

In the Layers palette, click on the blank layer beneath your grouped, top layer. Press B to switch to the Brush tool and click the Brush thumbnail in the Options Bar to open the Brush Picker, where you'll choose a soft-edged brush. Press D to set black as your Foreground color, and then begin to paint (on this blank layer) over the areas of the image that need a fill flash with your newly created "Fill Flash" brush. The areas you paint over will appear lighter, because you're "painting in" the lighter version of your image on this layer.

Step Five:

Continue painting until it looks as if you had used a fill flash. If the effect appears too intense, just lower the Opacity of the layer you're painting on by dragging the Opacity slider to the left in the Layers palette.

Before

After

Fixing Underexposed Photos

This is a tonal correction for people who don't like making tonal corrections (more than 60 million Americans suffer from the paralyzing fear of MTC [Making Tonal Corrections]). Since this technique requires no knowledge of tonal corrections (like using Levels), it's very popular; and even though it's incredibly simple to perform, it does a pretty incredible job of fixing underexposed photos.

Step One:

Open an underexposed photo that could've used either a fill flash or a better exposure setting. Make a copy of the Background layer by pressing Control-J. This will create a layer titled "Layer 1."

SCOTT KELBY

Step Two:

In the Layers palette, change the blend mode of this new layer from Normal to Screen to lighten the entire photo.

Step Three:

If the photo still isn't properly exposed, press Control-J again to duplicate this Screen layer, and keep duplicating it until the exposure looks about right (this may take a few layers, but don't be shy about it—keep going until it looks good).

Step Four:

There's a good chance that at some point you'll duplicate the Screen layer again and the image will look overexposed. What you need is "half a layer"—half as much lightening. Here's what to do: Lower the Opacity of your top layer to "dial in" the perfect amount of light, giving you something between the full intensity of the layer (at 100%) and no layer at all (at 0%). For half the intensity, try 50%. (Did I really even have to say that last line? Didn't think so.) Once the photo looks properly exposed, click the More flyout menu at the top right of the Layers palette and choose Flatten Image.

Before

After

Automatic Red-Eye Removal

Photoshop Elements 4 brought some serious new red-eye removal features to the table by automating the entire process. Sure, you still have the old Red Eye Removal tool, but this might be even better, especially if you know in advance that you've got a lot of photos that need a red-eye fix (you shot photos of people in low-light situations using your on-camera flash). You can actually set up Elements 5 to automatically remove red eye as the images are imported into the Organizer, or you can do it on a case-by-case basis. Either way—life is good.

Step One:
First, we'll start with the fully automatic version, which you can use when you're importing photos into the Organizer. Here's how it works: When importing photos, the Adobe Photoshop Elements Photo Downloader dialog appears. On the right side of the dialog, under the Advanced Options section, there's a checkbox for Automatically Fix Red Eyes. This checkbox (shown circled here) is on by default, so if you think some of the photos you're about to import will have red eye, just click the Get Photos button to start the importing—and the red-eye correction.

Step Two:
Once you click the Get Photos button, the Getting Photos dialog will appear. At the bottom of the dialog, a status bar indicates how many photos are being "fixed." Then, it shows you a preview of which photos it determined have red eye as they're being corrected.

Step Three:
Once the process is complete, it gives you an onscreen report of how many it actually fixed, and it automatically groups the original with the fixed version (in a Version Set), so if you don't like the fix (for whatever reason), you still have the original. You can see both versions of the file by Right-clicking on the photo (in the Organizer) and in the contextual menu, under Version Set, choosing Reveal Items in Version Set.

Step Four:
Here is one of the photos with red eye and with it automatically removed.

Step Five:
This really isn't a step; it's another way to get an Auto Red Eye Fix, and that's by opening an image in the Editor or even in Quick Fix, and then going under the Enhance menu and choosing Auto Red Eye Fix. You can also use the keyboard shortcut Control-R. Either way, it senses where the red eye(s) is and removes it automatically. See, I told you life was good.

Instant Red-Eye Removal

When I see a digital camera with the flash mounted directly above the lens, I think, "Hey, there's an automated red-eye machine." In studio situations, you don't have to deal with this as much, because your flash probably wouldn't be mounted directly above your lens—you're using bounce flash, holding the flash separately, you've got studio strobes, or one of a dozen other techniques. Elements has had instant red-eye removal for a while now, but the red-eye removal in this version gives significantly better results.

Step One:
Open a photo where the subject has red eye.

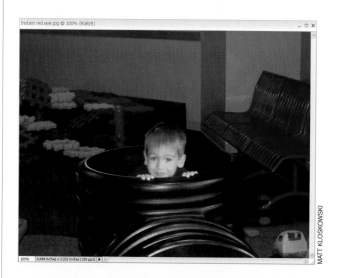

Step Two:
Press Z to switch to the Zoom tool (it looks like a magnifying glass in the Toolbox) and drag out a selection around the eyes (this zooms you in on the eyes). Now, press the letter Y to switch to the Red Eye Removal tool (its Toolbox icon looks like an eye with a tiny crosshair cursor in the left corner). There are two different ways to use this tool: click or click-and-drag. We'll start with the most precise, which is click. Take the Red Eye Removal tool and click it once directly on the red area of the pupil. It will isolate the red in the pupil and replace it with a neutral color. Instead, now you have "gray" eye, which doesn't look spectacular, but it's a heck of a lot better than red eye.

Step Three:
If the gray color that replaces the red seems too "gray," you can adjust the darkness of the replacement color by going to the Options Bar and adjusting the Darken Amount. To get better results, you may have to adjust the Pupil Size setting so that the area affected by the tool matches the size of the pupil. This is also done in the Options Bar when you have the Red Eye Removal tool selected. Now, on to the other way to use this tool (for really quick red-eye fixes).

Step Four:
If you have a lot of photos to fix, you may opt for this quicker red-eye fix—just click-and-drag the Red Eye Removal tool over the eye area (putting a square selection around the entire eye). The tool will determine where the red eye is within your selected area (your cursor will change to a timer), and it removes the red. Use this "drag" method on one eye at a time for the best results.

Before

After

Repairing Keystoning

Keystoning is often found in photos with tall objects such as buildings, where the objects appear as if they're falling away from the viewer (giving the impression that the tops of these tall objects are narrower than their bases). Here's how to use Elements' Free Transform function, and one simple filter, to fix the problem fast.

Step One:
Open an image that has a keystoning problem, where a tall object seems to be leaning away from the viewer.

Step Two:
Make sure you're in Maximize Mode by going under the Window menu, under Images, and choosing Maximize Mode. Now we're going to create a guide that we can use to help us align our building. Click on the Foreground color swatch (at the bottom of the Toolbox) to bring up the Color Picker. In the R (red) field enter 74, for G (green) enter 132, and in the B (blue) field enter 244, then click OK to set your Foreground color to a light blue.

Step Three:

Switch to the Line tool (press U to cycle through the Shape tools until you get the Line tool). Go up in the Options Bar and set the Weight to 2 pixels. Then, hold the Shift key and draw a vertical, blue, 2-pixel line from the top of your image down to a corner at the base of your tall object. This will add a Shape layer in your Layers palette. (*Note:* If it's not positioned where you want it, you can drag it with the Move tool [V]. If this layer is locked, click on the Lock icon near the top center of the Layers palette to unlock it.) This blue line will act as your visual guide. Now, in the Layers palette, click back on the Background layer. Press Control-A to put a selection around your entire photo, and then press Control-Shift-J to cut your image from the Background layer and put it on its own separate layer.

Step Four:

With your image's layer active, press Control-T to bring up the Free Transform bounding box.

Step Five:

Go to the Options Bar and you'll see a grid that represents the bounding box around the photo. Click the bottom-center box so any transformation you apply will have the bottom center locked in place.

Continued

Step Six:

Hold Control-Alt-Shift and drag either the top-left and/or top-right corner points of the bounding box outward until the top corner of the object aligns with your guide.

Step Seven:

Making this correction can sometimes make your object look a bit "smushed" and "squatty" (my official technical terms), so release the Control-Alt-Shift keys, grab the top-center point, and drag upward to stretch the photo back out to fix the "squattyness" (another technical term).

Step Eight:

When your object looks right, press Enter to lock in your transformation. Now you can go to the Layers palette, click on your blue-line Shape layer, and drag it onto the Trash icon at the top of the Layers palette to delete it. Then click on your image's layer and press Control-E to merge your image layer with the Background layer. There's still one more thing you'll proba-bly have to do to complete this repair job.

Step Nine:

If after making this adjustment the object looks "round" and "bloated," you can repair that problem by going under the Filter menu, under Distort, and choosing Pinch. Drag the Amount slider to 0%, and then slowly drag it to the right (increasing the amount of Pinch), while looking at the preview in the Pinch dialog, until you see the roundness and bloating go away. When it looks right, click OK to complete your keystoning repair.

Before: In the original photo, the building appears to be "falling away."

After: The same photo after repairing the keystoning and bloating.

Fixing Problems Caused by Your Camera's Lens

In Elements 5, Adobe introduced a new filter called the Correct Camera Distortion filter. It is pretty much a one-stop shop for repairing the most common problems caused by the camera's lens, including pincushion and barrel distortion, horizontal and vertical perspective problems, and edge vignetting.

Problem One: Perspective Distortion

Step One:
The first problem we're going to tackle is perspective distortion. In the example shown here, the base of the building looks larger than the top, which gives the photo an almost cartoon-like perspective.

Step Two:
To fix this problem (caused by the lens), go under the Filter menu, under Distort, and choose Correct Camera Distortion. When the dialog appears, turn off the Show Grid checkbox at the bottom right of the preview window (it's on by default), then go to the Perspective Control section (on the center-right side of the dialog) and drag the Vertical Perspective slider to the left until the building starts to look straight and not so top-heavy. When you make this correction, the filter pinches the bottom third of your photo inward, which leaves transparent gaps along the bottom and lower-side edges of your photo (you can see the checkerboard in these areas).

Step Three:
The Scale slider at the bottom of the dialog in the Edge Extension section lets you deal with these edge gaps caused by the perspective repair. Move the slider to the right to increase your image size in the frame, covering those gaps, so you don't have to crop your photo later.

Before: The base of the building is larger than the top.

After: The perspective distortion is corrected.

Continued

Problem Two: **Barrel Distortion**

Step One:
Another common lens correction problem is called barrel distortion, which makes your photo look bloated or rounded. So, open the Correct Camera Distortion filter again, but this time you're going to drag the Remove Distortion slider (in the top right of the dialog) slowly to the right to "pucker" the photo inward from the center, removing the rounded, bloated look. To remove pincushion distortion, in which the sides of your photo appear to curve inward, drag the slider to the left.

Step Two:
When you click OK, the correction will leave gaps around the edges, so get the Crop tool (C) and crop the image to hide the missing edges. It's hard to see the difference in the small images on the next page, but try this technique, and you'll see the difference.

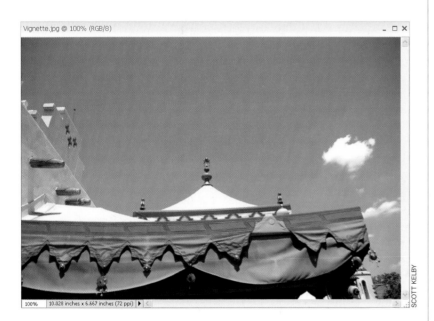

Before	*After (removing the bloating caused by barrel distortion)*

Problem Three: Lens Vignetting

Step One:
Vignetting is a lens problem where the corners of your photo appear darkened. To remove this problem, go back to the Correct Camera Distortion filter.

Continued

Step Two:

In the Vignette section at the center-right side of the dialog, drag the Amount slider to the right, and as you do you'll see the edges brighten. Keep dragging the slider until the edges match the brightness of the rest of the photo. The Midpoint slider (just below the Amount slider), determines how far into the photo your corner brightening will extend. In this case, you have to extend it just a little bit by dragging the slider to the left (as shown here), then click OK.

Before: You can see the dark vignetted areas in the corners.

After: The vignetting is completely removed.

The Mask
selection techniques

One of the problems with people is you can't always get them to stand in front of a white background so you can easily select them and place them on a different background in Elements 5. It's just not fair. If I were elected president, one of my first priorities would be to sign an executive order requiring all registered voters to carry with them a white, seamless roll at all times. Can you imagine how much easier life would be? For example, let's say you're a sports photographer and you're shooting an NFL *Monday Night Football* game with one of those Canon telephoto lenses that are longer than the underground tube for a particle accelerator; and just as the quarterback steps into the pocket to complete a pass, a fullback comes up from behind, quickly unfurls a white, seamless backdrop, and lets you take the shot. Do you know how fast you'd get a job at *Sports Illustrated*? Do you know how long I've waited to use "unfurl" in a sentence and actually use it in the proper context? Well, let's just say at least since I was 12 (three long years ago). In this chapter, you'll learn how to treat everyone, every object, every thing, as though it were shot on a white, seamless background.

Selecting Square, Rectangular, or Round Areas

Selections are an incredibly important part of working in Elements 5. That's because without them, everything you do, every filter you run, etc., would affect the entire photo. By being able to "select" a portion of your image, you can apply these effects only to the areas you want, giving you much greater control. Believe it or not, the most basic selections (squares, rectangles, circles, and ovals) are the ones you'll use the most, so we'll start with them.

Step One:

To make a rectangular selection, choose (big surprise) the Rectangular Marquee tool by pressing the M key. Adobe's word for selection is "marquee." (Why? Because calling it a marquee makes it more complicated than calling it what it really is—a selection tool— and giving tools complicated names is what Adobe does for fun.)

Step Two:

We're going to start by selecting a rectangle shape, so click your cursor in the upper left-hand corner of the doorway and drag down and to the right until your selection covers the entire shape, then release the mouse button. That's it! You've got a selection, and anything you do now will affect only the area within that selected rectangle (in other words, it will only affect the church doorway).

Step Three:

To add another area to your current selection, just press-and-hold the Shift key, and then draw another rectangular selection. In our example here, you'll want to select the darker area of the wall to the left of the doorway, so hold the Shift key, drag out a rectangle around it, and release the mouse button. Now both areas are selected.

Step Four:

Now let's make an adjustment and you'll see that your adjustment will only affect your selected areas. Go under the Enhance menu, under Adjust Color, and choose Adjust Hue/Saturation. When the dialog appears, drag the Hue slider to the right (or left), and you'll see the color of the two areas change as you drag. More importantly, you'll see that nothing else changes color—just those areas. This is why selections are so important—it's how you tell Elements you only want to adjust a specific area. You can also drag the Saturation or Lightness sliders to get the color you want. To deselect (making your selection go away), just press Control-D.

Continued

Step Five:

Okay, you've got rectangles, but what if you want to make a perfectly square selection? It's easy—the tool works the same way—but before you drag out your selection, you'll want to hold the Shift key down. Let's try it: Open another image, get the Rectangular Marquee tool, hold the Shift key, and then draw a perfectly square selection (around the black area inside of this fake Polaroid frame, in this case).

Step Six:

While your selection is still in place, open a photo that you'd like to appear inside your selected area and press Control-A (this is the shortcut for Select All, which puts a selection around your entire photo at once). Then press Control-C to copy that photo into Elements' memory.

Step Seven:

Switch back to the Polaroid image, and you'll notice that your selection is still in place. Go under the Edit menu and choose Paste Into Selection. The image held in memory will appear pasted inside your square selection. If the photo is larger than the square you pasted it into, you can reposition the photo by just clicking-and-dragging it around inside your selected opening with the Move tool (V).

Step Eight:

You can also use Free Transform (press Control-T) to scale the pasted photo in size. Just grab a corner point, press-and-hold the Shift key, and drag inward or outward. When the size looks right, press the Enter key and you're done. (Well, sort of—you'll need to press Control-D to deselect, but only do this once you're satisfied with your image, because once you deselect, Elements flattens your new image into your Background layer, meaning there's no easy way to adjust this image.) Now, on to oval and circular selections...

Step Nine:

Open an image with a circle shape you want to select, and then press M to switch to the Elliptical Marquee tool (pressing M toggles you between the Rectangular and Elliptical Marquee tools by default). Now, just click-and-drag a selection around your circle. Press-and-hold the Shift key as you drag to make your selection perfectly round. If your round selection doesn't fit exactly, you can reposition it by moving your cursor inside the borders of your round selection and clicking-and-dragging to move it into position. If you want to start over, just press Control-D to deselect, and then drag out a new selection. *Hint:* With circles it helps if you start dragging before you reach the circle, so try starting about ¼" to the top left of the circle.

Continued

Step Ten:

We'll change the circle's color (like we did in the previous rectangle project), so go under the Enhance menu, under Adjust Color, and choose Adjust Hue/Saturation. Turn on the Colorize checkbox at the bottom right. Then, move the Hue slider to the left until it reads +111 and move the Saturation slider to the right until it reads 50. This should give you a green sign. Now press Control-D to deselect.

Step Eleven:

This isn't really a step; it's more of a recap: To make rectangles or ovals, you just grab the tool and start dragging. However, if you need to make a perfect square or a circle (rather than an oval), you press-and-hold the Shift key before you start dragging. You're starting to wish you'd paid attention in geometry class now, aren't you? No? Okay, me either.

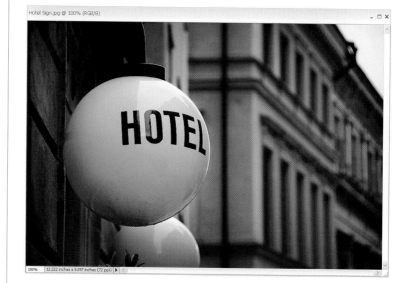

Saving Your Selections

If you've spent 15 or 20 minutes (or even longer) putting together an intricate selection, once you deselect it, it's gone. (Well, you might be able to get it back by choosing Reselect from the Select menu, as long as you haven't made any other selections in the meantime, but don't count on it. Ever.) Here's how to save your finely-honed selections and bring them back into place anytime you need them.

SCOTT KELBY

Step One:
Open an image and then put a selection around an object in your photo using the tool of your choice. To save your selection once it's in place (so you can use it again later), go under the Select menu and choose Save Selection. This brings up the Save Selection dialog. Enter a name in the Name field and click OK to save your selection.

Step Two:
Now you can get that selection back (known as "reloading" by Elements wizards) at any time by going to the Select menu and choosing Load Selection. If you've saved more than one selection, they'll be listed in the Selection pop-up menu—just choose which one you want to "load" and click OK. The saved selection will appear in your image.

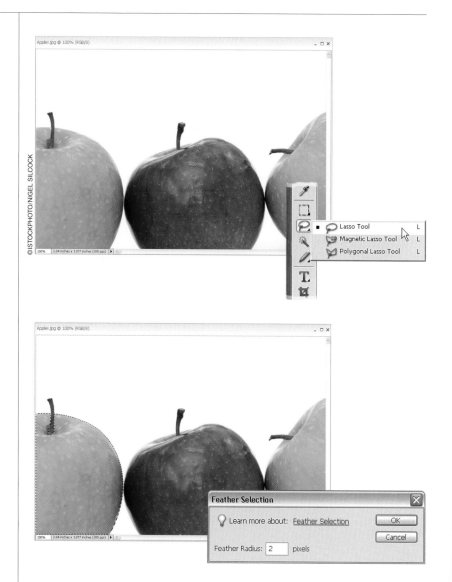

How to Select Things That Aren't Round, Square, or Rectangular

By now you know that selecting squares, rectangles, circles, ovals, etc., is a total no-brainer. But things get a little stickier when the area you want to select isn't square or rectangular or, well…you get the idea. Luckily, although it's not quite the no-brainer of the Marquee tools, making those selections isn't hard—if you don't mind being just a little patient. And making these "non-conformist" selections can actually be fun. Here's a quick project to get your feet wet:

Step One:
Open a photo with an odd-shaped object that's not rectangular, square, etc. This is what the Lasso tool was born for, so press the L key to access it from the Toolbox.

Step Two:
Click-and-hold the Lasso tool on the object you want to select (in this case, you'll be selecting the green apple on the left) and slowly (the key word here is *slowly*) drag the Lasso tool around the object, tracing its edges. If, after you're done, you've missed a spot, just hold the Shift key and click-and-drag around that missing area—it will be added to your selection. If you selected too much, hold the Alt key and click-and-drag around the area you shouldn't have selected.

Step Three:
When the object is fully selected, go under the Select menu and choose Feather (we're doing this to soften the edges of the selected area). Enter 2 pixels (just a slight bit of softening), and then click OK. Now that our edges are softened, we can make adjustments to the object without "getting caught."

Step Four:

In the example here, we're going to make the green apple red. Press Control-U to bring up the Hue/Saturation dialog. Drag the Hue slider (the top one) to the left until the apple turns red. When you do this, you'll quickly see if you made an accurate selection or not. If you see little slivers of green, you missed those spots when you were doing your tracing with the Lasso tool. If you want to try again, just press Control-D to deselect, and then press Control-Z (undo) a few times until the original color comes back. Now you can try again, making sure you've got the entire apple accurately selected. Also, try moving the Saturation slider to the left a little until the color is close to the red apple in the middle. Click OK.

Step Five:

Now select the green apple on the right using the Lasso tool. Press Control-U to bring up the Hue/Saturation dialog again and adjust the right apple's color the same way you adjusted the color of the left apple.

Step Six:

Click OK in the dialog and press Control-D to deselect. Remember, these adjustments affect only the left and right apples, not the whole photo, because you selected them with the Lasso tool *before* you altered the color.

Softening Those Harsh Edges

When you make an adjustment to a selected area in a photo, your adjustment stays completely inside the selected area. That's great in many cases, but when you deselect, you'll see a hard edge around the area you adjusted, making the change look fairly obvious. However, softening those hard edges (thereby "hiding your tracks") is easy—here's how:

Step One:

Let's say you want to brighten the area around the white flower, so it looks almost like you shined a soft spotlight on it. Start by drawing an oval selection around the flower using the Elliptical Marquee tool (press M until you have it). Make the selection big enough so the entire flower and the surrounding area appear inside your selection. Now, we're going to darken the area around the flower, so go under the Select menu and choose Inverse. This inverses the selection so you'll now have everything *but* the flower selected (you'll use this trick often).

Step Two:

Now press Control-L to bring up Levels. When the dialog appears, drag the bottom right-hand Output Levels slider to the left until it reads 140 and click OK. Now press Control-D to deselect. You can see the harsh edges around the oval, and it looks nothing like a soft spotlight—it looks like a bright oval. That's why we need to soften the edges so there's a smooth blend between the bright oval and the dark surroundings.

Step Three:

Press Control-Z two times so your photo looks like it did at the end of Step One (your inversed selection should be in place—if not, drag out another oval and inverse it). With your selection in place, go under the Select menu and choose Feather. When the Feather Selection dialog appears, enter 20 pixels (the higher the number, the more softening effect on the edges) and click OK. That's it—you've softened the edges. Now, let's see what a difference that makes.

Step Four:

Press Control-L to bring up Levels again, drag the bottom-right Output Levels slider to 140, and click OK. Deselect by pressing Control-D, and you can see that the edges of the area you adjusted are soft and blending together smoothly so it looks more like a spotlight. Now, this comes in really handy when you're doing things like adjusting somebody with a face that's too red. Without feathering the edges, you'd see a hard line around your person's face where you made your adjustments, and it would be a dead giveaway that the photo had been adjusted. But add a little bit of feather (with a face, it might only take a Feather amount of 2 or 3 pixels), and it will blend right in, hiding the fact that you made an adjustment at all.

Selecting Areas by Their Color

So, would you select an entire solid-blue sky using the Rectangular Marquee tool? You probably wouldn't. Oh, you might use a combination of the Lasso and Rectangular Marquee tools, but even then it could be somewhat of a nightmare (depending on the photo). That's where the Magic Wand tool comes in. It selects by ranges of color, so instead of clicking-and-dragging to make a selection, you click once and the Magic Wand selects things in your photo that are fairly similar in color to the area you clicked on. The Magic Wand tool is pretty amazing by itself, but you can make it work even better.

Step One:
Open a photo that has a solid-color area that you want to select (in this case, it's a red car). Start by choosing the Magic Wand tool from the Toolbox (or press the W key). Then, click it once in the solid-color area in your photo. You can see that much of the car body is selected, but probably not all of it (because, although the body is red, there are all different shades of red on it, caused by shadows and reflections. That's why this is such a good example—sometimes one click is all it takes and the whole object will be selected, but more often than not, you'll need to do a little more Magic Wanding to get the full car body).

Step Two:
As you can see above, the first click didn't select the entire area, so to add these areas to what you already have selected, just press-and-hold the Shift key, and then click on those parts of the car body that aren't selected. Keep holding down the Shift key and clicking on all the areas that you want to select until the entire body is selected (don't select the door handle, mirror, etc.—just the red parts), as shown here. It took about 15 Shift-clicks with the Magic Wand for me to get this entire car body selected.

© ISTOCKPHOTO/CRISTIAN LUPU

Step Three:

Now you can use the Adjust Hue/Saturation command (Control-U) to change the color of the car body, just like you did in previous techniques, by dragging the Hue slider until the body looks the way you want it. Press Control-D to deselect and see your final change.

TIP: If you click in an area with the Magic Wand and not all of that area gets selected, then deselect (Control-D), go to the Options Bar, increase the Tolerance setting, and try again. The higher the setting, the wider the range of colors it will select; so as a rule of thumb: if the Magic Wand doesn't select enough, increase the Tolerance amount. If it selects too much, decrease it.

Making Selections Using a Brush

A lot of people are more comfortable using brushes than using Marquee tools. If you're one of those people (you know who you are), then you're in luck—you can make your selections by painting over the areas you want selected. Even if this sounds weird, it's worth a try—you might really like it (it's the same way with sushi). A major advantage of painting your selections is that you can choose a soft-edged brush (if you like) to automatically give you feathered edges. Here's how it works:

Step One:
Choose the Selection Brush tool from the Toolbox (press the A key). Before you start, you'll want to choose your brush size by clicking on the Brush thumbnail in the Options Bar to open the Brush Picker. If you want a soft-edged selection (roughly equivalent to a feathered selection), choose a soft-edged brush in the Picker or change your brush's Hardness setting in the Options Bar: 0% gives a very soft edge, while 100% creates a very hard edge.

Step Two:
Now you can click-and-drag to "paint" the area you want selected. When you release the mouse, the selection becomes active. *Note:* You don't have to hold down the Shift key to add to your selection when using this brush—just start painting somewhere else and it's added. However, you can press-and-hold the Alt key while painting to deselect areas.

Once you have one or more objects on a layer, putting a selection around everything on that layer is a one-click affair. What's especially great about this ability is that not only does it select the hard-edged areas in a layer, but it also selects the soft-edged areas, such as drop shadows. It'll make sense in a moment.

Selecting Everything on a Layer at Once!

Step One:
Open a layered image in which one layer contains elements you want to select and alter. To instantly put a selection around everything on that layer, just Control-click on that layer's thumbnail in the Layers palette (not its name; its thumbnail).

Step Two:
For one example of why you might want to do this, while your selection is still in place, click the Create a New Layer icon. Now, choose a Foreground color and press Alt-Backspace to fill your selected area with that color. Next, change the blend mode of this new layer (at the top of the Layers palette) to Color, so now you have colored the layer's object(s). Lower the Opacity in the Layers palette to add a slight colored cast to your layer. Press Control-D to deselect.

Getting Elements to Help You Make Tricky Selections

If you've tried the Lasso tool for making selections, then you know two things: (1) it's pretty useful, and (2) tracing right along the edge of the object you're trying to select can be pretty tricky. But you can get help in the form of a tool called (are you ready for this?) the Magnetic Lasso tool! If the edges of the object you're trying to select are fairly well defined, this tool will automatically snap to the edges (as if they're magnetic), saving you time and frustration (well, it can save frustration if you know this technique).

Step One:
Click-and-hold for a moment on the Lasso tool in the Toolbox and a menu will pop up where you can choose the Magnetic Lasso tool (or just press the L key until you have it). Then, open an image in which you want to make a selection. Click once near the edge of the object you want to select. Without holding the mouse button, move the Magnetic Lasso tool along the edge of the object, and the selection will "snap" into place. Don't move too far away from the object; stay close to it for the best results.

Step Two:
As you drag, the tool lays down little points along the edge. If you're dragging the mouse and it misses an edge, just press Backspace to remove the last point and try again. If it still misses, hold the Alt key and then hold down the mouse button, which temporarily switches you to the regular Lasso tool. Drag a Lasso selection around the trouble area, then release the Alt key and the mouse button, and BAM—you're back to the Magnetic Lasso tool to finish up the job. *Note:* You can also click the Magnetic Lasso tool to add selection points if needed.

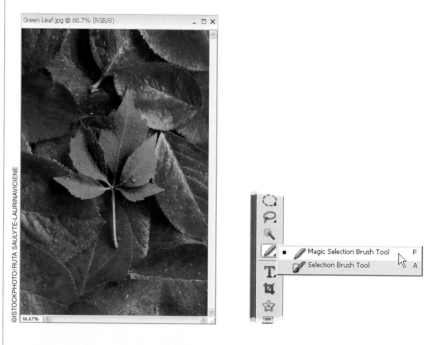

Easier Selections with the Magic Selection Tool

This is another one of those tools in Photoshop Elements 5 that makes you think, "What kind of math must be going on behind the scenes?" because this is some pretty potent mojo for selecting an object (or objects) within your photo. What makes this even more amazing is that I was able to inject the word "mojo" into this introduction, and you didn't blink an eye. You're one of "us" now…

Step One:
Open the photo that has an object you want to select (in this example, we want to select the green leaf). Go to the Toolbox and choose the Magic Selection Brush tool (or just press the F key).

Step Two:
By default, the Magic Selection Brush tool "paints" in red. If the object you're trying to select is also red, you can choose a different color for your brush. Go up to the Options Bar and click on the down-facing arrow to the right of the Color swatch. A palette of colors will appear, so you can choose a color that will contrast well with what you're trying to select to make it easier to see.

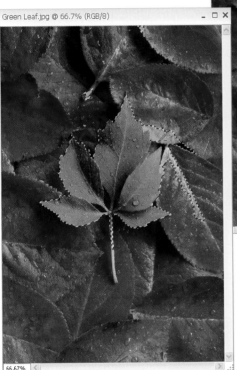

Step Three:

Take the Magic Selection Brush tool and simply paint a "squiggly" line around what you want to select. You don't have to be precise, and that is what's so great about this tool—it digs squiggles. It *longs* for the squiggles. It *needs* squiggles. So squiggle.

Step Four:

Once you release the mouse button, the Magic Selection Brush makes your selection for you, based on the area that you squiggled over. If the selection includes areas you don't want, such as the highlights on the red leaves to the right of the green leaf in this image, simply press-and-hold the Alt key and squiggle over the unwanted part. This removes it from your selection.

Step Five:

Now that we've got it selected, we might as well do something to it, eh? How about this: let's leave the leaf green, and make the background black and white. You start by going under the Select menu and choosing Inverse (which inverses your selection so you've got everything selected but the leaf). Go under the Enhance menu, under Adjust Color, and choose Remove Color. That's it. Now you can deselect by pressing Control-D.

Removing Backgrounds

One of the most requested selection tasks is how to remove something (or someone) from a background. Luckily, this task has been made dramatically easier thanks to a fairly amazing tool called the Magic Selection Brush tool (and you know if they use the word "magic" it must be true, thanks to rigid enforcement of the truth in advertising laws).

Step One:

You'll find the Magic Selection Brush tool in the Toolbox (as you might expect) nested with the Selection Brush tool (or you can press F to get it).

Step Two:

Here's how it works: Just take the brush and drag it over the object you want to select (in this case, I wanted the door and ornamental entry around it, so I dragged from the bottom-left corner diagonally to the top-right corner). The first time I tried it, it almost selected the entire object. The key word here is "almost." Sometimes, it does a perfect job (and the title "magic" is appropriate), and other times, well…magic might not come to mind, but more often than not, it really works wonders. Now, if you paint a line over an area, and it doesn't get the entire door, just hold the Shift key and paint over (or just click on) any area it missed the first time. So, be prepared to Shift-drag one or more lines to get the whole door. If you get part of the wall in your selection, press-and-hold the Alt key and paint over the area you want removed.

©ISTOCKPHOTO/NEIL SETCHFIELD

Step Three:

Here the doorway is selected after just two little strokes (my initial stroke, then I held the Shift key and painted over the step on the bottom). *Hint:* You can paint a line, paint a squiggle (you know—a squiggle), or click with the tool, and it'll do the rest. Just don't freak out if it doesn't work perfectly the first time; take a deep breath, hold the Shift key, and paint another stroke. If it selects too much, just undo (Control-Z) and try a slightly different area to stroke.

Step Four:

Well, now that we've got a selection, we might as well have some fun with it. Open a different image (in this case, a grassy field with lots of blue sky), then go back to your selected door image (make sure you're in Cascade viewing mode by going under Window, under Images). Press V to get the Move tool, and drag your selected door right over onto the field photo. If the door is too big, press Control-T to bring up the Free Transform bounding box, then hold the Shift key, grab a corner handle, and drag inward to scale it down to size. Press Enter to lock in your resizing. *Note:* If you can't see the corner handles, press Control-0 (zero).

©ISTOCKPHOTO/ANDRZEJ TOKARSKI

Continued

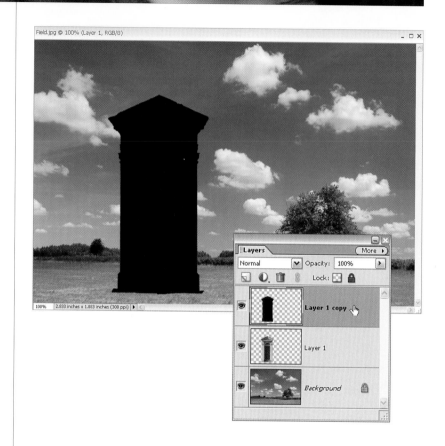

Step Five:

Press Control-J to duplicate your door layer (so now you have a door, then a duplicate right on top of it in the Layers palette). We're going to turn this duplicate into a cast shadow, and to do that we have to start by filling the duplicate door layer with black. So, press the letter D to set your Foreground color to black, and then press Alt-Shift-Backspace to fill your duplicate door with black.

Step Six:

Now we're going to turn this layer into a cast shadow. Start by pressing Control-T to bring up Free Transform again. When the Free Transform bounding box appears, press-and-hold the Control key, and then drag the top-center point down and to the left so the door looks like it's lying down. When it looks like the one shown here, press Enter to lock in your transformation.

Step Seven:
Go to the Layers palette and click-and-drag this shadow layer directly below the door layer, so the shadow appears behind the door (not in front of it).

Step Eight:
To soften the shadow (so the edges aren't so harsh), go under the Filter menu, under Blur, and choose Gaussian Blur. When the dialog appears, enter 3 for the Radius (the higher the number, the blurrier the edges will be), and then click OK.

Step Nine:
Your shadow is solid black, so to make it look more realistic, we're going to lower the Opacity so you can see through the shadow a bit. Go to the Layers palette, click on the shadow layer, and then lower the Opacity to around 65% (actually, you can choose any Opacity setting you want—if you want the shadow lighter, choose something less than 65%).

Continued

Step Ten:

Since you're a photographer, you've probably already noticed a problem. The entryway around the door looks "too red" for the surroundings, so we'll have to remove some red to make it look like the door is really in the field. Click on the door image layer in the Layers palette. Go under the Filter menu, and under Adjustments, choose Photo Filter. From the Filter pop-up menu, choose Cooling Filter (80). Reduce the Density a little, and your doorway will better match the cool tones of the field photo. Click OK and you're done.

Head Games
retouching portraits

This should be called "The Kevin Ames Chapter." Actually, it really should be called the "I Hate Kevin Ames Chapter" because I already had this entire chapter written, until I stopped by Kevin's studio in Atlanta one night to show him the rough draft of the book. What should have been a 15-minute visit went on until after midnight with him showing me some amazing portrait retouching tricks. So I had to go back home and basically rewrite, update, and tweak the entire chapter. Which, I can tell you, is no fun once you think a chapter is done and you're about a week from deadline. But the stuff he showed me was so cool, I literally couldn't sleep that night because I knew his techniques would take this chapter to the next level. And even though Kevin was incredibly gracious to let me share his techniques with my readers (that's the kind of guy Kevin is), there was no real way I was going to name this chapter "The Kevin Ames Chapter." That's when it became clear to me—I would have to kill him. But then I remembered Kevin had mentioned that Jim DiVitale had developed some of the techniques that he had showed me, so now it was going to be a double murder. I thought, "Hey, they both live in Atlanta, how hard could this be?" but the more I thought about it, what with having to fly back up there and having to fly on Delta (stuffed in like human cattle), I figured I'd just give them the credit they deserve and go on with my life. Thus far, it's worked out okay.

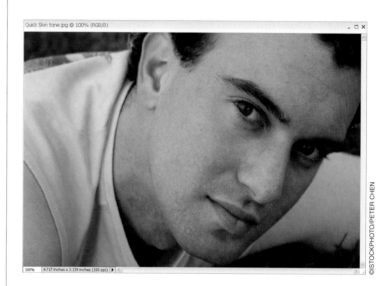

Quick Skin Tone Fix

In photos of people, the most important thing is that the skin tone looks good. That's because it's really hard for someone looking at your photo to determine if the grass is exactly the right shade of green or if the sky is the right shade of blue; but if the skin tone is off, it sticks out like a sore thumb (which would be red if it were really sore). Here's a quick fix to get your skin tones patched up in a hurry:

Step One:
Open an image in which the flesh tone looks like it needs adjusting. In the example shown here, the skin tone looks bluish and a little bit pale, so it definitely needs a fix to look right.

Step Two:
Go under the Enhance menu, under Adjust Color, and choose Adjust Color for Skin Tone.

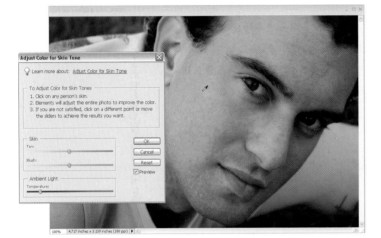

Step Three:
When the Adjust Color for Skin Tone dialog appears, move your cursor over an area of skin tone and click once to set the skin tone for the image. If you don't like your first results, click in a different area of skin tone until you find a skin-tone adjustment you're happy with.

Step Four:
You can also manually tweak the skin tone by using the Tan and Blush sliders, and you can control the overall tint of the light by dragging the Temperature slider to the left to make the skin tones cooler or to the right to make them warmer. *Note:* This skin-tone adjustment affects more than just skin—it usually warms the entire photo. If that creates a problem, use one of the selection tools (even the Lasso tool) to put a selection around the skin-tone areas first, add a 2-pixel Feather (under the Select menu), and then use the Adjust Color for Skin Tone command.

Before   *After*

Removing Blemishes

When it comes to removing blemishes, acne, or any other imperfections on the skin, our goal is to maintain as much of the original skin texture as possible. That way, our retouch doesn't look pasty and obvious. Here are three techniques I use that work nicely.

TECHNIQUE #1

Step One:
Open a photo containing some skin imperfections you want to remove.

Step Two:
Choose the Clone Stamp tool from the Toolbox (or press the S key). From the Brush Picker (which you access by clicking on the Brush thumbnail in the Options Bar), choose a soft-edged brush that's slightly larger than the blemish you want to remove.

TIP: Once you're working, if you need to quickly adjust the brush size, use the Bracket keys on your keyboard: the Left Bracket key ([) makes your brush smaller; the Right (]) larger.

Step Three:

In the Options Bar, change the Mode pop-up menu of the Clone Stamp tool to Lighten. With its Mode set to Lighten, the Clone Stamp will affect only pixels that are darker than the area you're going to sample. The lighter pixels (the regular flesh tone) will pretty much stay intact, and only the darker pixels (the blemish) will be affected.

Step Four:

Press the letter Z to access the Zoom tool and zoom in if needed, and then switch back to the Clone Stamp tool. Find an area right near the blemish that's pretty clean (no visible spots, blemishes, etc.), hold the Alt key, and click once. The Clone Stamp will now sample the skin from that area. Try to make sure this sample area is very near the blemish so the skin tones will match. If you move too far away, you risk having your repair appear in a slightly different color, which is a dead giveaway of a repair.

Step Five:

Now, move your cursor directly over the blemish and click just once. Don't paint! Just click. The click will do it—it will remove the blemish instantly, while leaving the skin texture intact. But what if the blemish is lighter than the skin, rather than darker? Simply go to the Options Bar and change the Mode of the Clone Stamp tool to Darken instead of Lighten—it's that easy. On to Technique #2.

Continued

TECHNIQUE #2

Step One:

Press L to switch to the Lasso tool. Find a clean area (no blemishes, spots, etc.) near the blemish that you want to remove. In this clean area, use the Lasso tool to make a selection that is slightly larger than the blemish. (*Note:* If you make a mistake and need to add to your selection, press-and-hold the Shift key while selecting with the Lasso tool; if you need to remove parts of your selection, press-and-hold the Alt key.)

Step Two:

Once your selection is in place, go under the Select menu and choose Feather. When the Feather Selection dialog appears, enter 2 pixels as your Feather Radius and click OK. Feathering blurs the edges of our selected area, which will help hide the traces of our retouch. Feathering (softening) the edges of a selection is a very important part of facial retouching, and you'll do this quite a bit to "hide your tracks," so to speak.

Step Three:

Now that you've softened the edges of the selection, hold Control-Alt, and you'll see your cursor change into two arrowheads—a white one with a black one overlapping it. This is telling you that you're about to copy the selected area. Click within your selection and drag this clean skin area right over the blemish to completely cover it. When the clean area covers the blemish, release the keys (and the mouse button, of course) to drop this selected area down onto your photo. Now, press Control-D to deselect. The blemish is gone. Best of all, because you dragged skin over from a nearby area, the full skin texture is perfectly intact, making your repair nearly impossible to detect.

TECHNIQUE #3
Step One:
Get the Spot Healing Brush tool from the Toolbox (or just press the J key). We'll use it on the blemishes—and you'll see it works brilliantly.

Step Two:
Just move over the blemish, and click the tool once. That's it. You've got to love a technique that only has two steps.

Before

After, using all three techniques

Lessening Freckles or Facial Acne

This technique is popular with senior class portrait photographers who need to lessen or remove large areas of acne, pockmarks, or freckles from their subjects. This is especially useful when you have a lot of photos to retouch and don't have the time to use the methods shown previously, where you deal with each blemish individually.

Step One:
Open the photo that you need to retouch. Make a duplicate of the Background layer by going to the Layer menu, under New, and choosing Layer via Copy (or just pressing Control-J). We'll perform our retouch on this duplicate of the Background layer, named "Layer 1."

Step Two:
Go under the Filter menu, under Blur, and choose Gaussian Blur. When the Gaussian Blur dialog appears, drag the slider all the way to the left, then drag it slowly to the right until you see the freckles blurred away. The photo should look very blurry, but we'll fix that in just a minute, so don't let that throw you off—make sure it's blurry enough that the freckles are no longer visible. Click OK.

Step Three:
Press-and-hold the Control key and click once on the Create a New Layer icon at the top of the Layers palette. This creates a new blank layer (Layer 2) directly beneath your current layer (the blurry Layer 1).

Step Four:
Now, in the Layers palette, click back on the top layer (the blurry Layer 1), then press Control-G to group the blurry layer with the blank layer beneath it (Layer 2). Doing this removes all the blurriness from view (and that's exactly what we want to do at this point).

Step Five:
In the Layers palette, click on the middle layer (the blank Layer 2), as you're going to paint on this layer. Press the letter D to set your Foreground color to black. Press the letter B to switch to the Brush tool, then click on the Brush thumbnail in the Options Bar, and from the Brush Picker choose a soft-edged brush.

Continued

Step Six:

Lower the Opacity setting of your brush in the Options Bar to 50%, and change the Mode pop-up menu from Normal to Lighten. Now when you paint, it will affect only the pixels that are darker than the blurred state. Ahhh, do you see where this is going?

Step Seven:

Now you can paint over the freckle areas, and as you paint you'll see them diminish quite a bit. If they diminish too much, and the person looks "too clean," undo (Control-Z), then lower the Opacity of the brush to 25% and try again.

Before

After

Here's a quick technique for removing the dark circles that sometimes appear under a person's eyes—especially after a hard night of drinking. At least, that's what I've been told.

Removing Dark Circles under Eyes

Step One:
Open the photo that has the dark circles you want to lessen. Select the Clone Stamp tool in the Toolbox (or press the S key). Then, click on the Brush thumbnail in the Options Bar to open the Brush Picker and choose a soft-edged brush that's half as wide as the area you want to repair. *Note:* Press the letter Z to switch to the Zoom tool and zoom in if needed.

Step Two:
Go to the Options Bar and lower the Opacity of the Clone Stamp tool to 50%. Then, change the Mode pop-up menu to Lighten (so you'll only affect areas that are darker than where you'll sample from).

Continued

Step Three:

Press-and-hold the Alt key and click once in an area near the eye that isn't affected by the dark circles. If the cheeks aren't too rosy, you can click there, but more likely you'll click (sample) on an area just below the dark circles under the eyes.

Step Four:

Now, take the Clone Stamp tool and paint over the dark circles to lessen or remove them. It may take two or more strokes for the dark circles to pretty much disappear, so don't be afraid to go back over the same spot if the first stroke didn't work. *Note:* If you want the dark circles to completely disappear, try using the Healing Brush tool (J) from the Toolbox. Simply Alt-click the Healing Brush in a light area under the dark circles, and then paint the circles away.

Before

After

Removing or Lessening Wrinkles

This is a great trick for removing wrinkles, with a little twist at the end (courtesy of my buddy Kevin Ames) that helps make the technique look more realistic. His little tweak makes a big difference because (depending on the age of the subject) removing every wrinkle would probably make the photo look obviously retouched (in other words, if you're retouching someone in their 70s and you make them look as if they're 20 years old, it's just going to look weird). Here's how to get a more realistic wrinkle removal:

Step One:
Open the photo that needs some wrinkles or crow's-feet lessened or removed.

Step Two:
Duplicate the Background layer by going to the Layer menu, under New, and choosing Layer via Copy (or pressing Control-J). You'll perform your "wrinkle removal" on this duplicate layer, named "Layer 1" in the Layers palette.

Step Three:
Get the Healing Brush tool from the Toolbox (or press the J key). Then, choose a soft-edged brush from the Brush Picker (which opens when you click the Brush thumbnail in the Options Bar). Choose a brush size that's close to the size of the wrinkles you want to remove.

Continued

Step Four:

Find a clean area that's somewhere near the wrinkles (perhaps the upper cheek if you're removing crow's-feet, or if you're removing forehead wrinkles, perhaps just above or below the wrinkle). Hold the Alt key and click once to sample the skin texture from that area. Now, take the Healing Brush tool and paint over the wrinkles. As you paint, the wrinkles will disappear, yet the texture and detail of the skin remains intact, which is why this tool is so amazing.

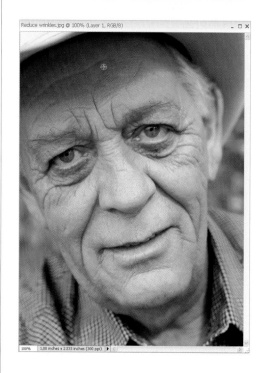

Step Five:

Now that the wrinkles are gone, it's time to bring just enough of them back to make it look realistic. Simply go to the Layers palette and reduce the Opacity of this layer to bring back some of the original wrinkles. This lets a small amount of the original photo (the Background layer, with all its wrinkles still intact) show through. Keep lowering the Opacity until you see the wrinkles, but not nearly as prominent as before.

Before

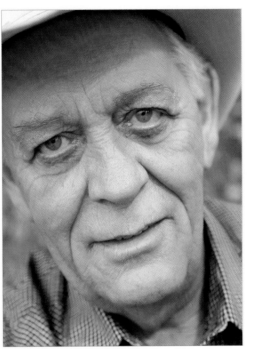

After

Whitening the Eyes

This is a great little technique for quickly whitening the whites of the eyes, and it has the added benefit of removing any redness in the eye along the way. *Note:* By redness, I mean the "bloodshot-I-stayed-up-too-late" type of redness, not the "red-eye-from-a-flash-mounted-above-the-lens" type of redness, which is addressed in Chapter 5.

Step One:
Open the photo where the subject's eyes need whitening. Press the letter Z to switch to the Zoom tool and zoom in if needed.

Step Two:
Choose the Lasso tool from the Toolbox (or press the L key) and draw a selection around one side of whites in one of the eyes. Press-and-hold the Shift key and draw selections around the other area of whites in the same eye and the whites of the other eye, until all the whites are selected in both eyes.

Step Three:
Go under the Select menu and choose Feather. You'll need to use Feather to soften the edges of your selection so your retouch isn't obvious. In the Feather Selection dialog, enter 2 pixels and click OK.

Step Four:
Go under the Enhance menu, under Adjust Color, and choose Adjust Hue/Saturation. When the Hue/Saturation dialog appears, choose Reds from the Edit pop-up menu at the top (to edit just the reds in the selection). Now, drag the Saturation slider to the left to lower the amount of saturation in the reds (which removes any bloodshot appearance in the whites of the eyes).

Step Five:
While you're still in the Hue/Saturation dialog, from the Edit menu switch back to Master. Drag the Lightness slider to the right to increase the lightness of the whites of the eyes. Click OK in the Hue/Saturation dialog to apply your adjustments, and then press Control-D to deselect and complete the enhancement.

Continued

Before   *After*

This is another one of those 30-second miracles for enhancing the eyes. This technique makes the eyes seem to sparkle by accentuating the catch lights, and generally draws attention to the eyes by making them look sharp and crisp (crisp in the "sharp and clean" sense, not crisp in the "I-burned-my-retina-while-looking-at-the-sun" sense).

Making Eyes that Sparkle

Step One:
Open the photo that you want to retouch. Make a duplicate of the Background layer by going under the Layer menu, under New, and choosing Layer via Copy (or pressing Control-J), which creates a new layer named "Layer 1." *Note:* Press the Z key to switch to the Zoom tool and zoom in if needed.

Step Two:
Go under the Enhance menu and choose Unsharp Mask. (It sounds like this filter would make things blurry, but it's actually for sharpening photos.) When the Unsharp Mask dialog appears, enter your settings. (If you need some settings, go to the first technique, named "Basic Sharpening," in Chapter 11, or you can use my favorite all-around sharpening settings of Amount: 85%, Radius: 1, and Threshold: 4 for now.) Then click OK to sharpen the entire photo.

Continued

Step Three:

After you've applied the Unsharp Mask filter, apply it again using the same settings by pressing Control-F, and then apply it one more time using the same keyboard shortcut (you'll apply it three times in all). The eyes will probably look nice and crisp at this point, but the rest of the person will be severely oversharpened, and you'll probably see lots of noise and other unpleasant artifacts.

Step Four:

Hold the Control key and click once on the Create a New Layer icon at the top of the Layers palette. This creates a new blank layer directly beneath your sharpened layer. Now, in the Layers palette, click back on the top layer (the sharpened layer), then press Control-G to group the sharpened layer with the blank layer beneath it. This removes all the visible sharpness (at least for now). In the Layers palette, click on the middle layer (the blank layer), as you're going to paint on this layer.

Step Five:
Press the letter D to set your Foreground color to black. Then, press B to switch to the Brush tool. Click on the Brush thumbnail in the Options Bar to open the Brush Picker, and choose a soft-edged brush that's a little smaller than your subject's eyes. Now paint over just the irises and pupils of the eyes to reveal the sharpening, making the eyes really sparkle and completing the effect.

Before

After

Enhancing Eyebrows and Eyelashes

Let's face it—not every face is perfect, so we sometimes resort to using makeup to enhance our facial features. So what happens when the model for your photo shoot forgets to wear mascara—or worse yet—has transparent eyebrows? Well, don't browbeat her (okay, that was lame)—just fix it in Elements.

Step One:
Open the photo that you want to enhance.

©ISTOCKPHOTO/AMANDA ROHDE

Step Two:
Go to the Layers palette and choose Levels from the Create Adjustment Layer pop-up menu (it's the half-white/half-black circle icon at the top of the palette).

Step Three:

When the Levels dialog appears, drag the shadow Input Levels slider to the right to darken the image. The entire image will darken, but don't worry, we'll fix that later—just focus on the eyebrows and eyelashes as you drag the slider. When the eyebrows and eyelashes look good to you, click OK.

Step Four:

Press the letter X until your Foreground color is black. Then, press Alt-Backspace to fill your adjustment layer mask with black. This hides the Levels adjustment you just made, revealing your original Background layer.

Step Five:

Now, press the letter B to switch to the Brush tool. Click on the Brush thumbnail in the Options Bar and in the resulting Brush Picker choose a small, soft-edged brush that's the same size as the largest area of the eyebrows. Press the X key again to switch your Foreground color to white and begin painting over the eyebrows. As you get to smaller areas of the eyebrows, press the Left Bracket key ([) to decrease the size of your brush.

Continued

Step Six:

If the eyebrows are too dark, don't sweat it—we'll fix that later. Now let's move on to the eyelashes, so press the Left Bracket key ([) to decrease the size of your Brush tool. (You may have to press the Bracket key several times to make the brush the size of the eyelashes.)

Step Seven:

With your small Brush tool, lightly paint over the eyelashes on both eyes. *Note:* If needed, press the Z key to switch to the Zoom tool and zoom into the image for a better look. Then, press the B key to switch back to the Brush tool and begin painting.

Step Eight:
Now the effect may be too intense, so lower the Opacity in the Layers palette to around 65% or until the effect looks natural.

Before

After

Colorizing Hair

This technique (that I learned from Kevin Ames) gives you maximum control and flexibility while changing or adjusting hair color, and because of the use of an adjustment layer, you're not "bruising the pixels." Instead, you're following the enlightened path of "non-destructive retouching."

Step One:
Open the photo you want to retouch. Choose Hue/Saturation from the Create Adjustment Layer pop-up menu at the top of the Layers palette.

Step Two:
When the dialog appears, turn on the Colorize checkbox (in the bottom right-hand corner of the dialog) and then drag the Hue slider to the approximate color you'd like for the hair. Doing this will colorize the entire image, but don't let that throw you—just focus on the hair color. You may also have to drag the Saturation slider to the right a bit to make the color more vibrant. Now, click OK and the entire photo will have a heavy color cast over it.

Step Three:
Press the letter X to change your Foreground color to black, and then press Alt-Backspace to fill the layer mask of the Hue/Saturation adjustment layer with black. Doing so removes the colorized tint from the photo.

Step Four:
Press B to switch to the Brush tool. Choose a soft-edged brush from the Brush Picker (by clicking on the Brush thumbnail in the Options Bar). Press X again to set your Foreground color to white and begin painting over the hair. As you paint, the tint you added with Hue/Saturation is painted back in. Once the hair is fully painted, change the layer blend mode of your Hue/Saturation adjustment layer to Color, then lower the Opacity in the Layers palette until the hair color looks natural.

Before

After

Whitening and Brightening Teeth

This really should be called "Removing Yellowing, Then Whitening Teeth" because almost everyone has some yellowing, so we remove that first before we move on to the whitening process. This is a simple technique, but the results have a big impact on the overall look of the portrait, and that's why I do this to every single portrait where the subject is smiling.

Step One:
Open the photo you need to retouch. Press Z to switch to the Zoom tool and zoom in if needed.

©ISTOCKPHOTO/MARCIN BALCERZAK

Step Two:
Press L to switch to the Lasso tool, and carefully draw a selection around the teeth, being careful not to select any of the gums or lips. If you've missed a spot, press-and-hold Shift while using the Lasso tool to add to your selection, or press-and-hold Alt and drag the Lasso to remove parts of the selection.

Feather Selection

Learn more about: Feather Selection

Feather Radius: 1 pixels

OK
Cancel

Step Three:
Go under the Select menu and choose Feather. When the Feather Selection dialog appears, enter 1 pixel and click OK to smooth the edges of your selection. That way, you won't see a hard edge along the area you selected once you've whitened the teeth.

Hue/Saturation

Learn more about: Hue/Saturation

OK
Cancel
Help

Edit: Yellows

Hue: 0

Saturation: -75

Lightness: 0

15°/45°   75°\105°

Colorize
Preview

Step Four:
Go under the Enhance menu, under Adjust Color, and choose Adjust Hue/Saturation. When the dialog appears, choose Yellows from the Edit pop-up menu at the top. Then, drag the Saturation slider to the left to remove the yellowing from the teeth.

Continued

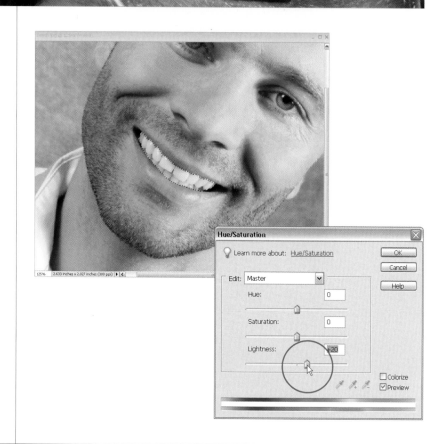

Step Five:

Now that the yellowing is removed, switch the Edit pop-up menu back to Master, and drag the Lightness slider to the right to whiten and brighten the teeth. Be careful not to drag it too far, or the retouch will be obvious. Click OK in the Hue/Saturation dialog and your enhancements will be applied. Press Control-D to deselect and see your finished retouch.

Before

After

If you've ever had to deal with hot spots (shiny areas on your subject's face caused by uneven lighting or the flash reflecting off shiny surfaces, making your subject look as if they're sweating), you know they can be pretty tough to correct. That is, unless you know this trick.

Removing Hot Spots

Step One:
Open the photo that has hot spots that need to be toned down. Press the Z key to switch to the Zoom tool and zoom in if needed. Select the Clone Stamp tool in the Toolbox (or press the S key). Go to the Options Bar and change the Mode pop-up menu from Normal to Darken and lower the Opacity to 50%. By changing the Mode to Darken, we'll only affect pixels that are lighter than the area we're sampling, and those lighter pixels are the hot spots.

Step Two:
Choose a medium, soft-edged brush from the Brush Picker (found by clicking the Brush thumbnail in the Options Bar), then hold the Alt key and click once in a clean area of skin (an area with no hot spots). This will be your sample area, or reference point, so Elements knows to affect only pixels that are lighter than this.

Continued

Step Three:

Start gently painting over the hot spot areas with the Clone Stamp tool, and as you do, the hot spots will fade away.

Step Four:

As you work on different hot spots, you'll have to resample (Alt-click) on nearby areas of skin so the skin tone matches. For example, when you move on to another hot spot, sample an area of skin near the new hot spot that you'll be working on.

Hot spots.jpg @ 100% (RGB/8)

100%   7.861 inches x 11.778 inches (72 ppi)

Step Five:
It's amazing what you can do in 60 seconds of hot-spot retouching using this technique. Notice how the hot spots are now gone as I paint them away. Much of this was done with brush strokes, but just clicking once or twice with the Clone Stamp tool (as I'm doing here) often works, too.

Before

After

Digital Nose Job

This is a very simple technique for decreasing the size of your subject's nose by 15% to 20%. The actual shrinking of the nose is a breeze and only takes a minute or two—you may spend a little bit of time cloning away the sides of the original nose, but since the new nose winds up on its own layer, it makes this cloning a lot easier. Here's how it's done:

Step One:
Open the photo that you want to retouch. Press the Z key to switch to the Zoom tool and zoom in if needed. Press L to switch to the Lasso tool, and draw a loose selection around your subject's nose. Make sure you don't make this selection too close or too precise—you need to capture some flesh-tone area around the nose as well.

Step Two:
To soften the edges of your selection, go under the Select menu and choose Feather. When the Feather Selection dialog appears, for Feather Radius enter 10 pixels (for high-res, 300-ppi images, enter 22 pixels), then click OK. Now, go under the Layer menu, under New, and choose Layer via Copy. This will copy just the selected area to a new layer (Layer 1).

Step Three:
Press Control-T to bring up the Free Transform bounding box. Hold Control-Alt-Shift, then grab the upper right-hand corner point of the bounding box and drag inward to add a perspective effect to the nose. Doing this gives the person a pug nose, so release all the keys, then grab the top-center point and drag straight downward to undo the "pug effect" and make the nose look natural again, but now it's smaller.

Step Four:
When the new size looks about right, press Enter to lock in your changes. If any of the old nose peeks out from behind the new nose, go to the Layers palette, click on the Background layer, and then use the Clone Stamp tool (S) to clone away those areas: Sample an area next to the nose by Alt-clicking, and then clone right over the old nose, completing the effect.

Continued

Before   *After*

This is a pretty slick technique for taking a photo where the subject was frowning and tweaking it just a bit to add a pleasant smile—which can often save a photo that otherwise would've been ignored.

Transforming a Frown into a Smile

Step One:
Open the photo that you want to retouch.

Step Two:
Go under the Filter menu, under Distort, and choose Liquify. When the Liquify dialog appears, choose the Zoom tool (it looks like a magnifying glass) from the Liquify Toolbox (found along the left edge of the dialog). Click it once or twice within the preview window to zoom in closer on your subject's face. Then, choose the Warp tool (it's the top tool in the Liquify Toolbox).

Continued

Step Three:

In the Tool Options on the right side of the dialog, choose a brush size that's roughly the size of the person's cheek. Place the brush at the base of a cheek and click-and-"tug" slightly up. This tugging of the cheek makes the corner of the mouth turn up, creating a smile.

Step Four:

Repeat the "tug" on the opposite side of the mouth, using the already tugged side as a visual guide as to how far to tug. Be careful not to tug too far, or you'll turn your subject into the Joker from *Batman Returns*. Click OK in Liquify to apply the change, and the retouch is applied to your photo.

Before   *After*

Glamour Skin Softening

This is a technique I learned from Chicago-based retoucher David Cuerdon. David uses this technique in fashion and glamour photography to give skin a smooth, silky look, and it's also popular in shots of female seniors (not high school seniors—the other seniors).

Step One:

Open the photo to which you want to give the glamour skin-softening effect and duplicate the Background layer by going under the Layer menu, under New, and choosing Layer via Copy (or pressing Control-J).

Step Two:

Go under the Filter menu, under Blur, and choose Gaussian Blur. When the dialog appears, enter from 3 to 6 pixels of blur (depending on how soft you want the skin) to put a blur over the entire photo. When it looks good to you, click OK in the dialog.

Step Three:
Next, lower the Opacity of this layer by 50%. At this point, the blurring effect is reduced and now the photo has a soft glow to it. In some cases, you may want to leave it at this, with an overall soft, glamorous effect (you sometimes see portraits of people over 60 with this overall softening), so your retouch is complete. If this is too much softening for your subject, go on to the next steps.

Step Four:
What really pulls this technique together is selectively bringing back details in some of the facial areas. Press E to switch to the Eraser tool, choose a soft-edged brush from the Brush Picker in the Options Bar, and erase over the facial areas that are supposed to have sharp detail, such as eyebrows, lips, and teeth. What you're doing is erasing the blurriness, and thereby revealing the original features on the Background layer beneath your blurry layer.

Continued

Step Five:

David completes his retouch at Step Four, leaving the subject's clothes, hair, etc., with the soft glow. I prefer to switch to a larger, soft-edged Eraser tool and erase over everything else except the skin—so I erase over the hair, the clothes, etc., so everything has sharp detail except the skin. This is totally a personal preference, so I recommend trying both and seeing which fits your particular needs.

Before

After

Slimming and Trimming

This is an incredibly popular technique because it consistently works so well, and because just about everyone would like to look about 10 to 15 pounds thinner. I've never applied this technique to a photo and (a) been caught, or (b) not had clients absolutely love the way they look. The most important part of this technique may be not telling the client you used it.

Step One:
Open the photo of the person that you want to put on a quick diet.

Step Two:
Maximize your view if needed by going under Window, under Images, and choosing Maximize Mode or click the Maximize button in the upper right-hand corner of the image window. Now, press Control-A to put a selection around the entire photo. Then, press Control-T to bring up the Free Transform command. The Free Transform handles will appear at the corners and sides of your photo.

Continued

Step Three:

Grab the right-center handle and drag it horizontally toward the left to slim the subject. The farther you drag, the slimmer the subject becomes.

Step Four:

How far is too far (in other words, how far can you drag before people start looking like they've been retouched)? Use the Width field in the Options Bar as a guide. You're pretty safe to drag inward to around 95%, although I've been known to go to 94% or even 93% once in a while (it depends on the photo).

Step Five:

Press Enter to lock in your transformation and press Control-D to deselect. Now that you've moved the image area over a bit, you'll have to use the Crop tool (C) to crop away the background area that is now visible on the right side of your photo. After you drag out your cropping border over your image, press the Enter key to complete your crop. You can see how effective this simple little trick is at slimming and trimming your subject. Also, notice that because we didn't drag too far, the subject still looks very natural.

Before   *After*

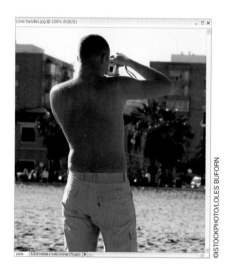

Removing Love Handles

This is a very handy body-sculpting technique, and you'll probably be surprised at how many times you'll wind up using it. It uses Liquify, which many people first dismissed as a "toy for giving people bug-eyes and huge lips," but it didn't take long for professional retouchers to see how powerful this tool could really be.

Step One:
Open the photo that has a love handle repair just waiting to happen.

Step Two:
Go under the Filter menu, under Distort, and choose Liquify. When the Liquify dialog appears, click on the Zoom tool in the Toolbox on the left-hand side of the dialog, and then drag out a selection around the area you want to work on to give you a close-up view for greater accuracy.

Step Three:

Get the Shift Pixels tool from Liquify's Toolbox (it's the seventh tool down or just press S). Choose a relatively small brush size using the Brush Size field near the top-right of the Liquify dialog. With it, paint an upward stroke starting just below and outside of the love handle on the right and continuing upward (as shown here). The pixels will shift back in toward the body, removing the love handle as you paint. (*Note:* When removing the love handle on the left, paint downward rather than upward. Why? That's just the way it works.) When you click OK, the love handle repair is complete, and you'll see the difference a quick 30-second retouch can make.

Before

After

Take Me Away
removing unwanted objects

Is "Take Me Away" a perfect title for a chapter about removing unwanted objects from your photos or what? I've heard the song (by Christina Vidal from Disney's *Freaky Friday* soundtrack) a couple of thousand times now, because my son likes to listen to it (over and over again) on the way to school each morning. Not only have I unconsciously memorized the words, I've actually begun to like the song. It happened around the 13-hundredth time I heard it. By my 14-hundredth listen, I started developing my own background harmonies, and by the 15-hundredth time, I went out and bought the sheet music. This is highly embarrassing stuff, so don't tell anyone. Anyway, this chapter shows you how to remove things that ruin otherwise

beautiful photos. For example, let's say you got married, and you've got some great photos from your wedding, but then a year or so later, you get divorced. You looked really great in your wedding dress, so you want to keep the photos, but you hate seeing your ex in there. Well, this chapter will show you how to remove him. Well, it doesn't show you exactly that—how to remove your ex from your wedding photos—but it does show you how to remove any annoying thing, so really you could apply these techniques to your wedding photos. But I gotta tell ya, if you spend your time removing your ex from your wedding photos, perhaps learning new Elements techniques shouldn't be your biggest concern.

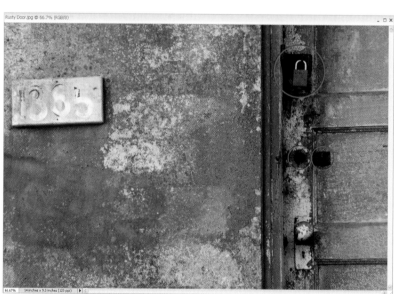

Cloning Away Unwanted Objects

The Clone Stamp tool has been the tool of choice for removing distracting or other unwanted objects in photos for years now. Although the Healing Brush in many ways offers a better and more realistic alternative, there are certain situations where the Clone Stamp tool is still the best tool for the job. Here's an example of how this workhorse removes unwanted objects:

Step One:
Nothing ruins old-world charm like a new padlock from Home Depot and the rusty hardware from a previous lock. The hole in the door next to the rusty hardware doesn't help much either, and since we're going to remove the padlock and rusty hardware, we may as well cover the hole at the same time, eh? (The three offending objects are circled here.) Let's do it.

Step Two:

Press S to get the Clone Stamp tool. In the Options Bar, click on the Brush thumbnail to the left of the Size pop-up menu and choose a medium, soft-edged brush in the Picker. Now, hold the Alt key and click once in an area of the door just above the rusty lock hardware. This is called "sampling." You just sampled a door area, and in the next step, you're going to clone that door area over the rusty hardware to completely cover it. (By the way, when you sample, a little "target" cursor appears letting you know you're sampling.)

Step Three:

Move directly down and begin painting with the Clone Stamp tool. As you paint over the rusty hardware, the door you sampled is cloned right over it, so it looks like the hardware has disappeared. Paint a little in this area to get a feel for how the Clone Stamp works (at least, if it's your first time cloning; if it's not, then you know what to do—start cloning over that hardware). As you can see here, that hardware is now gone! The key technique to remember is to sample in an area where the basic light and texture are the same (above the hardware), then move straight down to the object. *Note:* The little plus-sign cursor (the area where you sampled) is immediately above the circular brush cursor (where you're painting now). By keeping them side-by-side, you're making sure you don't pick up patterns or colors from other parts of the photo that would make your cloning look obvious.

Continued

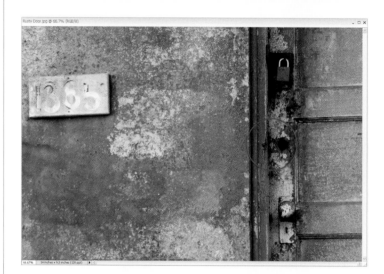

Step Four:

Now, we're going to clone over the hole in the door left by the old lock. To do that, start by pressing the Left Bracket ([) key to make your brush smaller and Alt-clicking in an area that has similar tone and texture to that part of the door. In the example shown here, I Alt-clicked on the left side of the door (right next to the hole).

Step Five:

Look at the plus-sign cursor (to the left of the hole in the previous step). That's where I sampled, and now you can start painting over the hole to clone over it (as shown on the top), but it's important to understand why you have to sample from an area that has similar color and texture. For example, try this: Alt-click over where you sampled in Step Two, then go back and start cloning over the hole. Look how much lighter (and more obvious) the cloning looks (as shown on the bottom). That's why you usually have to sample very close to where you clone. If not, it's a dead giveaway.

TIP: One of the tricks to removing objects realistically is to sample often (by Alt-clicking) in different but nearby areas so that your cloning appears random, therefore avoiding repeating patterns.

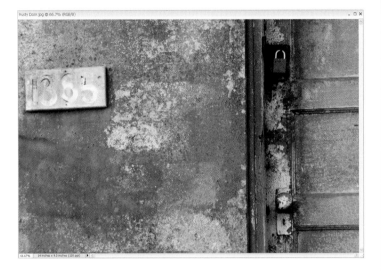

Step Six:

In the example shown here, I've chosen a different spot and Alt-clicked. Then, I started cloning away more of the hole. During the process of removing something with only a small area of similar color and texture to sample from (or when removing something large), you may want to Alt-click in slightly different areas several times, so your cloning looks natural and random. Just keep in mind that wherever you Alt-click, make sure the tone and texture are the same as the area you're cloning into (in other words, it should look the same as the area that currently surrounds the hole).

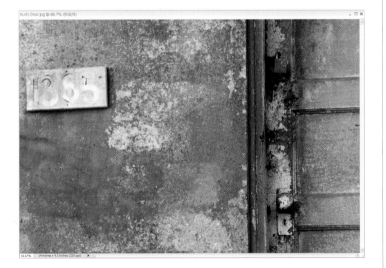

Step Seven:

Alt-click the Clone Stamp tool on the door area above the padlock, then paint right over the padlock and rusty hasp. Again, you will probably have to sample several areas to cover the entire lock and complete this technique.

Continued

Before   *After*

This is an incredibly handy little trick I learned from Rich Harris, who contributes some great tutorials to our magazine, *Photoshop User* (www.photoshopuser.com), and I've found no better way to clone away objects that need to be straight (like horizons, walls, etc.). Thanks to Rich for sharing this technique with us.

Removing Things in a Straight Line

SCOTT KELBY

Step One:

Open your image, and then press S to get the Clone Stamp tool. Now press-and-hold the Alt key, and take a look at your cursor (shown here enlarged in the white box). See the horizontal and vertical lines inside the circle? That's the key. You must position the cursor's center "target" line (either horizontal or vertical) on the straight edge that you want to clone in your image (in this case, the horizontal edge of a building). With the Alt key held down, click once when the target (called the "sample cursor") is aligned on the edge in your image.

Step Two:

Drag directly to the right while pressing-and-holding the Alt key, but don't click. With this key held down, align the sample cursor's horizontal center line along the edge in your image.

Continued

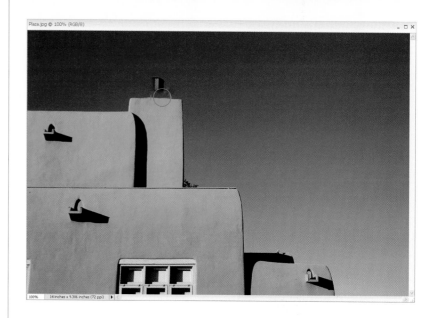

Step Three:

With the horizontal line positioned along the edge in your photo, release the Alt key and start cloning. As you clone, paint along the same straight line. It's all about making sure that the cursor's horizontal line is aligned with the edge in your image *before* you start painting.

Step Four:

After using a smaller brush to clone away part of your object along a straight line, you may need to switch to a larger brush to start cloning away other areas of the object. Then, get your smaller brush again to finish cloning along the line. Here is the finished image.

If there are just one or two annoying things that are messing up your otherwise lovely photo, here's a quick way to get rid of them while maintaining maximum texture and authenticity (because you're using another part of the photo to cover what you don't want visible, so the grain, texture, and well—everything—is right on the money).

Covering Unwanted Elements

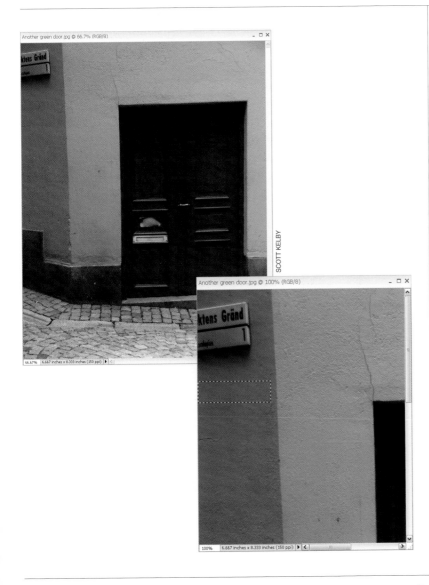

SCOTT KELBY

Step One:

In this example, we have another charming "old-world" door, but the street sign around the corner pulls the charming "old-world" feel right out of the photo. So...the sign has to go. We could use the Clone Stamp tool, but this method makes the removal perfect because you're actually going to cover the sign with a chunk of the wall close to it, which is an even more realistic fix and is as fast as, if not faster than, the alternative.

Step Two:

Press Z to get the Zoom tool and zoom in on the area with the offensive sign. Now press M to get the Rectangular Marquee tool, and drag out a selection below the sign and its shadow.

Continued

Step Three:

You'll need to put a feather on your selection so the edges will be soft and blend in perfectly, hiding the fact that you did anything to the photo at all. So, go under the Select menu and choose Feather. When the Feather Selection dialog appears, enter 1–3 pixels (depending on your percentage of zoom) for the Feather Radius and click OK.

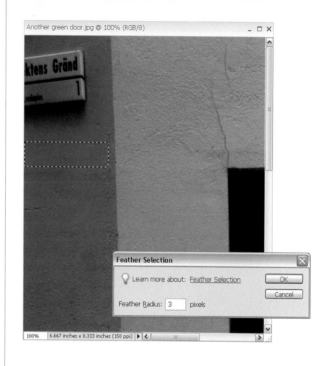

Step Four:

Pressing-and-holding the Control and Alt keys, click-and-drag the selected area over part of the sign or its shadow. This makes a copy of the selected area, so you're really dragging along a copy of the rectangular chunk of the wall. Press Control-D to deselect and see the results. By the way, you won't see any harsh edges to give you away because you feathered those edges in the previous step.

Step Five:
Move to another clean area of wall, make a selection, feather the selection, and copy-and-drag it over more of your sign. Do this until the entire sign and the shadows around it are covered.

Step Six:
Below is a before and after. You can see what a difference removing that one little area made.

TIP: If you press-and-hold Control-Alt and the Shift key, your selected area will remain perfectly in line as you drag. Also, if you're covering a small object, you can drag your first selection around the object, then move that selection to a clean area, feather it, copy it, and you're done.

Before

After

Removing Spots and Other Artifacts

In Elements 3, Adobe added the Spot Healing Brush tool, which is just about the perfect tool for getting rid of spots and other artifacts. (By the way, the term "artifacts" is a fancy "ten-dollar" word for spots and other junk that wind up in your photos.) Believe it or not, it's even faster and easier to use than the regular Healing Brush, because it's pretty much a one-trick pony—it fixes spots.

Step One:
Open a photo that has spots (whether they're in the scene itself or are courtesy of specks or dust on either your lens or your camera's sensors). In the photo shown here, there are all sorts of distracting little spots in the sky.

Step Two:
Press Z to get the Zoom tool and zoom in on an area with lots of spots (in this case, I zoomed in on the area of sky with the contrails). Now get the Spot Healing Brush tool from the Toolbox (or just press the letter J).

Step Three:
Position the Spot Healing Brush directly over the spot you want to remove and click once. That's it—you don't have to sample an area or Alt-click anywhere first—you just move it over the spot and click—the spot is gone.

Step Four:
You remove other spots the same way—just position the Spot Healing Brush over them and click. I know it sounds too easy, but that's the way it works. So, just move around and start clicking away on the spots. Now you can "de-spot" any photo, getting a "spotless" version in about 30 seconds, thanks to the Spot Healing Brush.

Before

After

Removing Distracting Objects (Healing Brush)

The Healing Brush is ideal for removing spots, little rips, stains, and stuff like that because it keeps more of the original texture and the fixes look more realistic, but it isn't as good as the Clone Stamp tool at removing larger, unwanted objects. For example, if the thing you want to remove is all by itself (it's not overlapping or touching anything else in your photo), then it works great. If not, it "frays" the ends and looks messy. So you'll see how it works, why it doesn't always work, and a great trick for making it work most of the time (with some help from the Clone Stamp tool).

Step One:

In this photo, the distracting objects (to me anyway) are what looks like a utility box and its wire on the left side of the building. So, we're going to use a combination of the Healing Brush and a little bit of the Clone Stamp tool to remove these objects, while maintaining as much of the original texture and grain as possible.

Step Two:

First we'll look at how the Healing Brush works, and then you'll see what the limitation of the Healing Brush is. Start by pressing Z to get the Zoom tool and zoom into an area you want to remove (in this case, we're going to remove a little spot on the building that appears below the top windows). Press J until you get the Healing Brush, and then Alt-click in an area near that spot. At this stage, the Healing Brush works kind of like the regular Clone Stamp tool, so click-and-drag over that little spot. See, it's gone. Piece of cake so far.

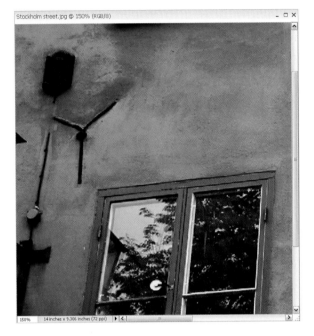

Step Three:

Now you're going to find the main limitation of the Healing Brush—and that's when objects touch. Look at the utility wire on the left. See how it touches the Y-shaped fixture? That's trouble. Go ahead and Alt-click near that intersection and try to use the Healing Brush to remove that area of the wire. Ahh, now you see the problem: Where the edge of the wire meets the rest of the building, it's all smudged. As bad as it looks here, believe it or not, this is pretty mild compared to what often happens when the area you're patching isn't isolated. The Healing Brush only gives you a clean removal if you can paint around the entire object without hitting an edge.

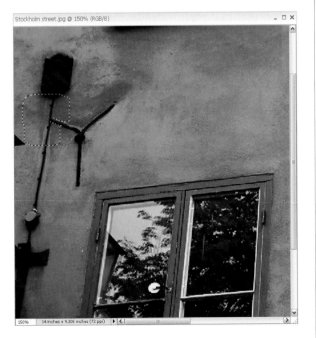

Step Four:

Undo your healing by pressing Control-Z. Now we'll try getting around that limitation: The first thing we want to do is make sure we don't accidentally remove any part of the Y-shaped fixture, so get the Lasso tool (press L until you have it). You're going to use it to box in the area with a selection, which will protect the fixture because you can only clone inside your selected area. Draw carefully around the end of the Y shape, pressing Shift to add to the selection or Alt to subtract from it.

Continued

Step Five:

Press S to get the Clone Stamp tool from the Toolbox, and then Alt-click once just to the left of the wire. Now paint a stroke right over the wire to remove it. In the example here, the plus-sign cursor shows where I sampled, and the circular brush cursor shows where I've painted over the wire. Having that selection in place prevents you from accidentally cloning over any of the Y-shaped fixture, because you can only clone inside the selected area.

Step Six:

Once you've cloned over enough area so the wire is no longer touching the fixture, you can press Control-D to deselect. You'll see part of the wire has been removed, but without all the smudging, thanks to using the Clone Stamp tool.

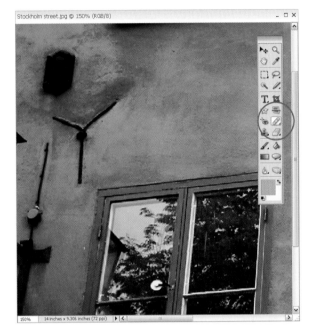

Step Seven:
Now switch back to the Healing Brush (as shown in the Toolbox), and Alt-click above the window (unlike the Clone Stamp tool, you don't have to Alt-click right next to the area where you'll be healing—just pick a spot, any spot, that has a similar texture).

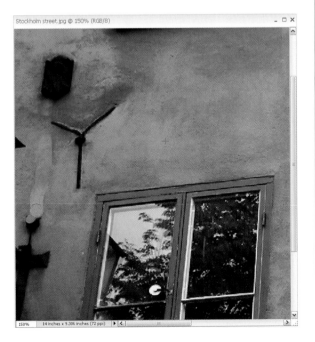

Step Eight:
Begin painting over the rest of the wire to remove it. Don't let it throw you off that the tone looks a bit funny as you're painting. The final healing doesn't take place until you release the mouse button, so there's a second or two where your healing looks bad, but just be patient for a moment.

Continued

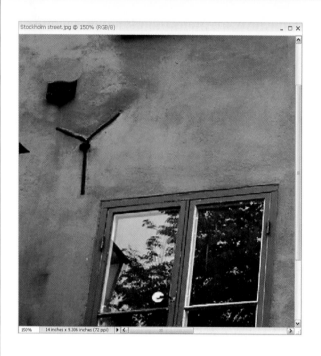

Step Nine:

If you can't get the wire and the utility box in just one stroke—don't sweat it. Just Alt-click in a different area (again, I'd try somewhere above the window), and paint another stroke until the entire wire and the utility box have been removed. So, in short, if you don't mind using the Clone Stamp just a little bit, you can turn the Healing Brush into a real tool for removing larger, unwanted objects.

Before   *After*

Exposure: 1/125   Focal Length: 52mm   Aperture Value: ƒ/5.6

38 Special
photographic special effects

This is where the fun begins. Okay, I don't want to discount all the immeasurable fun you've had up to this point, but now it gets really fun. This is where we get to play around in Elements and change reality, and then send the client an invoice for our "playtime." Did the model wear a blouse that was the wrong color? No sweat, change it in Elements. Was it an overcast day when you shot the exterior of your client's house? Just drop in a new sky. Do you want to alter a photo to make it look like you shot it with a soft focus filter on your lens? Now you can do it digitally. Do you want to take your income to the next level? Just shoot a crisp shot of a $20 bill, retouch it a bit, print out a few hundred sheets on your color laser printer and head for Vegas. (Okay, forget that last one, but you get the idea.) This is where the rubber meets the road, where the nose gets put to the grindstone, where the meat meets the potatoes... (Where the meat meets the potatoes? Hey, it's late.)

Creating Drama with a Soft Spotlight

This is a great technique that lets you focus attention by using dramatic soft lighting. The technique I'm showing you here I learned from famous nature photographer Vincent Versace. I had been getting a similar look by filling a layer with black, making an oval selection, feathering the edges significantly, and then knocking a hole out of the layer (as you'll see in the next technique), but Vincent's technique, using the Lighting Effects filter, is so much easier that it's just about all I use now.

Step One:

Open the RGB photo to which you want to apply the soft spotlight effect. In this example, I want to focus attention on the flower in the center by darkening the area around it. Next, press Control-J to duplicate the Background layer.

Step Two:

Go under the Filter menu, under Render, and choose Lighting Effects. I have to tell you, if you haven't used this filter before, it's probably because its interface (with all its sliders) looks so complex, but luckily there are built-in presets (Adobe calls them "Styles") that you can choose from, so you can pretty much ignore all those sliders. Once you ignore the sliders, the filter is much less intimidating, and you can really have some fun here. The small preview window on the left side of the dialog shows you the default setting, which is a large oval light coming from the bottom right-hand corner.

Step Three:
For this effect, we're going to use a very soft, narrow beam, so go under the Style pop-up menu at the top of the dialog (this is where the presets are) and choose Flashlight.

Step Four:
Once you choose Flashlight, look at the preview window and you'll see a small spotlight in the center of your image. Click on the center point (inside the circle) and drag the light into the position where you want it. If you want the circle of light a little bit larger, just click on one of the side points and drag outward. When you click OK, the filter applies the effect, darkening the surrounding area and creating the soft spotlight effect you see here.

Continued

Step Five:

If the Lighting Effect filter seems too intense, you can remedy it immediately after the fact by dragging the Opacity slider in the Layers palette to the left to reduce the effect of the filter. The farther you drag, the less the intensity of the effect. Then, while in the Layers palette, change the blend mode of this layer to Darken, so the flashlight effect doesn't make the colors seem too saturated.

Before   *After*

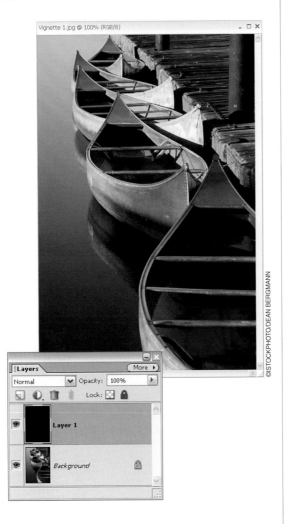

If you want to focus attention on something within your image, applying a wide vignette that acts like a soft light is a great way to do this (which is really an alternative to the previous tutorial). What you're really doing is creating a dark border that will burn in the edges of your image. Here's how to do just that:

Burned-In Edge Effect (Vignetting)

Step One:
Open the photo to which you want to apply a burned-in edge effect. Just so you know, what we're doing here is focusing attention through the use of light—we're burning in all the edges of the photo (not just the corners, like lens vignetting, which I usually try to avoid), leaving the visual focus in the center of the image.

Step Two:
Go to the Layers palette and add a new layer by clicking on the Create a New Layer icon at the top of the palette. Press the letter D to set your Foreground color to black, and then fill your new layer with black by pressing Alt-Backspace.

Continued

Step Three:

Press M to get the Rectangular Marquee tool and drag a selection about 1" inside the edges of your photo. Then, to greatly soften the edges of your selection, go under the Select menu and choose Feather. When the dialog appears, enter 50 pixels for a low-res photo (or 170 pixels for a high-res, 300-ppi photo), and click OK.

Step Four:

Now that your edges have been softened, all you have to do is press Backspace, and you'll knock a soft hole out of your black layer, revealing the photo on the Background layer beneath it. Now press Control-D to deselect. *Note:* If the edges seem too dark, you can go to the Layers palette and lower the Opacity of your black layer (in the example shown here, I lowered the Opacity to around 80%).

Before

After

Using Color for Emphasis

This is a popular technique for focusing attention by the use of color (or really, it's more like the use of less color—if everything's in black and white, anything that's in color will immediately draw the viewer's eye). As popular as this technique is, it's absolutely a breeze to create. Here's how:

Step One:
Open a photo containing an object you want to emphasize through the use of color. Go under the Layer menu, under New, and choose Layer via Copy (or just press Control-J). This will duplicate the Background layer onto its own layer (Layer 1).

Step Two:
Press B to get the Brush tool from the Toolbox and choose a medium, soft-edged brush from the Brush Picker in the Options Bar (just click on the arrow next to the Brush thumbnail to open the Picker). Also in the Options Bar, change the Mode pop-up menu to Color for the Brush tool.

Step Three:

Set your Foreground color to black by pressing the letter D and begin painting on the photo. As you paint, the color in the photo will be removed. The goal is to paint away the color from all the areas *except* the areas you want emphasized with color.

TIP: If you make a mistake while painting away the color or later decide that there was something else that you really wanted to keep in color, just switch to the Eraser tool by pressing the E key, paint over the "mistake" area, and the original color will return as you paint. (What you're really doing here is erasing part of the top layer, which is now mostly black and white, and as you erase, it reveals the original layer, which is still in full color.)

Before   *After*

Soft Focus Effect

This is a quick way to emulate the effect of a soft focus filter on your lens. Besides being quick and easy, what I like about this effect is the soft glow it gives your images. Try this technique on a sharp photo of some trees and you'll love what it does for the image.

Step One:
Open the photo to which you want to apply a soft focus effect. Duplicate the Background layer by pressing Control-J. By default, this duplicate layer is named Layer 1.

Step Two:
Go under the Filter menu, under Blur, and choose Gaussian Blur. For low-res images, enter about 6–10 pixels (for high-res images, try 20 pixels instead) and click OK.

Step Three:

That amount of Gaussian Blur will blur the entire image so much that it'll be hard to see any detail. So, to bring back the detail, go to the Layers palette and lower the Opacity setting of this blurred layer to 50%. Lowering the Opacity setting allows the detail to come back, but along with it comes a soft glow that gives the image a dreamy, almost painted look, which completes the effect.

Before

After

Changing an Object's Color

Have you ever wanted to change the color of an object (such as a shirt, a car, etc.) in a photo? You have? Then here's perhaps the fastest, easiest way to change the color of, well…whatever.

Step One:
Open a photo containing an element that needs to be a different color.

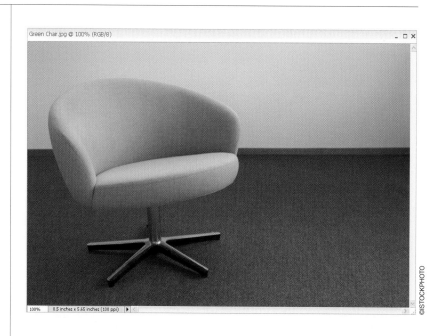

Step Two:
Choose the Color Replacement tool, which is found in the Brush tool's flyout menu in the Toolbox (or press the B key until you have it).

TIP: You can adjust the Color Replacement tool's settings by going to the Options Bar, clicking the down-facing arrow next to the word "Brush," and choosing your settings in the Picker that appears.

Step Three:

Open another image that has the color you want to use. Alt-click the Color Replacement tool on the color you want to sample within that image. (In this example, I'm sampling the color from an old telephone.) Your cursor will temporarily switch to the Eyedropper tool.

Red Phone.jpg @ 100% (RGB/8)

©ISTOCKPHOTO/MARK EVANS

100%   2.69 inches x 1.983 inches (300 ppi)

Continued

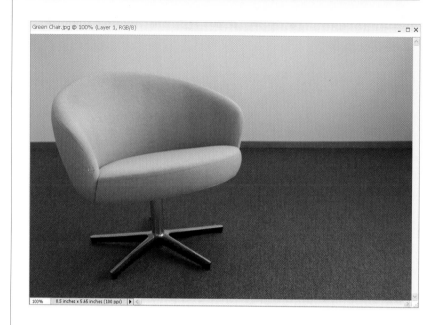

Step Four:

Now return to the photo you want to colorize and start painting with the Color Replacement tool using the sampled color, completing the effect. *Hint:* If you make a mistake, just press Control-Z to undo and try again.

Before

After

When shooting outdoors, there's one thing you just can't count on—the sun. Yet, you surely don't want to take a photo of your house on a dreary day, or shoot a photo of your car on a gray overcast day. That's why it's so important to have the ability to replace a gloomy gray sky with a bright sunny sky. Is it cheating? Yes. Is it easy? You betcha. Do people do it every day? Of course.

Replacing the Sky

Step One:
Open the photo that needs a new, brighter, bluer sky.

Step Two:
You have to make a selection around the sky. Usually, you can click in the sky area with the Magic Wand tool (W) to select most of it, and then choose Similar from the Select menu to select the rest of the sky—but as usual, it likely selected other parts of the image besides just the sky. So use the Lasso tool (L) while holding the Alt key to deselect any excess selected areas on your image. If needed, hold the Shift key while using the Lasso tool to add any unselected areas of the sky. You can use any combination of selection tools you'd like—the key is to select the entire sky area.

Continued

Step Three:

Shoot some nice blue skies and keep them handy for projects like this, or steal a sky from another photo. Simply open one of those "blue sky" shots, and then go under the Select menu and choose All to select the entire photo, or use the Magic Wand or Lasso tools as you did in the previous step to select just the sky you want. Then, press Control-C to copy this sky photo into memory.

Step Four:

Switch back to your original photo (the selection should still be in place). Create a new layer by clicking on the Create a New Layer icon at the top of the Layers palette, then go under the Edit menu and choose Paste Into Selection. The new sky will be pasted into the selected area in your new layer, appearing over the old sky. Press Control-D to deselect.

Step Five:

If the sky seems too bright for the photo, simply lower the Opacity of the layer in the Layers palette to help it blend in better with the rest of the photo. That's it—newer, bluer sky.

Before

After

Neutral Density Gradient Filter

One of the most popular lens filters for outdoor photographers is the neutral density filter, because often (especially when shooting scenery, like sunsets) you wind up with a bright sky and a dark foreground. A neutral density gradient lens filter reduces the exposure in the sky by a stop or two, while leaving the ground unchanged (the top of the filter is gray, and it graduates down to transparent at the bottom). Well, if you forgot to use your ND gradient filter when you took the shot, you can create your own ND effect in Photoshop Elements.

Step One:
Open the photo (preferably a landscape) where you exposed for the ground, which left the sky too light. Press the letter D to set your Foreground color to black. Then, go to the Layers palette and choose Gradient from the Create Adjustment Layer pop-up menu (it's the half-white/half-black circle icon) at the top of the palette.

Step Two:
When the Gradient Fill dialog appears, click on the little, black downward-facing arrow (it's immediately to the right of the Gradient thumbnail) to bring up the Gradient Picker. Double-click on the second gradient in the list, which is the gradient that goes from Foreground to Transparent. Don't click OK yet.

Step Three:
By default, this puts a dark area on the ground (rather than the sky), so click on the Reverse checkbox to reverse the gradient, putting the dark area of your gradient over the sky and the transparent part over the land. Your image will look pretty awful at this point, but you'll fix that in the next step, so just click OK.

Step Four:
To make this gradient blend in with your photo, go to the Layers palette and change the blend mode of this adjustment layer from Normal to Overlay. This darkens the sky, but it gradually lightens until it reaches land, and then it slowly disappears. So, how does it know where the ground is? It doesn't. It puts a gradient across your entire photo, so in the next step, you'll basically show it where the ground is.

Continued

Step Five:

In the Layers palette, double-click on the thumbnail for the Gradient Fill adjustment layer to bring up the Gradient Fill dialog again. To control how far down the darkening will extend from the top of your photo, just click once on the Gradient thumbnail at the top of the dialog. This brings up the Gradient Editor. Grab the top-right white color stop above the gradient ramp near the center of the dialog and drag the color stop to the left; the darkening will "roll up" from the bottom of your photo, so keep dragging to the left until only the sky is affected, and then click OK in the Gradient Editor.

Step Six:

By default, the gradient you choose fills the entire image area, smoothly transitioning from a dark gray at the top center to transparent at the very bottom. It's a smooth, "soft-step" gradient. However, if you want a quicker change from black to transparent (a hard step between the two), you can lower the Scale amount in the Gradient Fill dialog.

Step Seven:
Also, if the photo you're working on doesn't have a perfectly straight horizon line, you also might have to use the Angle control by clicking on the line in the center of the Angle circle and dragging slowly in the direction that your horizon is tilted. This literally rotates your gradient, which enables you to have your gradient easily match the angle of your horizon. When it looks good to you, click OK to complete the effect.

Before: Exposing for the ground makes the sky too light.

After: The ground is the same, but the sky is now bluer and more intense.

Putting One Photo Inside Another

Putting a photo inside another is a fairly popular collaging technique. But in the technique you're going to do here, you'll realistically put one image inside another, matching the angles of the photo. Here's how it's done:

Step One:

Open the photo that you want to put inside another photo. Press Control-A to put a selection around your entire photo, then press Control-C to copy that photo into memory. Next, open the image that you want the copied photo to appear within.

Step Two:

Press the L key until you get the Polygonal Lasso tool from the Toolbox (this tool draws perfectly straight selections; if your object doesn't have straight sides, use another selection tool to create a selection within your image's object). Click the Polygonal Lasso tool once on the bottom-left corner of your object, and then move your cursor up to the top-left corner and click again (a straight line is drawn between your two clicks). Keep clicking at each corner until you have all sides of the object selected (as shown here).

Step Three:
Now go under the Edit menu and choose Paste Into Selection, and the photo you had in memory will be pasted into your selection. But there's a problem—the object is likely angled and your photo probably isn't, so it looks fake. Here's how to fix it: Press Control-T to bring up the Free Transform command. Hold the Control key, grab the bottom-left corner point, and move it to where it touches the bottom-left corner of your object. You'll do the same with the other corners—dragging each one to the corresponding corner of your object.

Step Four:
When all four corners are lined up, and your photo has been transformed to fit perfectly within the object, press Enter to lock in your changes, and then press Control-D to deselect, which completes the effect.

Simple Depth-of-Field Effect

If you want to create a quick depth-of-field effect (where the part of the subject closest to the camera is in sharp focus and the background is out of focus), I don't know of a faster, easier way than this.

Step One:
Open the photo that you want to apply the depth-of-field effect to. Press Control-J to duplicate the Background layer to create a new layer that will be named "Layer 1."

Step Two:
Go under the Filter menu, under Blur, and choose Gaussian Blur. When the dialog appears, change the Radius to about 4 pixels (or more if you're using a high-res photo) and click OK to put a blur over the entire image.

Simple depth of field1.jpg @ 100% (Layer 1, RGB/8)

100%   8 inches x 5.986 inches (72 ppi)

Step Three:
Press the E key to switch to the Eraser tool and choose a large, soft-edged brush from the Brush Picker (which is found by clicking the Brush thumbnail in the Options Bar). Start erasing over the parts of the image that appear in the foreground. Erasing on this blurred layer reveals the original, unblurred image on the Background layer. By leaving these areas sharp and the background areas blurry, it creates a simple depth-of-field effect as if you had shot it that way with your camera.

Before

After

Creating Photo Montages

Here's a great way to blend any two (or more) photos together to create a photo montage (often referred to as a collage).

Step One:

Open the photo that you want to use as your base photo—this will serve as the background of your collage. (*Note:* Make sure you're not in Maximize Mode by deselecting it under the Window menu, under Images.) Now open the first photo that you want to collage with your background photo.

Step Two:
Press V to switch to the Move tool, and then click-and-drag the photo from this document right onto your background photo, positioning it where you want it. It will appear on its own layer (Layer 1) in the Layers palette of your background image.

Step Three:
Hold the Control key and at the top of the Layers palette, click on the Create a New Layer icon. This creates a layer directly beneath your current layer (Layer 1). Now, click back on the top layer, then press Control-G to group your photo with the blank layer beneath it. Press the letter D to set your Foreground color to black.

Step Four:
Switch to the Gradient tool by pressing G, and then press Enter to bring up the Gradient Picker (it appears below the Gradient thumbnail in the Options Bar). Choose the second gradient in the Picker (this is the Foreground to Transparent gradient).

Continued

Step Five:

Click on the middle (blank) layer in the Layers palette to make it active. Although you can't see your top photo, try to click the Gradient tool near the center of this photo and drag toward the center of the document. The point where you first clicked on the top layer will be at 100% opacity, and the point where you stop dragging will be totally transparent. Everything else will blend in between. If you want to start over—easy enough—just press Control-Z to undo and click-and-drag again. (Be careful: If you drag beyond the image's border, your Foreground color will appear in the gradient.)

Step Six:

If you want to blend in another photo, click-and-drag that image onto your montage, click on the top layer in the Layers palette, then start again from Step Three. Add as many images as you'd like.

©ISTOCKPHOTO/BRADLEY L. MARLOW

Here's how to create the classic soft-edged vignette that was originally made popular decades ago by portrait photographers, and still remains popular for wedding photos and portraits of children. A rectangular version is often used for photos used in print ads of high-priced items such as fine homes, jewelry, perfume, etc.

Creating the Classic Vignette Effect

Step One:
Open the photo to which you want to apply the classic vignette effect.

Step Two:
Press M until you get the Elliptical Marquee tool from the Toolbox and draw an oval-shaped selection around the part of the photo you want to remain visible.

Continued

Step Three:

To soften the edge of your selection, go under the Select menu and choose Feather. When the Feather Selection dialog appears, enter 35 or more pixels (the higher the number, the softer the edge) and click OK.

Step Four:

Here's the thing—you have your subject in a circular selection, and that's the part you want to keep intact. However, you want everything else deleted, so go under the Select menu and choose Inverse. Doing this selects everything except the area you want to keep intact.

Step Five:
Now, press Backspace to remove the background areas, and then press Control-D to deselect. Because you feathered the oval in Step Three, the edges are soft, completing the vignette effect.

TIP: If you'd like to use this soft-edged vignette for collaging with other photos, you'll need the white areas outside the edge to be transparent and not solid white. To do that, just before Step Two, double-click on the Background layer in the Layers palette. A dialog will appear; just click OK to change your Background layer to Layer 0, and then go on to Step Two.

Before

After

Fake Duotone

The duotone tinting look is all the rage right now, but creating a real two-color duotone, complete with curves, that will separate in just two colors on press is a bit of a chore. However, if you're outputting to an inkjet printer, or to a printing press as a full-color job, then you don't need all that complicated stuff—you can create a fake duotone that looks at least as good (if not better).

Step One:
Open the color RGB photo that you want to convert into a duotone (again, I'm calling it a duotone, but we're going to stay in RGB mode the whole time). Now, the hard part of this is choosing which color to make your duotone. I always see other people's duotones, and think, "Yeah, that's the color I want!" but when I go to the Foreground color swatch and try to create a similar color in the Color Picker, it's always hit or miss (usually miss). That's why you'll want to know this next trick.

Step Two:
If you can find another duotone photo that has a color you like, you're set. So I usually go to a stock-photo web-site (like iStockphoto.com) and search for "duotones." When I find one I like, I return to Elements, press I to get the Eyedropper tool, click-and-hold any-where within my image area, and then (while keeping the mouse button held down) I drag my cursor outside Elements and onto the photo in my Web browser to sample the color I want. Now, mind you, I did not and would not take a single pixel from someone else's photo—I'm just sampling a color.

Step Three:
Return to your image in Elements. Go to the Layers palette and click on the Create a New Layer icon. Then, press Alt-Backspace to fill this new blank layer with your sampled color. The color will fill your image area, hiding your photo, but we'll fix that.

Step Four:
While still in the Layers palette, change the blend mode of this sampled color layer to Color.

Step Five:
If your duotone seems too dark, you can lessen the effect by clicking on the Background layer, and then going under the Enhance menu, under Adjust Color, and choosing Remove Color. This removes the color from your RGB photo without changing its color mode, while lightening the overall image. Pretty sneaky, eh?

Getting the Polaroid™ Look

This is a quick technique that lets you turn any photo into what looks like a Polaroid snapshot. This is an ideal effect to apply when you really want that "scrapbook" feel, or you're looking for that spontaneous "my-family-on-vacation" feel. Give this one a try—it's much, much easier than it looks.

Step One:
Open the photo you want to turn into a Polaroid. Press D to set your colors to the default black and white. Now, press Control-A to put a selection around the entire image. Go under the Layer menu, under New, and choose Layer via Cut (or press Control-Shift-J) to remove the photo from the Background layer and put it on a separate layer (Layer 1) above the background.

Step Two:
To create this effect, you'll need a little more working room around your photo, so go under the Image menu, under Resize, and choose Canvas Size. When the Canvas Size dialog appears, ensure the Relative checkbox is turned on, then add at least 2 inches of space to both the Width and Height. Choose Background in the Canvas Extension Color pop-up menu, and click OK.

Step Three:

Create a new blank layer directly beneath your current layer by Control-clicking on the Create a New Layer icon at the top of the Layers palette (the new layer will be titled "Layer 2"). Press the M key to switch to the Rectangular Marquee tool, and on this layer draw a selection that's about a ½-inch larger than your photo on all sides. This will act as the border for your Polaroid image.

Step Four:

Click on the Foreground color swatch in the Toolbox, choose a very light gray in the Color Picker (I used R=232, G=232, B=232), and then fill your selection with this light gray by pressing Alt-Backspace. Now you can deselect by pressing Control-D. In the Layers palette, click on your top layer (your photo layer) and press Control-E to combine (merge) your photo with the gray rectangle layer below it, creating just one layer.

Step Five:

Make a duplicate of this merged layer by dragging it to the Create a New Layer icon at the top of the Layers palette (this copied layer will be titled "Layer 2 copy"). Press the D key to set your Foreground color to black. Then, press Alt-Shift-Backspace to fill your copied layer with black. Now, in the Layers palette, drag the black layer directly beneath your photo layer. You're going to "bend" this black-filled layer and use it as the shadow for the Polaroid.

Continued

Step Six:

Go under the Filter menu, under Distort, and choose Shear. When the Shear dialog appears, click on the center of the line that appears vertically at the center of the grid. This adds a point to the line. Click-and-drag this point to the left. The bottom of the dialog shows a preview of how your shear will look. When it looks good to you, click OK.

Step Seven:

With the "shadow" layer still active in the Layers palette, press the V key to switch to the Move tool. Then drag this black, sheared layer directly to the right until the corners are peering out, giving the impression that the Polaroid's shadow is bent.

Step Eight:

To soften the edges of your shadow (and make them look, well...shadow-like), go under the Filter menu, under Blur, and choose Gaussian Blur. Enter a Radius of 6 and click OK (enter a Radius of 14 for high-res, 300-ppi images).

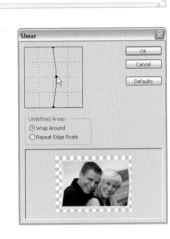

Step Nine:

Now that the shadow is soft, you'll need to lower its opacity to make it appear more subtle. Go to the Layers palette and lower the Opacity setting to around 65%. (You can go lower if you like—it's up to you.) Now that your shadow is finished, to make the effect look more realistic, you'll have to bend the edges of the photo itself.

Step Ten:

In the Layers palette, click on your photo layer (Layer 2) to make it active. Then, go under the Filter menu, under Distort, and choose Shear. When the Shear dialog appears, it will still have the last settings you applied in the grid. Click-and-drag the center point on the line to the right to bend your photo in the opposite direction of the shadow. When it looks good to you, click OK. Now use the Move tool to reposition your image above the shadow.

Step Eleven:

Merge the shadow layer and the photo layer into one layer by pressing Control-E. Then, press Control-T to bring up the Free Transform bounding box. Move your cursor outside the bounding box, then click-and-drag upward to rotate the Polaroid. Press Enter to lock in your transformation, giving you the final effect.

Photo to Sketch in 60 Seconds Flat

I learned this technique from Rich Harris, the former creative guru over at Wacom Technologies. He sent me a bunch of PDFs with some special effects he had come up with, and this one just blew me away, so I asked Rich if I could include it in the book. It does the best job I've seen yet of converting a photo into a color pencil sketch.

Step One:

Open the photo you want to convert into a color sketch. Duplicate the Background layer by going to the Layer menu, under New, and choosing Layer via Copy (or by pressing Control-J). Hide this duplicate layer (Layer 1) by going to the Layers palette and clicking on the Eye icon to the left of this layer. Now click on the Background layer.

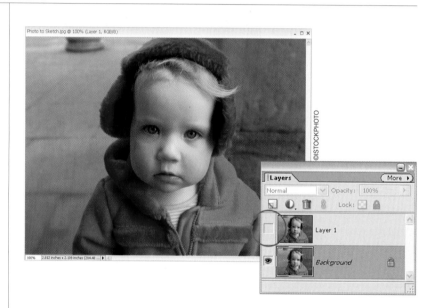

Step Two:

Press Control-Shift-U to remove the color from the Background layer (technically, this is called "desaturating," but in Elements it's the Remove Color command, which is found under the Enhance menu's Adjust Color submenu). Then press Control-J to duplicate the gray Background layer (this copied layer is titled "Background copy").

Step Three:
With the Background copy layer active, press Control-I to invert the photo (giving you a photo-negative look).

Step Four:
Go to the Layers palette and change the layer blend mode for the layer to Color Dodge. This turns your photo white (it looks like a blank document, but in the next step, you'll bring back the photo).

Step Five:
Go under the Filter menu, under Blur, and choose Gaussian Blur. When the dialog appears, drag the Radius slider all the way to the left, and then slowly drag it back to the right, and as you do your sketch will begin to appear. Click OK when the lines look dark, and the photo doesn't look too blurry.

Continued

Step Six:
Go to the Layers palette and make the top layer (the color layer) visible again by clicking in the empty box where the Eye icon used to be. Now lower the Opacity of this layer to 20% to bring back a hint of the original color of the photo.

Step Seven:
To add some texture to your sketch, go under the Filter menu, under Texture, and choose Texturizer. When the Texturizer dialog appears, you'll use the default settings (which are: Texture pop-up menu set to Canvas, Scaling set at 100%, Relief at 4, and Light set to Top). Click OK to apply your canvas texture. Now press Control-F to apply the filter again to make the effect a little more intense, completing the technique.

Before

After

If you've taken the time to get your pano set up right during the shoot (in other words, you used a tripod and overlapped the shots by about 15% to 20% each), then you can have Elements 5's Photomerge feature automatically stitch your panorama images together. If you handheld your pano shoot, you can still use Photomerge: it's just going to be much more manual with you doing most of the work rather than Elements doing it for you.

Automated Pano Stitching with Photomerge™

Step One:
Open the photos that you want Photomerge to stitch together as one panoramic image (you can also open individual images or a folder of images directly from within the Photomerge dialog if you like). In the example shown here, I had four shots already open in Elements.

Step Two:
Go under the File menu, under New, and choose Photomerge™ Panorama.

Continued

Step Three:

When you choose Photomerge, a dialog appears asking which files you want to combine into a panorama. Any files you have open will appear in the window, or you can click the Browse button and navigate to the photos you need to open. Control-click to select individual files in the Open dialog or if the files are contiguous, click on the first file, press-and-hold the Shift key, then click on the last file. Now click Open and then click OK in the Photomerge dialog.

Step Four:

If your pano images were shot correctly (as I mentioned in the introduction of this technique), Photomerge will generally stitch them together seamlessly. If that's the case, click OK and your final panorama will appear as one image. Then you just use the Crop tool (C) to trim away any excess areas in your pano. This is what we call the "best-case scenario," when you've shot the panos on a tripod and overlapped them just like you should so Photomerge had no problems and did its thing right away. It was perfect the first time. But you know, and I know, life just isn't like that.

Step Five:

More likely what you'll get (especially if you handheld your camera or didn't allow enough overlap) is this warning dialog that lets you know that Photomerge "ain't gonna do it for you" (that's a technical phrase coined by Adobe's Alabama tech office). In other words—it's up to you.

Step Six:

Once you click OK in that warning dialog, Photomerge will at least try to merge as many segments together as possible. The segments it couldn't merge will appear in the "Lightbox" (that horizontal row across the top). Although Photomerge didn't do all the work for you, it still can help—just make sure the Snap to Image checkbox on the right-hand side is turned on.

Step Seven:

Get the Select Image tool (it looks like the Move tool) from the Toolbox on the left of the dialog and drag the image's thumbnail from the Lightbox down to your work area near the first image. Slightly overlap the image above the other merged images, release your mouse button, and if Photomerge detects a common overlapping area, it will snap them together, blending any visible edges. It actually works surprisingly well. If you need to rotate a segment to get it lined up, click on it with the Select Image tool first, then switch to the Rotate tool and click-and-drag within the segment to rotate. See, it's not that bad (especially using the Snap to Image option).

Converting to Black and White

One of my favorite new features in Elements 5 is its new black-and-white conversion tool. Well, it's not really a tool, it's more like a dialog where you decide how you want your color photo converted into black and white. It's a very visual way to make the jump from color to black and white, and if you can point-and-click, you can do it. Here's how it's done:

Step One:

Open the color photo you want to convert to black and white (yes, you need to start with a color photo), and then go under the Enhance menu and choose Convert to Black and White (as shown here).

Step Two:

When you choose Convert to Black and White, a dialog appears and your photo (behind the dialog) is converted to black and white on the spot (in other words, you get a live preview of your changes). At the top of the dialog is a before and after, showing your color photo on the left, and your black-and-white conversion on the right, which honestly is of little help, especially since you can see your full-sized photo behind the dialog. Anyway, your first step is to choose which style of photo you're converting from the list of styles on the lower-left side of the dialog. These styles are really just preset starting points that are fairly well-suited to each type of photo. The default setting is Scenic Landscape, which is a fairly non-exciting setting. Since I'm generally looking to create high-contrast, black-and-white photos with lots of depth, I recommend the Vivid Landscapes style, which is much punchier. Go ahead and choose that now, just so you can see the difference.

©ISTOCKPHOTO/VERA BOGAERTS

Step Three:

Whether you stay with the default Scenic Landscape, or try my suggested Vivid Landscapes (or any of the other styles to match the subject of your photo), these are just starting places—you'll need to tweak the settings to really match your photo, and that's done by simply clicking on one (or more) of the thumbnails found in the two rows in Section 3. So that's it—you're going to click on any thumbnail that looks better than your current image (either the one at the top of the dialog, or your actual photo which still appears behind it. By the way, if you have a big enough display, just drag the dialog over to the right so you can see more of your original photo. Bigger previews are better!

Step Four:

The final tweak of your photo comes from the Adjustment Intensity slider, which is found in Section 2. Now, you're probably wondering why I went out of order (I went 1, 3, and now 2, instead of 1-2-3. That's because I think this is the best method. Choose which photo thumbnail looks best, and then turn up the volume [so to speak] if you need to). If you make some changes that don't look good, just press the Reset button found in the upper-right corner of the dialog, right below the Cancel button. When your conversion looks good to you, just click the OK button, and your photo now appears in black and white. However, luckily, Elements 5 leaves your photo in RGB mode, so if you wanted to add a tint to your black-and-white photo (maybe to get a duotone effect), you can do just that using a Hue/Saturation adjustment layer found in the Layers palette. Just choose it, turn on the Colorize checkbox, and drag the Hue slider. That's it.

Get Back
photo restoration techniques

Okay, I know you're thinking, "Hey, this is supposed to be a book for digital photographers. Why are we restoring old damaged photos taken 50 years before digital cameras were invented?" Well, a secret loophole in my book contract enables me, once in every book, to cover a topic that doesn't fall within the general purview of the book. For example, in *The Photoshop CS2 Book for Digital Photographers*, I included a full chapter called "Underrated Breakfast Cereals." So when you're working your way through this chapter, keep thinking to yourself, "Hey, this could be another cereal chapter." Then you'll find not only does this chapter fit, but on some level it fits so well that it makes you want to fix yourself a huge bowl of Kellogg's® Smart Start®. Besides, there's another useful loophole: the theory that once a torn, washed-out, scratched photo of your great-grandfather is scanned, it then becomes a "digital," torn, washed-out, scratched photo of your great-grandfather. And once you open it in Elements 5 you'll be engulfed with a burning desire to repair that photo. If I hadn't included this chapter on how to repair and restore these old photos, then where would you be, Mr. "Hey-this-is-supposed-to-be-a-book-for-digital-photographers" frumpy-pants? Don't you feel just a little guilty? I thought so. Now put down your spoon and start restoring some photos.

Colorizing Black-and-White Photos

Once you've restored a black-and-white photo, you might want to consider colorizing (hand tinting) the photo to give it added depth. This particular technique doesn't take a lot of Elements skills; it just takes a bit of patience, because colorizing a photo can take some time.

Step One:
Open the black-and-white photo you want to colorize.

Step Two:
To colorize a photo, your Elements image has to be in a color mode, so if your photo is in Grayscale mode (it will say "Gray" up in your document's title bar), you'll have to convert it to RGB mode by going under the Image menu, under Mode, and choosing RGB Color.

Step Three:
Press L to switch to the Lasso tool and draw a selection around the first area within your photo that you want to colorize. Press-and-hold the Alt key to subtract from your selection or hold the Shift key to add to it. Then, go under the Select menu and choose Feather. When the dialog appears, enter 2 pixels to soften the edge of your selection just a tiny bit, and then click OK.

Step Four:
Now, you could do all of your colorization on the Background layer, but I recommend pressing Control-J to copy your selected area onto its own layer. That way, if a color you've applied winds up looking too intense, you can lower the layer's Opacity to "tone it down" a bit.

Step Five:
Go under the Enhance menu, under Adjust Color, and choose Adjust Hue/Saturation. When the Hue/Saturation dialog appears, click on the Colorize checkbox in the bottom right-hand corner, drag the Hue slider (at the top of the dialog) to the tint you'd like for this selected area (you can play with the Saturation and Lightness sliders too), and then click OK.

Continued

Step Six:
In the Layers palette, click on the Background layer to make it active and with the Lasso tool, select the next area to be colorized (in this case, the roof gable). Apply a feather to your selection (as you did in Step Three), and press Control-J to copy your selection to its own layer. Now apply your Hue/Saturation adjustment again (like you did in Step Five). When you're applying the color, if it looks too intense, drag the Saturation slider to the left to reduce the color's intensity, giving it a pastel look that's typical of color tinting. When it looks good to you, click OK.

Step Seven:
You'll basically repeat this process to colorize the rest of the photo. Each time you'll go to the Background layer, select an area to be colorized, add a slight feather, copy the selection to its own layer by pressing Control-J, apply the Hue/Saturation command, click the Colorize checkbox, and choose your desired color using the Hue and Saturation sliders. When you're finished, if any of the colors look too intense, just lower the Opacity in the Layers palette. Then choose Flatten Image from the Layers palette's More flyout menu to complete the effect. *Hint:* If you're tinting something like a person's face, you'll also be tinting the whites of their eyes, so you might want to grab the Eraser tool and just erase over the whites to remove that brownish tint.

Before *After*

Repairing Washed-Out Photos

If you've got an old photo that's washed out, lacking detail, and generally so light that it's just about unusable, try this amazingly fast technique to quickly bring back detail and tone.

Step One:
Open the washed-out photo.

Step Two:
Duplicate the Background layer by dragging it to the Create a New Layer icon at the top of the Layers palette. This creates a layer called "Background copy."

Step Three:
Change the layer blend mode of the Background copy layer by choosing Multiply from the pop-up menu at the top left of the Layers palette. As the name implies, this has a "multiplier" effect that darkens the photo and brings back some of the tonal detail.

Step Four:
If the image is still too blown out, continue making copies of this duplicate layer (which is already set to Multiply mode) by pressing Control-J until the photo no longer looks washed out. If the last layer that you add makes it too dark, just lower the Opacity setting of this layer until it looks right.

Continued

Step Five:

Now you may have a new problem—you've got a bunch of layers. The more layers you have, the larger your Elements file, and the larger your Elements file, the slower Elements goes, so there's no sense in having a bunch of extra layers. It just slows things down. So, once the photo looks good, go to the Layers palette, click on the More flyout menu, and choose Flatten Image to flatten all those layers down into one Background layer.

Before

After

Removing Spots and Other Little Junk

It's amazing how those little spots, specks, and well…junk that winds up on all photos can be so painstaking to remove. In most cases, it's not hard to get rid of spots; it just takes a while. But there is a tool that can greatly speed up the process, so you can spend more time on the important repairs, and less time cleaning up the junk.

Step One:
Open a photo that has some specks, spots, and stuff (if the photo has just a ton of spots all over it, you may want to skip this and turn to the next technique in this chapter, as this one's best suited to situations where you have 30 or 40 spots to remove—not 300). The main offenders in this photo are circled in red.

Step Two:
If needed, use the Zoom tool (Z) to zoom into your document. Then, go to the Toolbox and choose the Spot Healing Brush (or just press J until you have it).

Continued

Step Three:

What's nice about this tool is that you don't have to hold down any keys or do anything special—you just move your cursor over a spot, click once, and it's gone. Best of all, it retains as much of the original texture as possible. So, just move around your photo, position your cursor over a spot, and click. If you come to an area that has a streak or row of specks, you can just paint a stroke right over them, and when you release the mouse button—they're gone.

Step Four:

The Spot Healing Brush doesn't do well when a spot is touching or overlapping another object in the photo. For example, look in the capture in Step One, and you'll see a scratch that crosses the woman's belt. That's when you need to switch to the Clone Stamp tool (S), choose a small, soft-edged brush from the Brush Picker in the Options Bar, and then Alt-click in a clean area near the scratch and clone right over it. These two tools make this a 2-minute repair.

Before   *After*

Removing Lots of Specks, Dust, and Scratches

If you've used Elements' Dust & Scratches filter, you've probably already learned how lame the filter really is. That is, unless you use this cool workaround that takes it from a useless piece of fluff, to a...well...reasonably useful piece of fluff. This technique works brilliantly for removing these types of artifacts (that's Elements-speak for specks, dust, and other junk that winds up) on the background areas of your photos.

Step One:
Open the photo that needs specks, dust, and/or scratches repaired. Duplicate the Background layer by dragging it to the Create a New Layer icon at the top of the Layers palette. This creates a layer called "Background copy."

Step Two:
Go under the Filter menu, under Noise, and choose Dust & Scratches. When the Dust & Scratches dialog appears, drag both sliders all the way to the left, then slowly drag the top slider (Radius) back to the right until the specks, dust, and scratches are no longer visible (most likely this will make your photo very blurry, but don't sweat it—make sure the specks are gone, no matter how blurry it looks), and then click OK.

Step Three:

In the Layers palette, hold the Control key and click on the Create a New Layer icon to create a new blank layer beneath your current layer. Now, click back on the top layer and press Control-G to group your blurred layer with the blank layer beneath it. Doing this hides the effect of the Dust & Scratches filter you applied in Step Two.

Step Four:

Press the letter D to set your Foreground color to black. Press B to switch to the Brush tool, click on the Brush thumbnail in the Options Bar, and when the Brush Picker appears, choose a medium-sized, soft-edged brush. Now go to the Layers palette, click on your middle, blank layer, and change the layer blend mode pop-up menu from Normal to Darken for this image. (If your dust and scratches are darker than the background, change the blend mode to Lighten.) This causes the changes you make with the Brush tool to only affect the pixels that are lighter (or darker) than the area you're painting. *Note:* Another method for doing this is to change the Brush tool's blend mode to Darken in the Options Bar. However, I like the layer version better, because you can always change the layer's blend mode later if you don't like how it looks, and you don't get that "after-the-fact" option with the Brush tool.

Continued

Step Five:

With the middle, blank layer active, paint directly over the areas of your photo that have specks. As you paint, the specks and dust will disappear (you're actually revealing the blurred layer above, where you applied the Dust & Scratches filter). Again, this technique works best on background areas, but it can also be useful for cleaning detailed areas. Just use a very small brush to minimize any blurring that may occur, and rather than painting strokes, just move over the speck and click once or twice.

Before

After

If you have an old photo with a serious rip, tear, stain, or other major anomaly, there's a reasonable chance that one of these little nasties could affect a part of your photo's main subject (for example, if it's a photo of a person, a stain could cover a body part or facial feature, leaving you with quite a task). Here's how to repair missing or damaged parts—the easy way.

Repairing Damaged or Missing Parts

WORKMAN FAMILY ARCHIVE

Step One:
Open the photo that contains a damaged feature (in this case, part of his arm and part of his leg are missing because of a tear—plus, part of the street and ground are also missing).

Step Two:
Use one of Elements' selection tools (try the Lasso tool if you just need to make a loose selection like the one I did here) to select an undamaged part of the image that you can use to fix the damaged area. For instance, if you're trying to fix a person's left leg and the right leg is undamaged, select the right leg to use for the repair.

Continued

Step Three:

To keep from having a hard edge around the selected area, you'll need to apply a feather to the edges of your selection. Go under the Select menu and choose Feather. When the dialog appears, enter a Feather Radius. For low-res images, use a 1- to 2-pixel Radius. For high-res, 300-ppi images, you can use as much as 4 or 5 pixels.

Step Four:

You'll need to duplicate the selection, so go under the Layer menu, under New, and choose Layer via Copy (or press Control-J). This creates a new layer with a copy of your selected area on it.

Step Five:

You probably can't just drag this patch over to fill the empty space (because the person would end up with two right legs, leaving him looking slightly freakish). So, you'll need to flip the copied layer by going under the Image menu, under Rotate, and choosing Flip Layer Horizontal, which turns your patch layer into a mirror reflection of the original selection.

Step Six:

Now, switch to the Move tool by pressing the V key, and with the patch on its own layer, drag it over to where the tear is on the right side of the photo. (*Note:* If you lower the Opacity of the patch layer to about 60%, it may help you precisely position the patch because you'll be able to see some of the original image on the layer beneath it.) If your selection looks a little rough, you can press E to switch to the Eraser tool and erase a little bit along the edge to make it smoother. It probably looks a bit jaggy right now, but once you put some background behind it, you'll be amazed at how it blends right in. Go back to Step Two and repeat these steps to replace the left elbow.

Step Seven:

If your copied leg part doesn't match the color of your original leg, click on the copied leg layer (Layer 1) and press Control-L to bring up the Levels dialog. Since the right leg part was darker than the left leg it was copied onto, I dragged the Highlights Input Levels slider a little to the left until they matched.

Continued

Step Eight:

Go to the Layers palette and click on the Background layer. Now we're going to start fixing the missing grass and pavement to the right of his left elbow. Start by pressing S to get the Clone Stamp tool, and then Alt-clicking in the clean area of background to the left and above the tear (you'll see the plus-sign cursor showing the spot where you Alt-clicked). Then move over to the white area to the right of his left elbow and thigh and start painting (okay, cloning) over that entire area of the photo. The background then will be cloned into that white area. You might have to Alt-click a time or two in different spots so you don't "run out of room" and start cloning other areas.

Step Nine:

Now onto the curb area to the right of the leg. Start by pressing M to get the Rectangular Marquee tool and select a clean rectangular area of the curb on the left side of the image (make sure you're on the Background layer). To soften the edges of your selection (to help hide any hard edges so your fix won't be a dead giveaway), go under the Select menu and choose Feather. When the dialog appears, enter 2 pixels (or higher for high-res, 300-ppi images) and click OK.

Step Ten:
Press Control-J to put that area on its own separate layer. Now get the Move tool, and click-and-drag that copied layer up, positioning it so it covers the white area. Again, if the copied area is a little too dark, do a Levels adjustment to lighten it. To finish, you'll switch back to the Clone Stamp tool, go to the Layers palette, click on the Background layer, and clone in any white areas left in the pavement. The final results are complete in a few quick minutes.

Before

After

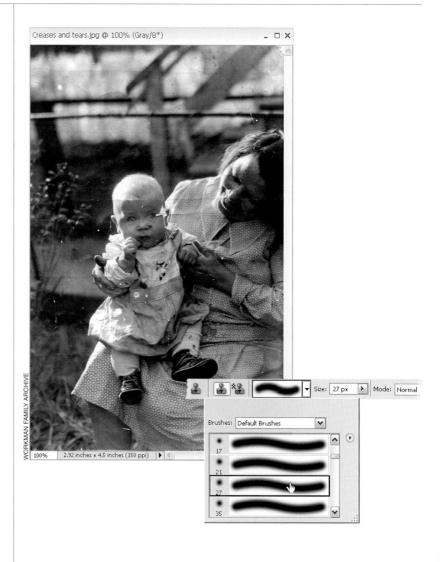

Repairing Rips and Tears

There are few things worse than rips, tears, or cracks from a photo being bent, especially when it happens to old family photos you really care about. Here's a simple technique that lets you hide these nasty rips by "covering" them up.

Step One:
Scan a photo that has rips, tears, or bends, and open it in the Elements Editor. The photo here has tears from being bent.

Step Two:
The plan is to clone over the cracks using noncracked, nearby areas. Start by getting the Clone Stamp tool from the Toolbox (or press the S key). Choose a medium to small, soft-edged brush by clicking on the Brush thumbnail in the Options Bar to open the Brush Picker.

Step Three:
Press-and-hold the Alt key and click in a "clean" area near the cracked area. (By clean, I mean Alt-click in an area that has no cracks or other visible problems. To help ensure that your repair doesn't look obvious, it's important to click near the tear, but not too far away from it.)

Step Four:
Move the Clone Stamp tool over the rip and click a few times over the crack. Don't paint strokes—just click. As you click, you'll see two cursors: your brush cursor where you're painting and a cross-hair cursor over the area you sampled. This lets you see the area you're cloning from (the crosshair) and the area you're cloning to (the brush cursor). This will be your basic strategy for repairing these rips—Alt-click the Clone Stamp tool in a clean area near the crack, then move your cursor over the crack and click a few times until the crack is covered by the cloned areas. For really large cracks, you can paint some small strokes, but be careful not to pick up any repeating patterns that might give you away.

Continued

Step Five:

Now start working on other areas. Press the Z key to switch to the Zoom tool, zoom in if needed, and then switch back to the Clone Stamp tool. (*Note:* You also might want to try the Healing Brush tool [use it the same way—Alt-click before you start healing] using a similar technique, depending on the photo, as it may work just as well, if not better.) The final result is worth a few minutes of cloning.

Before

After

Sharp Dressed Man
sharpening techniques

You're about to learn some of the same sharpening techniques used by today's leading digital photographers and retouchers. Okay, I have to admit, not every technique in this chapter is a professional technique. For example, the first one, "Basic Sharpening," is clearly not a professional technique, although many professionals sharpen their images exactly as shown in that tutorial (applying the Unsharp Mask to the RGB composite—I'm not sure what that means, but it sounds good). There's a word for these professionals—"lazy." But then one day, they think, "Geez, I'm kind of getting tired of all those color halos and other annoying artifacts that keep showing up in my sharpened photos," and they wish there was a way to apply more sharpening, and yet avoid these pitfalls. Then, they're looking for professional sharpening techniques that will avoid these problems—and the best of

those techniques are in this chapter. But the pros are busy people, taking conference calls, getting pedicures, vacuuming their cats, etc., and they don't have time to do a series of complicated, time-consuming steps. So, they create advanced functions that combine techniques. For some unexplainable sociological reason, when pros do this, it's not considered lazy. Instead, they're seen as "efficient, productive, and smart." Why? Because life isn't fair. How unfair is it? I'll give you an example. A number of leading professional photographers have worked for years to come up with these advanced sharpening techniques, which took tedious testing, experimentation, and research, and then you come along, buy this book, and suddenly you're using the same techniques they are, but you didn't even expend a bead of sweat. You know what that's called? Cool.

Basic Sharpening

After you've color corrected your photos and right before you save your files, you'll definitely want to sharpen them. I sharpen every digital camera photo, either to help bring back some of the original crispness that gets lost during the correction process, or to help fix a photo that's slightly out of focus. Either way, I haven't met a digital camera (or scanned) photo that didn't need a little sharpening. Here's a basic technique for sharpening the entire photo:

Step One:
Open the photo that you want to sharpen. Because Elements displays your photo in different ways at different magnifications, it's absolutely critical that you view your photo at 100% when sharpening. To ensure that you're viewing at 100%, once your photo is open, double-click on the Zoom tool in the Toolbox, and your photo will jump to a 100% view (to see the actual percentage of zoom, look up in the image window's title bar or Options Bar, depending on your viewing mode, or look in the image window's bottom-left corner).

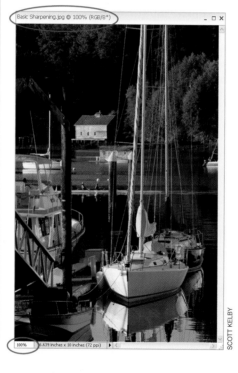

Step Two:
Go under the Enhance menu and choose Unsharp Mask. (If you're familiar with traditional darkroom techniques, you probably recognize the term "unsharp mask" from when you would make a blurred copy of the original photo and an "unsharp" version to use as a mask to create a new photo whose edges appeared sharper.)

Step Three:

When the Unsharp Mask dialog appears, you'll see three sliders. The Amount slider determines the amount of sharpening applied to the photo; the Radius slider determines how many pixels out from the edge that the sharpening will affect; and the Threshold slider determines how different a pixel must be from the surrounding area before it's considered an edge pixel and sharpened by the filter. Threshold works the opposite of what you might think—the lower the number, the more intense the sharpening effect. So, what numbers do you enter? I'll give you some great starting points on the following pages, but for now, we'll just use these settings: Amount: 125%, Radius: 1, and Threshold: 3. Click OK and the sharpening is applied to the photo.

Before

After

Continued

Sharpening Soft Subjects:

Here are the Unsharp Mask settings—
Amount: 150%, Radius: 1, Threshold: 10—
that works well for images where the
subject is of a softer nature (e.g., flowers,
puppies, people, rainbows, etc.). It's a subtle application of sharpening that is very
well suited to these types of subjects.

Sharpening Portraits:

If you're sharpening a close-up portrait
(head-and-shoulders type of thing), try
these settings—Amount: 75%, Radius: 2,
Threshold: 3—which applies another
form of subtle sharpening.

Moderate Sharpening:

This is a moderate amount of sharpening that works nicely on product shots, photos of home interiors and exteriors, and landscapes. If you're shooting along these lines, try applying these settings—Amount: 225%, Radius: 0.5, Threshold: 0—and see how you like it (my guess is you will).

Maximum Sharpening:

I use these settings—Amount: 65%, Radius: 4, Threshold: 3—in only two situations: (1) The photo is visibly out of focus and it needs a heavy application of sharpening to try to bring it back into focus; or (2) the photo contains lots of well-defined edges (e.g., buildings, coins, cars, machinery, etc.).

Continued

All-Purpose Sharpening:

These are probably my all-around favorite sharpening settings—Amount: 85%, Radius: 1, Threshold: 4—and I use these most of the time. It's not a "knock-you-over the-head" type of sharpening—maybe that's why I like it. It's subtle enough that you can apply it twice if your photo doesn't seem sharp enough after the first application (just press Control-F), but once will usually do the trick.

Web Sharpening:

I use these settings—Amount: 400%, Radius: 0.3, Threshold: 0—for Web graphics that look blurry. (When you drop the resolution from a high-res, 300-ppi photo down to 72 ppi for the Web, the photo often gets a bit blurry and soft.) I also use this same sharpening on out-of-focus photos. It adds some noise, but I've seen it rescue photos that I would have otherwise thrown away. If the effect seems too intense, try dropping the Amount to 200%.

SCOTT KELBY

Coming Up with Your Own Settings:
If you want to experiment and come up with your own custom blend of sharpening, I'll give you some typical ranges for each adjustment so you can find your own sharpening "sweet spot."

Amount:
Typical ranges go anywhere from 50% to 150%. This isn't a rule that can't be broken. It's just a typical range for adjusting the Amount, where going below 50% won't have enough effect, and going above 150% might get you into sharpening trouble (depending on how you set the Radius and Threshold). You're fairly safe to stay under 150%.

Radius:
Most of the time, you'll use just 1 pixel, but you can go as high as (get ready)—2. I gave you one setting earlier for extreme situations, where you can take the Radius as high as 4, but I wouldn't recommend it very often. I once heard a tale of a man in Cincinnati who used 5, but I'm not sure I believe it.

Continued

Threshold:

A pretty safe range for the Threshold setting is anywhere from 3 to around 20 (3 being the most intense, 20 being much more subtle. I know, shouldn't 3 be more subtle and 20 more intense? Don't get me started). If you really need to increase the intensity of your sharpening, you can lower the Threshold to 0, but keep a good eye on what you're doing (watch for noise appearing in your photo).

Before

After

Creating Extraordinary Sharpening

One of the problems we face when trying to make things really sharp is that things tend to look oversharpened, or worse yet, our photos get halos (tiny glowing lines around edges in our images). So, how do we get our images to appear really sharp without damaging them? With a trick, of course. Here's the one I use to make my photos look extraordinarily sharp without damaging the image:

Step One:
Open your image, and then apply the Unsharp Mask filter (found under the Enhance menu) to your image, just as we've been doing all along. (For this example, let's try these settings: Amount 120%, Radius 1, and Threshold 3, which will provide a nice, solid amount of sharpening.)

Step Two:
Press Control-J to duplicate the Background layer. Because we're duplicating the Background layer, the layer will be already sharpened, but we're going to sharpen this duplicate layer even more in the next step.

Continued

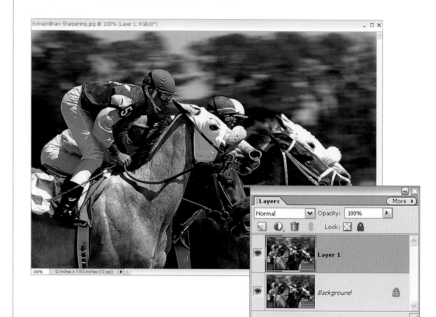

Step Three:

Now apply the Unsharp Mask filter again, using the same settings, by pressing Control-F. If you're really lucky, the second application of the filter will still look okay, but it's doubtful. Chances are that this second application of the filter will make your photo appear too sharp—you'll start to see halos or noise, or the photo will start looking artificial in a lot of areas. So, what we're going to do is hide this oversharpened layer, then selectively reveal this über-sharpening only in areas that can handle the extra sharpening (this will make sense in just a minute).

Step Four:

Go to the Layers palette, press-and-hold the Control key, and click on the Create a New Layer icon at the top of the Layers palette (holding the Control key makes the new layer appear below your currently active layer, rather than above it, like usual).

Step Five:

In the Layers palette, click on your oversharpened layer to make it the active layer (it should be your top layer, with that blank layer you just created appearing directly below it in the stack of layers). Now press Control-G. This groups your oversharpened layer with the empty one beneath it; thus it hides the oversharpened layer in that blank layer.

Step Six:

Here's the fun part—the trick is to paint over just a few key areas, which fool the eye into thinking the entire photo is sharper than it is. Here's how: Press B to get the Brush tool, and in the Options Bar, click on the Brush thumbnail to open the Brush Picker and choose a soft-edged brush. Press D to set your Foreground color to black. Now, in the Layers palette click on the blank layer, and then start painting on your image to reveal your sharpening. (*Note:* If you make a mistake, press E and erase your black brush stokes with the Eraser tool.) In this image, you'd paint over the jockey in the green helmet and his horse to make them super sharp, but stay away from their edges and just paint "inside the lines." That way, the edges don't get halos, but the overall image appears very sharp.

Before

After

Luminosity Sharpening

Okay, you've already learned that sharpening totally rocks, but the more you use it, the more discerning you'll become about it (you basically become a sharpening snob), and at some point, you'll apply some heavy sharpening to an image and notice little color halos. You'll grow to hate these halos, and you'll go out of your way to avoid them. In fact, you'll go so far as to use this next sharpening technique, which is fairly popular with pros shooting digital (at least with the sharpening-snob crowd).

Step One:
Open a photo that needs some moderate to serious sharpening.

Step Two:
Duplicate the Background layer by going under the Layer menu, under New, and choosing Layer via Copy (or pressing Control-J). This will duplicate the Background layer onto a new layer (Layer 1).

Step Three:
Go under the Enhance menu and choose Unsharp Mask. (*Note:* If you're looking for some sample settings for different sharpening situations, look at the "Basic Sharpening" tutorial at the beginning of this chapter.) After you've input your Unsharp Mask settings, click OK to apply the sharpening to the duplicate layer.

Step Four:
Go to the Layers palette and change the layer blend mode of this sharpened layer from Normal to Luminosity. By doing this, it applies the sharpening to just the luminosity (lightness details) of the image, and not the color. This enables you to apply a higher amount of sharpening without getting unwanted halos. You can now choose Flatten Image from the Layers palette's More flyout menu to complete your Luminosity sharpening.

Continued

Before   *After*

This is a sharpening technique that doesn't use the Unsharp Mask filter but still leaves you with a lot of control over the sharpening, even after it's applied. It's ideal to use when you have an image that can really hold a lot of sharpening (a photo with a lot of edges) or one that really needs a lot of sharpening.

Edge Sharpening Technique

Step One:
Open a photo that needs edge sharpening.

Step Two:
Duplicate the Background layer by going under the Layer menu, under New, and choosing Layer via Copy (or pressing Control-J). This will duplicate the Background layer onto a new layer (Layer 1).

Continued

Step Three:

Go under the Filter menu, under Stylize, and choose Emboss. You're going to use the Emboss filter to accentuate the edges in the photo. You can leave the Angle and Amount settings at their defaults (135° and 100%), but if you want more intense sharpening, raise the Height amount from its default setting of 3 pixels to 5 or more pixels (in the example here, I left it at 3). Click OK to apply the filter, and your photo will turn gray, with neon-colored highlights along the edges.

Step Four:

In the Layers palette, change the layer blend mode of this layer from Normal to Hard Light. This removes the gray color from the layer, but leaves the edges accentuated, making the entire photo appear much sharper.

Step Five:
If the sharpening seems too intense, you can control the amount of the effect by simply lowering the Opacity of this top layer in the Layers palette.

Before

After

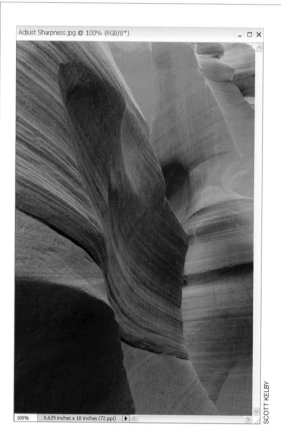

Advanced Sharpening Using Adjust Sharpness

I predict that Elements 5's new Adjust Sharpness control will actually replace the long-heralded Unsharp Mask as the sharpening filter of choice. Here's why: (1) it does a better job of avoiding those nasty color halos, so you can apply more sharpening without damaging your photo; (2) it lets you choose different styles of sharpening; (3) it has a much larger preview window so you can see your sharpening more accurately; (4) it has a More Refined feature that applies multiple iterations of sharpening; and (5) it's just flat out easier to use.

Step One:

Open the photo you want to sharpen using this new Adjust Sharpness control. (By the way, although most of this chapter focuses on using the Unsharp Mask filter, I only do that because it's the current industry standard. If you find you prefer the Adjust Sharpness control, from here on out, when I say to apply the Unsharp Mask filter, you can substitute the Adjust Sharpness control instead. Don't worry, I won't tell anybody.)

Step Two:
Go under the Enhance menu and choose Adjust Sharpness. When the dialog opens, you'll notice there are only two sliders: Amount (which controls the amount of sharpening—sorry, my editors made me say that) and Radius (which determines how many pixels the sharpening will affect). I generally leave this setting at 1 pixel, but if a photo is visibly blurry, I'll pump it up to 2. (Very rarely do I ever try to rescue an image that's so blurry that I have to use a 3- or 4-pixel setting.)

Step Three:
Below the Radius slider is the Remove pop-up menu, which lists the three types of blurs you can reduce using Adjust Sharpness. Gaussian Blur (the default) applies a brand of sharpening that's pretty much like what you get using the regular Unsharp Mask filter (it uses a similar algorithm). Another Remove menu choice is Motion Blur, but unless you can determine the angle of blur that appears in your image, it's tough to get really good results with this one. So, which one do I recommend? The other choice—Lens Blur. It's better at detecting edges, so it creates fewer color halos than you'd get with the other choices, and overall I think it just gives you better sharpening for most images. The downside? Choosing Lens Blur makes the filter take a little longer to "do its thing." A small price to pay for better-quality sharpening.

Continued

Step Four:

At the bottom of the dialog, there's a checkbox labeled "More Refined." It gives you (according to Adobe) more accurate sharpening by applying multiple iterations of the sharpening. I leave More Refined turned on nearly all the time. (After all, who wants "less refined" sharpening?) *Note:* If you're working on a large file, the More Refined option can cause the filter to process slower, so it's up to you if it's worth the wait. I've also found that with the Adjust Sharpness control I use a lower Amount setting than I would with the Unsharp Mask filter to get a similar amount of sharpening, so I usually find myself lowering the Amount to around 60% in most instances.

Before   *After*

The Show Must Go On
showing it to your clients

Okay, you've sorted and categorized the photos from the shoot; you've backed up your digital negs to CD; and you've color corrected, tweaked, toned, sharpened, and otherwise messed with your photo until it is, in every sense of the word, a masterpiece. But now it's time to show it to the clients. Hopefully, you'll get to show it to the clients in person, so you can explain in detail the motivation behind collaging a 4x4 monster truck into an otherwise pristine wedding photo. (Answer: Because you can.) There's a good chance they'll see the photo first onscreen, so I included some cool tricks on how to make your presentation look its very best (after all, you want those huge 122" tires to look good), and I even included some techniques on how to provide your own online proofing service using Elements (in case your clients smell bad, and you don't want them coming back to your studio and stinkin' up the place). I want you to really sop up the techniques (like you're using a big ol' flaky biscuit) because once you're done with this chapter, once you've come this far, there's no turning back. At this point, some people will start to scour their studio, searching for that one last roll of traditional print film, probably knocking around at the bottom of some drawer (or hidden in the back of the refrigerator, behind some left-over Moo Shoo Pork), so they can hold it up toward the light, smile, and begin laughing that hysterical laugh that only people truly on the edge can muster. These people are not Kodak shareholders.

Watermarking and Adding Copyright Info

This two-part technique is particularly important if you're putting your photos on the Web and want some level of copyright protection. In the first part of this technique, you'll add a see-through watermark, so you can post larger photos without fear of having someone download and print them. Secondly, you'll embed your personal copyright info, so if your photos are used anywhere on the Web, your copyright info will go right along with the file.

Step One:

We're going to start by creating a watermark template. Create a new blank document in the Elements Editor (go to File, under New, and choose Blank File) in RGB mode in your typical working resolution (72 ppi for low-res, 300 ppi for high-res, etc.). Click on the Foreground color swatch at the bottom of the Toolbox and choose a medium gray color in the Color Picker, then click OK. Now, press Alt-Backspace to fill the Background layer with medium gray. Press the letter D to set your Foreground color to black.

Step Two:

Press T to switch to the Horizontal Type tool. In the Options Bar, choose a font like Arial Bold from the font pop-up menus, and then click on the Center Text icon. Click the cursor on the gray background, press-and-hold the Alt key, type "0169" using your numeric keypad, and release the Alt key to create a copyright symbol. (*Note:* On a laptop, press-and-hold the Function key to access your keypad.) Then, press Enter to move your cursor to the next line and type the name you want for the copyright on the photo. If needed, adjust the leading (space between lines) by selecting all your text (Control-A) and choosing a point size in the Set the Leading pop-up menu in the Options Bar. Now hide the Background layer by clicking on its Eye icon in the Layers palette.

Step Three:

Highlight your name (but not the copyright symbol) with the Type tool and increase the size of your name by using the Set the Font Size pop-up menu in the Options Bar. When it's at the right size, highlight just the copyright symbol, and resize it upward until it's quite a bit larger than your name. Try the type at around 50 points and the copyright symbol at 200 points.

Continued

Step Four:

Go to the Artwork and Effects palette (if it's not visible, go under the Window menu and choose Artwork and Effects), and in the More flyout menu choose Large Thumbnail View. At the top of the palette, click on the Special Effects button (the one right in the middle). In the pop-up menu in the palette's upper left-hand corner, choose Filters. In the second pop-up menu, choose Stylize. Now double-click on the Emboss effect. A warning dialog will appear letting you know that the Type layer must be simplified. Click OK.

Step Five:

In the resulting Emboss dialog, set the Angle to 135°, Height to 3 pixels, and Amount to 100%. Click OK, and this will apply a beveled effect. To smooth the edges of the Type layer, go to the Layers palette and click on the Lock Transparent Pixels icon at the top of the palette (the second icon from the right). Then, from the Filter menu, choose Blur, and add a 2- or 3-pixel Gaussian Blur.

Step Six:

Go back to the Layers palette and change the blend mode of this Type layer from Normal to Hard Light. This will make the watermark transparent. Now you can make the Background layer visible again by going to the Layers palette and clicking in the empty box where the Eye icon used to be. You can now see the Emboss and blurring effects clearly.

Step Seven:
Open the photo you want to contain this transparent watermark. Make sure this photo and the document with your embossed watermark are both visible within Elements (if not, exit Maximize Mode by going under the Window menu, under Images, and choose Cascade).

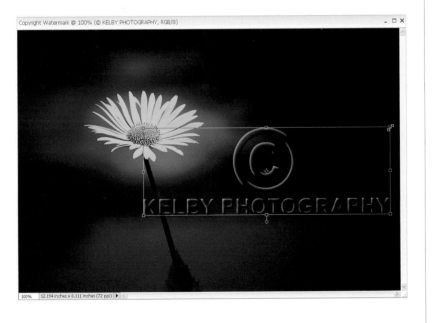

Step Eight:
Press V to switch to the Move tool, then click-and-drag the watermark's Type layer from the Layers palette (in the embossed watermark document) and drop it onto your photo (you're dragging a layer between documents). Once the watermark is in your new document, you can resize it as needed. Just press Control-T to bring up Free Transform and click-and-drag one of the corner handles. Add the Shift key to resize the type proportionately. Press Enter to complete your transformation.

Continued

Step Nine:

Now go to the Layers palette and lower the Opacity of your Type layer so it's clearly visible, but doesn't dominate the photo.

Step Ten:

Now for the second part—we'll embed your personal copyright info into the photo file itself. Go under the File menu and choose File Info. This is where you enter information that you want embedded. This embedding of info is supported by all the major file formats on the Windows platform (such as TIFF, JPEG, EPS, PDF, and Elements' native PSD file format).

Step Eleven:
In the dialog, change the Copyright Status pop-up menu from Unknown to Copyrighted. In the Copyright Notice field, enter your personal copyright info, and then under Copyright Info URL enter your full Web address. That way, when others open your file in Elements, they can go to File Info, click the Go To URL button, and it will launch their browser and take them directly to your site.

Step Twelve:
Click OK and the info is embedded into the file. Once copyright info has been embedded into a file, Elements automatically adds a copyright symbol before the file's name, which appears in the photo's title bar. That's it—you applied two levels of protection: one visible and one embedded.

Creating Your Own Custom Copyright Brush

If you want a quick way to apply your copyright watermark to an image, check out this trick I learned from portrait photographer (and guru) Todd Morrison. He showed me how to turn your copyright info into a brush, so you're only one click away from applying your mark to any photo. My thanks to Todd for letting me share his ingenious technique.

Step One:
Create a new document in the Elements Editor (go to File, under New, and choose Blank File), and then press U until you get the Custom Shape tool (it's in the flyout menu of Shape tools right below the Gradient tool in the Toolbox). Then, press the Enter key to bring up the Custom Shape Picker onscreen, and from the flyout menu in the top-right corner, choose Symbols. Now choose the Copyright symbol from the shapes in the Picker. Press the letter D to set black as your Foreground color and drag out a copyright symbol in the center of your document. Press-and-hold the Shift key as you drag to keep the symbol proportional.

Step Two:
Press T to switch to the Horizontal Type tool, and then type your copyright info. The Type tool will create a Type layer above the copyright Shape layer. (*Note:* When you set your type, go up to the Options Bar and make sure your justification is set to Center Text [click on the center of the three Align icons].) Then, type a few spaces between the copyright date and the name of your studio. This enables you to put the large copyright symbol in the center of your type.

Untitled-1 @ 100% (Copyright 2006   Spauldi, RGB/8)

Copyright 2006 ⓒ Spaulding 12

Brush Name

Learn more about: Brush Name

Name: Spaulding 12 Copyright

OK

Cancel

649

Size: 649 px   Mode: Color   Opa

Brushes: Default Brushes

48   Oil Heavy Flow Dry Edges
32   Oil Medium Wet Flow
55   Wet Sponge
100 Rough Round Bristle
75   Airbrush 75 Tilt Size and Angle
45   Airbrush Dual Brush Soft Round 45
649 Spaulding 12 Copyright

GREG SAVEL

Step Three:
Press M to get the Rectangular Marquee tool, and click-and-drag a selection around your type and your copyright symbol. Then, go under the Edit menu and choose Define Brush from Selection. When the Brush Name dialog appears, name your brush and click OK. This adds your type as a custom brush in your Brush Picker. Press Control-D to deselect. *Note:* Don't worry—the preview of the brush that appears in the Brush Name dialog may look squished, but the brush won't be.

Step Four:
Press B to get the Brush tool. In the Options Bar, click on the Brush thumbnail and in the resulting Brush Picker, scroll to the bottom of the brushes. The last brush in the set is the custom copyright brush you just created.

Step Five:
Now that you've created your copyright brush, it's time to put it to use. Open a photo that you want to use as a client proof. Click on the Create a New Layer icon at the top of the Layers palette, and then with the Brush tool, click once where you want your copyright info to appear. Lower the Opacity in the Layers palette so you can see through the copyright. Two things to keep in mind: (1) If the photo is dark, try white as your Foreground color; (2) you can use the Size slider (up in the Options Bar) to change the size of your Brush tool.

Poster Presentation

This technique gives your work the layout of a professional poster, yet it's incredibly easy to do.

Step One:
Open the photo you want to turn into a poster layout.

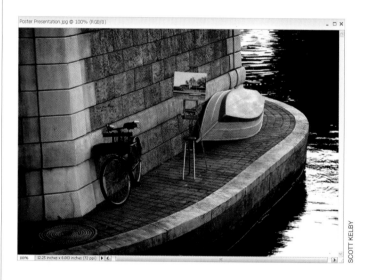

Step Two:
Go under the Image menu, under Resize, and choose Canvas Size. When the dialog appears, turn on the Relative checkbox, enter 1 inch for both the Width and the Height fields, and choose White in the Canvas Extension Color pop-up menu.

Step Three:
When you click OK, an inch of white canvas space will be added around your photo.

Step Four:
Now you're going to go back to the Canvas Size dialog under the Image menu, under Resize. Add another inch of white canvas but only to the bottom of your image. So, in the Canvas Size dialog enter 1 inch in the Height field, and then in the Anchor grid, click on the top-center anchor (which makes the area you're adding appear below the image).

Continued

Step Five:
Click OK and an additional inch of white canvas area is added below your photo.

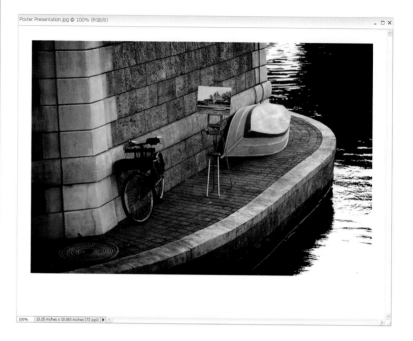

Step Six:
In this extra inch of white space, you'll add some type. Press D to set your Foreground to black, and then press T to get the Horizontal Type tool to add your type (i.e., the name of your studio, the name of the poster, whatever you'd like). I chose the font Gill Sans MT in all caps at a size of 20 points. You'll want to add extra space between the letters, which gives the type an elegant look. To do that, when you're typing in your text, just put an extra space (or two if you like) between each letter using the Spacebar.

Step Seven:
Once your type has been created and you have space between your letters (as mentioned in the previous step), choose the Move tool at the top of the Toolbox and position your type so it's centered below your photo.

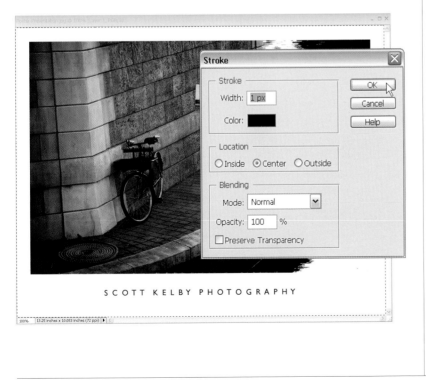

Step Eight:
Let's add a thin outside border. Click on the Create a New Layer icon in the top of the Layers palette, and then press Control-A to put a selection around your entire image area. Go under the Edit menu and choose Stroke (Outline) Selection. When the Stroke dialog appears, set black as your stroke Color, set the Width to 1 pixel, set the Location to Center, and click OK. Now you can press Control-D to deselect.

Continued

Step Nine:

To make the outside border thinner and less obtrusive, go to the Layers palette and lower the Opacity setting for this layer to around 30%, giving you the final poster layout shown here.

SCOTT KELBY PHOTOGRAPHY

This is a great technique for displaying your images in online galleries or in PDF presentations for clients. It gives your photos that finished "gallery" look, but without the time or costs involved in framing your prints and then shooting the framed work—it's totally a digital illusion created from scratch in Photoshop Elements 5.

Creating a Digital Frame

SCOTT KELBY

Step One:
Open the photo you want to frame digitally. Press D to set your Foreground and Background colors to their defaults. Press Control-A to put a selection around your entire photo, and then press Control-Shift-J to cut your photo from the Background layer and put it on its own separate layer (Layer 1).

Step Two:
Go under the Image menu, under Resize, and choose Canvas Size. When the dialog appears, turn on the Relative checkbox, set the Canvas Extension Color pop-up menu to White, and then enter 4 inches for both Width and Height. Click OK to add white space around your photo.

Continued

Step Three:

Press-and-hold the Control key and click on the Create a New Layer icon at the top of the Layers palette. By pressing this key, the new layer you're creating appears below your photo layer, rather than above it.

Step Four:

Press M to get the Rectangular Marquee tool. Draw a selection that's a couple of inches larger than your photo (this will be the edge of your frame, so you'll want to make this selection as big as you want your frame). Next, with your Foreground color still set to black, press Alt-Backspace to fill this selection with black. Do not deselect quite yet.

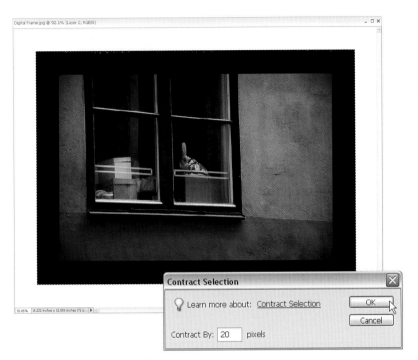

Step Five:
Now you're going to shrink your selection, so go under the Select menu, under Modify, and choose Contract. When the dialog appears, enter 20 pixels (this will determine the width of your frame, so if you want a thicker frame, use a higher number here) and click OK to shrink your selection.

Step Six:
Press Backspace to knock a hole out of your black rectangle, giving the impression of a black metal frame, and then press Control-D to deselect. Now to add some depth: Go to the Artwork and Effects palette (under the Window menu), and click on the Special Effects button (it's the one right in the middle at the top of the palette). From the top-left pop-up menu choose Layer Styles, and from the right pop-up menu choose Drop Shadows. When the shadow icons appear, double-click on Low to create a soft shadow on the top-left corner and bottom-right corner, which adds some depth.

Continued

Step Seven:

Go back to the Layers palette and click on the Create a New Layer icon. You're going to create a thin mat on this layer, so get the Rectangular Marquee tool again, but this time draw a rectangular selection that's just slightly larger than your image. Fill this selection with black by pressing Alt-Backspace. Don't deselect yet.

Step Eight:

Go under the Select menu, under Modify, and choose Contract. This time, contract just 2 pixels (again, depending on the size of the photo, you might need to make this number a little higher) and click OK, but don't deselect yet.

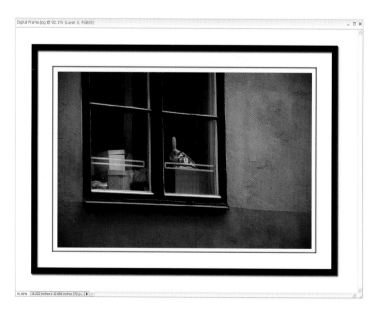

Step Nine:

Go under the Select menu and choose Feather (this is to soften the edges of your selection). When the dialog appears, enter 2 and click OK to slightly soften the edges. Press Backspace to knock a hole out of this black layer, and press Control-D to deselect. It will now appear as though there's an inner shadow all the way around your layer (as shown here), but that shadow is a little too dark to make a convincing mat.

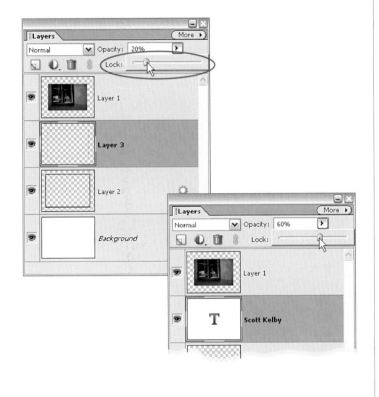

Step Ten:
Go to the Layers palette and lower the Opacity setting of this thin black layer to around 20%, creating the look of a mat surrounding your photo.

Step Eleven:
Press T to get the Type tool, and choose a script font that looks like handwriting, if possible, from the Font pop-up menu in the Options Bar (I used Monotype Corsiva). Add your signature just below the bottom-right corner of your photo, and then lower the Opacity of your Type layer to around 60% so it looks like you signed the photo in pencil.

Putting Your Photos Up on the Web

Elements has a built-in feature that not only automatically optimizes your photos for the Web, it actually builds a real HTML document for you, with small thumbnail images; links to large, full-size proofs; your email contact information; and more. All you have to do is upload it to the Web and give your friends (or clients) the Web address for your new site. In this section, we're going to look at how to create standard HTML webpages, but later in the book, we'll look at how to create flash-based interactive webpages. But that's later. For now, let's start here.

Step One:

In the Organizer, Control-click on all the photos that you want to appear on your webpage. Then, go to the task bar above the Timeline and click on the Create button, and in the menu that appears choose Photo Galleries.

Step Two:

When the Photo Galleries Wizard appears (shown here), the photos you selected a moment ago in the Organizer appear along the left side of the dialog, and in the center of the dialog is where you'll choose your Web gallery (HTML) template and individual style (of course, there are other types of website templates other than HTML here; you've got Flash and Interactive photo gallery templates as well, but as I mentioned in the intro above, we're just going to focus on the standard HTML Web galleries at this point).

Step Three:

Under the Choose a Template section, you'll choose which type of photo gallery you want from the pop-up menu. We're building a standard Web gallery, so choose Web Galleries from the pop-up menu. Then, you'll choose a template (from the top horizontal row). Each one has a different layout, and each gives you a small thumbnail preview, and a written description of the template below it. Click on the one that looks good to you, and then choose the color combination (style) from the lower horizontal row of thumbnails in the Choose a Style section.

Step Four:

Once you click on the template you want in the top horizontal list of templates (I chose the Left Filmstrip style, because I like the larger thumbnails and the vertical scrolling), and the style (color) for your template from the second horizontal row (I like the all black one called "Darkroom," so I chose it in the example you see here), you can click the Next Step button. This brings up another dialog where you can customize your HTML webpage (shown in the next step).

Continued

Step Five:

When this next dialog appears, you'll now see a preview of the page you're building in the top of the dialog. The Customize section along the left side is for customizing the text that will appear on your webpage. To customize your page, you can enter your text in the fields on the left side. As you enter text in these fields, you'll see your text appear live in the preview window, so you know exactly what you're getting.

Step Six:

This webpage template has a Slideshow feature (where your viewers can see an automated slide show online), so you get to choose how many seconds each slide is displayed on screen, and choose the custom transition that occurs between slides. Below that is a pop-up optimization menu that will customize your website for the type of viewers you feel will be visiting it. Below that, you can customize the colors used for just about everything (from the background, to the text, to borders, to...well...pretty much everything) on the site by simply clicking on the color swatch to the right of what you want to change, and choosing a new color from the Color Picker.

Step Seven:
Before you actually post this gallery to the Web, I would recommend previewing it in your Web browser, so click on the (you saw this one coming) Preview in Browser button, and it will launch your Web browser and preview the page you've just created. If your page looks the way you want it to, now you can move on to the final step, which is preparing the webpage for uploading either to your Web server, or to Adobe's new free Web service called "Photoshop Showcase," where Adobe will host your Web gallery for free.

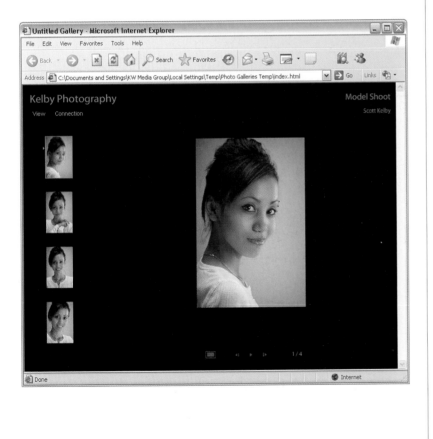

Step Eight:

The last things you need to do before uploading your page are to give your gallery a name and choose where you want to save it in the Save and Share section at the bottom of the dialog. Once you name the Gallery (in the Save Gallery As field), click the Browse button and pick a place on your hard disk where you want to save the file, then choose (from the Share To pop-up menu) where this site will be hosted (Adobe's free Photoshop Showcase, to your FTP site for uploading to the Web, to a CD, or you can choose not to share the site at all). Once you've chosen where to share your site to, all you have to do is press the Share/Burn/Save button, and Photoshop Elements takes care of the rest. It even saves a copy of your new Web gallery right into the Organizer at the top of the list of images, so you can find it again easily. That's it—you've created your custom HTML webpage.

TIP: If you chose not to share your new Web gallery because you plan to upload it to your server later, Elements automatically creates all the files and folders you'll need to upload it to the Web and saves them in the location you chose earlier in the Save and Share section of the Photo Galleries Wizard. These are the files and folders you need to put your photo gallery up live on the Web, including your HTML home page (index.html). Now all you have to do is upload them to a Web server and you're live!

I've often joked that we're now one click away from becoming a Sears Portrait Studio since Adobe invented the Picture Package feature, which lets you gang-print the standard, common photo sizes together on one sheet. With Picture Package, Elements does all the work for you. All you have to do is open the photo you want gang-printed, and then Elements will take it from there—except for the manual cutting of the final print, which is actually beyond Elements' capabilities. So far.

Getting One 5x7", Two 2.5x3.5", and Four Wallet-Size Photos on One Print

SCOTT KELBY

Step One:
Open the photo in the Elements Editor that you want to appear in a variety of sizes on one page, and then go under the File menu and choose Print Multiple Photos.

Step Two:
When the dialog appears, on the right-hand side choose which printer you want to use. Then in section 2, choose Picture Package from the pop-up menu. You'll get a printing warning letting you know that the image will be rendered at less than 220 dpi at the requested print size. Just click OK.

Continued

Step Three:

In the third section down, choose the sizes and layout for your Picture Package from the Select a Layout pop-up menu. In this example, I chose Letter (1) 5x7 (2) 2.5x3.5 (4) 2x2.5, but you can choose any combination you like.

Step Four:

Even though you've chosen a layout, only one photo will appear in the layout preview in the center of the dialog. You'll need to click the Fill Page With First Photo checkbox to place your image multiple times.

Step Five:
When you click Print, Elements 5 auto-matically resizes, rotates, and compiles your photos into one printable page that you can then cut. This is a simple use of Picture Package, but it's actually more flexible than it looks, as you'll see in the next step.

Step Six:
Another option you have is to add a custom frame around the photos in your Picture Package. To add a frame, just choose one from the Select a Frame pop-up menu and your choice will be immediately reflected in the preview.

Continued

Step Seven:

If you'd like to create more Picture Package layouts using your same settings, all you have to do is import another photo. You do that by first clicking on the Add button near the bottom left-hand corner of the dialog. This brings up the Add Photos dialog, where you can find the photo you want to import from the Photo Browser, the Catalog, etc. (Here I chose to add a photo from a selected Tag by clicking on the Tag radio button and then choosing the Jordan & Kira tag from the pop-up menu.) Just click on the checkbox to the left of the image's thumbnail in the dialog, and click Add Selected Photos. Once imported, a small thumbnail of your photo will appear in the list of photos on the left side of the Print Photos dialog (you can see here that I added a black-and-white photo of my daughter Kira). When you're finished adding photos, click Done.

Step Eight:

To see the layout with your new photo, click the right-facing arrow button just below the large preview in the center of the dialog. It will toggle you to a layout for your second photo. If you import several photos, you'll be able to toggle to a layout for each photo.

Step Nine:
If you're a more advanced user who understands Color Management options and assigning color profiles, you can click on the More Options button, located directly below the preview, and assign a color space to your photos before printing. But if you're not comfortable making these choices, just skip the More Options button.

Step Ten:
Click Print and here's how your additional Picture Package output will look.

Using Picture Package Layouts with More Than One Photo

Although the Picture Package feature is most often used for printing one photo multiple times on the same page, you can substitute different photos in different positions, and you can customize their location. Here's how:

Step One:

Once you have the Print Photos dialog open and you've selected Picture Package as your type of print (see previous tutorial), click the Add button (near the bottom left-hand corner of the dialog) to add additional photos from the Photo Browser, Catalog, etc., until you have a row of thumbnails appearing down the left side of the dialog. Make sure the Fill Page With First Photo checkbox (found on the right side of the dialog, just below the Select a Frame pop-up menu) is turned on.

Step Two:

To add a new photo to your Picture Package layout, just click on the image's thumbnail on the left and drag-and-drop it onto the preview area in the center of the dialog on the position you want it to appear. (*Note:* As you drag, you'll notice a highlight around the preset picture positions in the preview window.)

Step Three:
If you want to move a photo to another position, just click directly on the photo in the preview area and drag it to a new position. It will automatically resize if necessary.

Step Four:
You can have as many different photos as you have positions in your layout, so just continue dragging-and-dropping thumbnails from the left side of the dialog into position within the preview area.

Step Five:
If you'd prefer to just have all your imported photos appear on the page at once (rather than dragging-and-dropping them), turn off the Fill Page With First Photo checkbox and all imported photos on the left of the dialog will automatically flow into place.

Creating a PDF Presentation for a Client

In Elements 5 there's a feature that takes a group of images, creates a slide show (complete with transitions), and compresses it into PDF format so you can email it easily to a client for proofing. This is perfect for showing your portfolio to clients, sending clients proofs of wedding shots or portrait sittings, sending friends photos from a party, or one of a dozen other uses, none of which I can think of at this particular moment, but I'm sure it'll come to me later when I'm at the mall or driving to the office.

Step One:
Open the photos you want to use in your PDF presentation in the Editor, click on the Create button in the task bar above the Options Bar, and from the pop-up menu, choose Slide Show. (*Note:* You can also Control-click images in the Organizer, and then click the Create button.)

Step Two:
This brings up the Slide Show Preferences dialog, where you choose various options for your slide show. In this case, let's go with the default settings, so click the OK button near the bottom-right corner of the dialog.

Step Three:
Clicking OK brings up yet another dialog. At the bottom of the dialog are thumbnails of all the photos that will be included in your slide show. The thumbnails are arranged in the order in which they'll appear, but to change the order, just click-and-drag a thumbnail to where you'd like it to appear. If you want to remove an image, Right-click on its thumbnail and choose Delete Slide from the contextual menu. To add an image, click-and-hold on the Add Media button in the top center of the dialog, choose Photos and Videos from Folder, and browse for your image.

Step Four:
By default, Elements will provide a Fade transition between your slides, but you may want some variety. To choose a different transition, click on the tiny, right-facing arrow to the right of any transition's icon and select a new transition from the pop-up menu that appears. To play it safe, choose something that nearly always works, like Dissolve. To apply this to all of your slides, choose Apply to All from the same menu.

Continued

Step Five:
Along the right side of the dialog, in the Properties palette, you can customize your active slide by changing its background color, enabling effects, etc. In the Extras palette you can add graphics, text, or narration, but since we're doing a simple slide show here, I left the settings at their defaults and clicked the Output button near the top left of the dialog.

Step Six:
This brings up the Slide Show Output dialog, where you can save your slide show as a PDF. Choose Save As a File from the list of options on the left, and then on the right side of the dialog, turn on the PDF File option. Here's where you choose your slides' settings. I like to use Small (800x600), but you can choose any size you'd like from the Slide Size pop-up menu (or enter your own preferred size by choosing Custom from the menu). Click OK and Elements 5 will create a PDF file that's ready for you to email to your client.

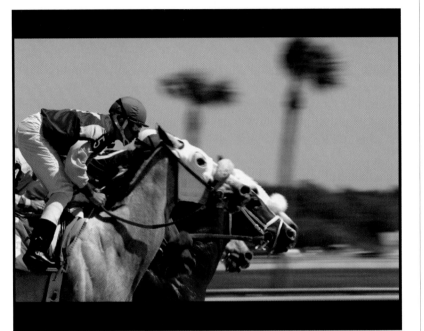

Step Seven:

When your client opens your emailed PDF, it automatically launches Adobe Reader in Full Screen mode (your photos appear centered on a black background), and the presentation begins. The capture here shows the first slide in a PDF presentation in Full Screen mode, right before it transitioned to the next photo. (*Note:* If for some strange reason your client/friend doesn't have Adobe Reader installed, he or she can download it free from Adobe's site at www.adobe.com.)

TIP: Are seven steps just too many for ya? Create a basic PDF slide show by opening your images in the Editor, and then clicking on the Share button in the task bar (its the one in the middle with the Earth and an envelope). From the pop-up menu, choose E-mail. (*Note:* You may get a dialog asking you to choose an email client as your default. Choose your email client from the pop-up menu and click Continue.) In the resulting dialog, choose Simple Slide Show (PDF) from the Format pop-up menu, and enter a File Name in the Choose Format section. Click the Add button in the bottom left-hand corner to navigate to your images and add any additional ones, then choose your images' size and quality (see the following tutorial for recommended settings). When you click the Next button, your default email software will launch with a new message—complete with a PDF slide show—ready for you to send.

How to Email Photos

Believe it or not, this is one of those most-asked questions, and I guess it's because there are no official guidelines for emailing photos. Perhaps there should be, because there are photographers who routinely send me high-res photos that: (a) get bounced back to them because of size restrictions, (b) take all day to download, or (c) never get here at all because there are no official guidelines on how to email photos. In the absence of such rules, consider these the "official" unofficial rules.

Step One:

Open the photo that you want to email in the Elements Editor. In the task bar, click on the Share button and choose E-mail. (*Note:* You may get an E-mail dialog asking you to choose an email client as your default. Choose your email client [Microsoft Outlook, etc.] from the pop-up menu and click Continue.)

Step Two:

This opens your photo in the Attach to E-mail dialog. The first decision to make is: Who do you want to email this photo to? (Adobe calls this simple task Select Recipients, because that makes it sound significantly more complicated and confusing.) To choose who will receive your photo by email, click in the checkbox beside the contacts (who are in your Contact Book. If a contact isn't in the list, click on the Edit Contacts button at the bottom center of the dialog to add a contact to the list).

Step Three:
In the Choose Format section, choose Individual Attachments. Then, in the Select Size and Quality section, choose the size at which you'd like to send your image. If you choose an image size other than the original size of the photo, you also get to choose a Quality setting. Remember: The higher the quality, the larger your file size will be, so try to find a happy medium. Try a 7 or an 8. Only go higher if you know the person to whom you're emailing this photo has a high-speed Internet connection.

Step Four:
If you'd like to add a message to your email (like "Here's where I'm on vacation. The weather is here, wish you were beautiful," etc.), enter that in the Message area in the bottom-right corner of the dialog.

Step Five:
Once your options are set, click the Next button in the bottom right-hand corner of the dialog. Clicking Next launches your default email application and your photo and message are automatically attached. All that's left to do now is click the Send button and it's on its way.

Create (or Die)
how to make presentations with your photos

Back in the old days, we'd edit a digital photo and then we'd just print it out. It was a simpler time. If we got the photo centered on the page, it was considered a minor miracle and people would come from local towns and villages just to see our centered prints. But now the young kids have these newfangled contraptions that let you take your photos and turn them into slide shows, webpages, wall calendars, and video CDs. Some folks call this progress, but I say it's just not right! It's not what photos were intended to do.

They're supposed to be still, lifeless, static, and centered on a white piece of paper. But then along comes Photoshop Elements 5, with its "creation" features, and all of a sudden every crackerjack with 2 gigs of RAM thinks he's Dennis Hopper (who coincidentally starred in the documentary *Create [or Die]*, which was released in 2003 to a worldwide audience, many of whom own digital cameras, yet most of whom were not able to adequately center their photos on a page). Leave stuff like centering photos to the pros, I say.

Creating with Your Photos

There is an entire area of Elements 5 dedicated to creating projects with your photos. By projects, I mean transforming your photos from just prints into "creations" like full-fledged slide shows, wall calendars, postcards, or Web photo galleries. Here's just one way to access Elements' Create feature:

Step One:

There are about half a dozen ways to get to the Create section of Elements, but the easiest and most visible way to get there is to just click on the Create button that appears above the Options Bar in the Elements Editor or just below the menu bar in the Organizer and a list of "creations" will appear (as shown here). *Note*: You don't have to have a photo open to build a creation—you can add the photo(s) after you've built the creation. I know, this sounds weird, but you'll see why this works in just a few moments.

Step Two:

When you choose a creation from that list, a new dialog appears where you can customize the way your final creation will look. This is generally a four-step process, where you start by choosing the size of your creation (from the pop-up menu at the top left). Then you choose whichever layout you'd like, and you get a preview of how each layout looks. In the third step, you have the option (this step is totally optional) to choose a custom theme that appears around your photo(s), and then finally you get to choose any additional options in the fourth and final step. If you just start at the top and work your way down, it's really pretty easy.

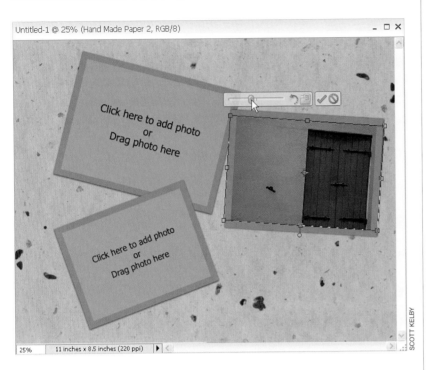

Untitled-1 @ 25% (Hand Made Paper 2, RGB/8)

Click here to add photo
or
Drag photo here

Click here to add photo
or
Drag photo here

25%   11 inches x 8.5 inches (220 ppi)

SCOTT KELBY

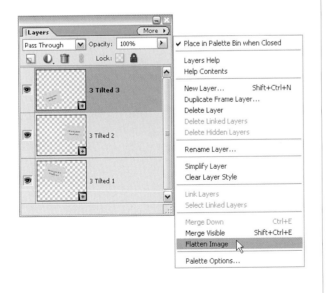

Step Three:
When you click OK, Elements 5 builds a new document using your custom settings, and it leaves a gray square where your photo(s) will appear. To get your photo in that gray square, you have two choices: (1) open the photo in Elements 5, then get the Move tool (V) from the Toolbox, click-and-drag the photo onto the gray square, and it automatically fits inside your layout. Or, (2) you can click on the gray square and the standard Open dialog appears asking you to find the photo on your hard disk that you want to open. Once you choose a photo (or drag-and-drop one onto the gray square), a small resizing slider appears in the upper-left corner of your placed photo. Drag this slider to change the size of your photo within the layout. When the size looks good to you, click the green Checkmark beside the slider. If you don't want to resize the photo, just click the red international symbol for "No!" (the circle with a slash through it). That's it!

Note: You can always go back later and resize or reposition the photo within that frame by double-clicking directly on the photo. Or you can replace the photo by simply dragging a photo from the Photo Bin and dropping it right on the existing photo. This makes swapping out photos very quick and easy.

TIP: If you don't choose a theme in Step Two, the layout you chose will appear on a transparent background (with a gray-and-white checkerboard pattern behind the photos). This enables you to drag-and-drop the photo layers onto the background of your choice, but if you prefer to have a white background, just go to the Layers palette and choose Flatten Image from the palette's More flyout menu.

Making Full-Blown Slide Shows

Earlier in the book, we looked at how to create a simple slide show from selected photos in the Organizer, but if you really want to create a slide show masterpiece, this is where you come.

Step One:

You start by clicking once on the Create button in either the Elements Organizer or the Editor, and from the pop-up menu that appears, choose Slide Show (as shown here). Choosing the Slide Show creation from the Editor will launch the Organizer because this particular feature is actually part of the Organizer. So, once the Organizer appears onscreen, the Slide Show Preferences dialog will also appear. This is where you choose how you want your slide show set up.

Step Two:

For example, at the top you choose how many seconds each slide will appear onscreen. Below that you choose the transition between slides (will it be a soft dissolve or a quick cut between photos?), and how long your transition will last. A popular transition effect is called Pan & Zoom (which slowly moves [pans] your images across the screen), and to turn this on, turn on the checkbox for Apply Pan & Zoom to All Slides.

Step Three:
Once you click OK, the Slide Show Editor appears, and this is where you'll create your magic (okay, "magic" is probably pushing it a bit, but this is where you'll "do your stuff"). If you opened photos in the Editor (or selected them in the Organizer) before you chose Slide Show, these photos will appear in the Slide Show Editor's Photo Bin at the bottom of the dialog, as shown here (which means you can skip Step Four). If not, you'll notice that the Photo Bin is empty, except for the prompt Click Here to Add Photos to Your Slide Show. So, click there (I know, that seems pretty obvious) to bring up the Add Photos dialog (shown in the next step).

Step Four:
Basically, here's where you choose which photos will wind up in your slide show. *Note*: Again, if you opened photos in the Editor (or selected them in the Organizer) before you chose Create's Slide Show option, you can skip this step, because photos will already be imported into your slide show—you'll only use Add Photos if either (a) you don't have any photos in your slide show, or (b) you want to add another photo (or more) to your existing slide show. Turn on the checkbox beside each photo you want in your slide show, then click the Add Selected Photos button at the bottom of the window and click Done.

Continued

Step Five:

To see a quick sample of what your slide show looks like at this point (before you start customizing it), click the Play button beneath the main preview window. You'll see a slide show of your imported photos in the order they were imported, with whichever transitions you chose in the Slide Show Preferences dialog. To stop, click the Pause button (which appears where the Play button used to be). If you're not thrilled with your slide show, it's probably because you're only seeing the default slide show. The slides aren't in order; there's no background music; you haven't customized the slide show your way. Well, that's about to change, because it's time to tweak your slide show.

Step Six:

The first thing to do is put the slides in the order you want them. To do that, just click on a thumbnail in the Photo Bin at the bottom of the dialog and drag it where you want it (the slides play from left to right, so if you want a particular slide to be first, drag that slide all the way to the left). As you drag slides around in the Photo Bin, you'll see a bar indicating where the slide will appear when you release the mouse button.

Step Seven:

With the slides in order, take a look directly beneath your photo thumbnails in the Photo Bin. You'll see "5 sec." That's telling you that this slide will stay onscreen for 5 seconds. If you want it onscreen for a shorter amount of time, just click directly on that number and a pop-up menu of duration times will appear. If you want to apply a particular duration to all your slides (for example, you want them all to appear onscreen for 3 seconds), after you choose 3 sec for one slide, click on the time again for that slide and choose Set All Slides to 3 sec. If you choose Custom, you can type any number in the Set Slide Duration dialog.

Step Eight:

Finally, the fun part—choosing your transitions. You can go with the one you originally chose in the Slide Show Preferences, or you can choose a new one. To do that, click directly on the little right-facing triangle that appears to the right of the square transition box (which is between your slides in the Photo Bin). This brings up a pop-up menu of transitions—just choose the one you want and it changes only that transition between those two slides. If you want that transition applied to all your slides, choose Apply to All at the top of the pop-up transition menu. (By the way, if you choose None, the international symbol for "No!" [a circle with a slash through it] will appear between your slides instead, but you can change that by clicking on the right-facing triangle next to it and choosing a transition from the pop-up menu.)

Continued

Step Nine:

If you want to change the duration of one (or more) of your slides or transitions, click on the slide or transition, then in the Properties palette (on the right side of the Slide Show Editor dialog), change the Slide or Transition time (which is measured in seconds) in the pop-up menu.

Step Ten:

Okay, what's even cooler than transitions? Pan & Zoom (in fact, you can have transitions and Pan & Zoom). Pan & Zoom brings movement to your slides, and this movement makes your slide show feel less static, as the photos move slowly left to right, top to bottom, while they slowly zoom in and out. That's why this effect is so popular. If you turned on the Apply Pan & Zoom to All Slides checkbox in the Slide Show Preferences (when you first opened your slide show), then all you have to do to edit a Pan & Zoom is click on a slide and the Pan & Zoom controls will appear in the Properties palette on the right side of the dialog.

Step Eleven:

If you didn't turn on Pan & Zoom for all slides from the start, it's easy to turn it on. Just click on the slide you want to apply it to, and then in the Properties palette turn on the checkbox for Enable Pan & Zoom. (Needless to say, to turn off the Pan & Zoom for any slide, just click on the slide and turn off the Enable Pan & Zoom checkbox in the Properties palette. I know, I said "needless to say," but then I said it anyway. It's a personality disorder.)

Step Twelve:

Once you've got Pan & Zoom turned on, you can tweak it in three very distinct ways: (1) When you turn on Pan & Zoom, a green square appears in the preview window, and the word "Start" appears in the bottom-right corner. You can reposition the location and size of this green square (shown here) to where you'd like the panning and zooming to start. In the Properties palette, if you click on the End thumbnail, you can position the panning end point by moving (and/or resizing) the red square. (2) You can swap the positions of these squares by using the three little buttons between the Start and End thumbnails in the Properties palette. (3) You can add an additional Pan & Zoom, which essentially duplicates your slide, and lets you add another Pan & Zoom segment, so you could have your photo pan from left to right, then in the second segment, zoom from large to small. To do this, click on the Add Another Pan & Zoom to This Slide prompt at the bottom of the Properties palette.

Step Thirteen:

Now, on to adding titles: If you want to add a title to the beginning of your slide show, click on the first slide in the Photo Bin, and then click the Add Text button at the top of the Slide Show Editor. This brings up the Edit Text dialog, in which you enter your text. As you begin typing, your text appears onscreen.

Continued

Step Fourteen:

Once you click OK in the Edit Text dialog, you can reposition your text by just clicking-and-dragging it where you want it. You can also now choose which font, size, style, opacity, and color you want for your text (and a host of other type tweaks) in the Properties palette on the right side of the dialog. If you need to edit your text, just click on the Edit Text button in the Properties palette or change your font, style, etc., in the bottom of the palette.

Step Fifteen:

If you want your title to appear over a blank slide, rather than over a photo, you can create your title over a blank background by clicking the Add Blank Slide button at the top of the dialog. This creates an empty black slide. Now you can either click the Add Text button to create the text that will appear over your black slide, or you can click on the Text icon in the Extras palette (on the top right of the window), which reveals a list of pre-designed type treatments, including text with shadows (which are about impossible to see over a black background, by the way).

Step Sixteen:

If you want to change the color of your blank slide (from the default black color), you can do that by clicking on the blank slide (in the Photo Bin), and then in the Properties palette you'll see a black color swatch named "Background Color." Click on it to bring up the Color Picker, where you can choose a different color. Once you've chosen a new color, click OK, and your currently selected slide's color will be changed.

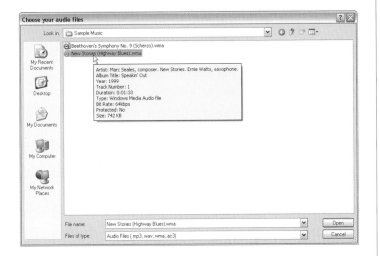

Step Seventeen:
All right, the slides are in order, the transitions have been chosen, and the titles have been created. Now, for the finishing touch—music. To add some background music to your slide show, click on the gray bar directly beneath the Photo Bin with the words "Click Here to Add Audio to Your Slide Show." This brings up a dialog prompting you to choose your audio file. You can browse for your own music files or choose from a list of music files in Elements' sample catalog. When you find a song you like, click on its name in the list, and then click the Open button.

Step Eighteen:
Now it's time to preview the finished slide show. Click the Full Screen Preview button on the top-right side of the Slide Show Editor's task bar, then sit back, relax, and enjoy the "magic." If, while watching your preview, you see something you want to change, just press the Escape key.

Step Nineteen:
When the show is tweaked to perfection (or your personal satisfaction, whichever comes first), it's time to output it into its final form. Click on the Output button in the Slide Show Editor's task bar to bring up the Slide Show Output dialog. Now you just click to choose what you want to do with your final show: save it as a file, burn it to CD or DVD, email your slide show to a friend (in which case, you'll choose either to create a PDF or a very compressed movie), or watch it on TV. As you click on your choice, some options for that choice will appear on the right side of the dialog. When you're done, click OK.

Creating Postcards or Greeting Cards

If you're interested in cheating Hallmark out of a few bucks, here's a great way to do it—create your own greeting cards. But it's not just about the money—it's about the personalization that can only come from using one of your own photos that makes the card really special (and cheap!). Here's how to do the holidays on a budget (kidding):

Step One:
Start by going to the Organizer and choosing the photo you want to use on the front of your greeting card. Then, click once on the Create button in the task bar at the top of the Organizer, and from the menu that appears choose Greeting Card. *Note*: Once again, you don't have to start by choosing a photo; you can have the Organizer create the greeting card first, then you can either drag-and-drop a photo onto your greeting card, or you can add your photo by clicking on the blank gray photo box that will appear on your greeting card.

Step Two:
When the New Greeting Card dialog appears, you're going to (1) choose the size you want for your greeting card, then (2) choose how you want your photo to appear on the page in the Select a Layout section. The first three layouts are for one-photo cards, but if you want to have more than one photo on your card, you can choose one of the layouts that has more than one gray box (you can have up to 22 photos on one card, which is quite a few for a 4x6" or 5x7" card. If you choose the 22-photo layout, you might want to send a magnifying glass along with the card. Hey, I'm just saying...).

Step Three:
Once you've decided on how many photos will appear on your card (please don't choose 22—I'm begging you), then you have the option of choosing a theme. Just as an example, choose the 2 Tilted as your layout, then under Select a Theme scroll down to Winter, and you get a preview of how your layout will look. Don't let it throw you that it doesn't show your photos in the preview; instead it displays two sample photos just to give you an idea of how your layout will look.

Continued

Step Four:

In the Additional Options section at the bottom-left side of the dialog, it gives you the choice of automatically filling those two photo boxes with photos you've pre-selected in the Organizer (of course, providing you actually chose two or more photos in the Organizer before you got this far), and you get the option of including captions for your photos. If you want either of these options, just turn on the checkbox.

Step Five:

When you click the OK button, it creates a new greeting card document for you (as shown here). Now, since we only selected one photo in the Organizer before we started building our greeting card, we see that photo but we also see the dreaded gray photo box (okay, it's not dreaded—just annoying). So, let's put a photo in that box by either (your choice); clicking on the box and choosing a photo from your hard disk, or using my preferred method of opening a photo in the Editor, and dragging-and-dropping that photo onto the square box. Whichever method you choose, you will have the option of resizing the photo once it's in place by using the little sizing slider that appears on the upper-left corner of the photo. Also, if you want to reposition the photo inside the frame, just click inside the frame and drag the photo where you want it.

Step Six:

Okay, let's say you've got two photos all in place, but then you decide that you don't like one of the photos and want to replace it with a different photo? Easy enough—just Right-click on the photo you want to replace and a contextual menu will appear. Choose (big shock coming up) Replace Photo. This brings up the Open dialog, where you can choose a different photo to replace the existing one. By the way, you can also replace photos as soon as you import one. For example, let's say you dragged-and-dropped a photo onto the gray box, and you know right then, before resizing or positioning it, that it's the wrong photo. Just click on the little Folder icon that appears to the right of the sizing slider and it brings up an Open dialog where you can choose a different photo. How convenient is that? (That's a rhetorical question. It's plenty convenient.)

Step Seven:

There is one particular option that's kind of hidden that I particularly like (like the way I worked the word "particular" twice into one sentence? I was particularly pleased with that). Anyway, here's what it does: instead of forcing your photo to fit the frame size (which usually means your photo will be cropped somewhat), instead it resizes the frame to fit your photo. To get to this feature, just Right-click on the photo in the greeting card layout, then choose "Fit Frame To Photo" from the contextual menu (as shown here). Well, that's pretty much it—your own custom greeting card, with hopefully less than 22 photos.

Creating Photo Book Pages

This is one of my favorite things in Elements 5 because Adobe did such a slick job with it. They've created some great-looking templates for photo book pages and digital scrapbooking—all you have to do is choose which layout you want and it does the rest. Here's how to start using this way-cool feature:

Step One:

Start by going to the Organizer and choosing the photo (or photos) you want to appear on your photo book page(s). Then, click once on the Create button in the task bar at the top of the Organizer and choose Photo Book Pages from the menu. *Note:* Once again, you don't have to start by choosing a photo; you can have the Organizer create the photo book pages first, then you can either drag-and-drop photos onto your photo pages, or you can add your photos by clicking on the blank gray photo boxes that will appear on your photo pages.

IMPORTANT: The Photo Book Pages feature is really designed to create pages that will become an actual hardcover book. You use Adobe's online services to upload your finished pages (a minimum of 20 pages), and once uploaded, Kodak assembles them into a professionally-printed, hardcover photo book and ships the finished book directly to you. Pretty sweet, eh? However, if you don't want to go that route, you can simply choose Create's Album Pages feature to create the pages (as many or as few as you want) and print them on your own printer, or save them as PDFs and email them to friends.

Step Two:

When the New Photo Book Pages dialog appears, start by choosing the size of your final book from the Select a Size pop-up menu. If you didn't select photos before you started your creation, then this is a good time to go down to the bottom of the dialog and choose how many pages you want in your photo book. Remember, if you plan on ordering a hardcover book from Kodak, you need a minimum of 20 pages. Otherwise, choose as many (or as few) as you like. By the way, if you choose 8 pages, you're going to create eight new pages that look exactly alike (well, they won't have the same photo on each page, but the layout you choose will appear on all eight pages, so keep that in mind when choosing how many pages you want). For example, if you think you might want six pages that have one large single photo, then choose 6 for your page count and you'll get six full-page documents.

Step Three:

Next choose which layout you'd like for your photo book pages by choosing a layout from the list of layouts. As you click on a layout, it gives you a preview of that style on the right.

Continued

Step Four:

Now you have the option to add a theme for your photo book pages (like different frames, edges, and album styles) from the list of themes. This is a totally optional choice—you don't have to choose a theme if you don't want to.

Step Five:

In the fourth section, you have a choice of two additional options: (1) If you selected photos in the Organizer before you started your creation, the checkbox for Auto-Fill with Selected Images from the Organizer will be turned on. Your only option is then to turn off that checkbox if you've changed your mind and want to add photos manually after the pages are complete. Otherwise, you'll just leave that checkbox checked. Or, (2) you can choose to include photo captions on your pages. By the way, if your photos already include captions (in other words, you added captions earlier when your photos were in the Organizer), and you turn on the Include Photo Captions checkbox, those captions will automatically appear as text with each photo.

SCOTT KELBY

Step Six:

Once you have made all your design decisions (page size, how many pages, your layout, and theme [if any]), just click OK, and your photo book pages will be created as one single document (you can move between pages by using the left and right arrow buttons at the bottom of the document window). If you chose photos in the Organizer before you started creating, each document will have a photo already in it. If not, the pages will have gray boxes, and you can either open photos and drag-and-drop them into those gray boxes (using the Move tool), or you can click on the boxes and then choose which photo you'd like to appear in each box by choosing them in the resulting Open dialog.

Step Seven:

Now, before you can send the book to Kodak, you have to save this newly created multi-page document, and give it a name. Easy enough. Go under the File menu and choose Save As. When the Save As dialog appears, simply type in a name, and save your file someplace where you'll be easily able to find it again (like your My Pictures folder, eh?). Now that you've saved your file, go to the task bar in either the Organizer or Editor (doesn't matter which) and click once on the icon that looks like the world with a tiny postcard in front of it (as shown here) and a list of online services will appear. Choose Order Kodak Photo Book from the pop-up menu.

Continued

Step Eight:

This brings up the Order Kodak Photo Book window. If your document(s) containing your photo book pages were open in the Elements 5 Editor, then you'll see all the individual pages displayed here. If not, you can add other saved multi-page documents by clicking on the Add Photos button in the top-left corner, right under the words "Step 1." By the way, when you saved your multi-page document, it automatically added it to your Organizer, so if you click the Add Photos button, the Add Photos dialog lets you choose that document from photos currently visible in the Organizer. Pretty handy.

Step Nine:

Once the photo pages are all open, then it's time to put them into the exact order you want them in. Luckily, this is simple—just click, hold, and drag the pages into the order you want them to appear in your hardcover book. When it looks about right, click the Next Step button and then you'll see the individual pages at a larger preview size. You can use the arrow buttons on the right and left sides of each photo page to move backward and forward through your pages. When you're done, click the Done button. This converts your book into an Adobe PDF document, ready for uploading to Kodak. Lastly, the Kodak/Adobe Photoshop Services window will appear asking you to create an online account (there's no charge for setting up an account), then it asks how many books you want, where you want them shipped, and how you'll be paying. Once complete, it uploads your book file, and within a few days your hardcover book will arrive. How cool is that!

Once you've created just about any layout (well, except the ones you have to create online, so let's rephrase that opening sentence to, "Once you've created a layout and it appears in the Elements Editor"), you can customize that layout with just one click using the Artwork and Effects palette. Now, if you're an Elements 3 or 4 user, you probably remember the Styles and Effects palette. Well, this is that on steroids, because new theme templates and an Artwork section have been added, making this a one-click bonanza with literally hundreds of different looks just one click away.

Customizing Your Layouts with Just One Click

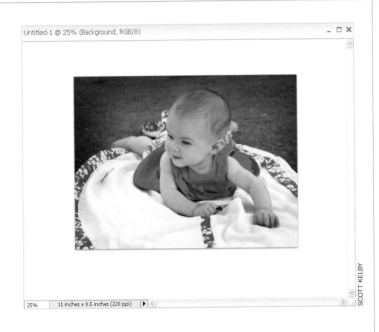

Step One:
Start by making one of the creations (like Photo Book Pages, or a CD or DVD Jacket, or a CD/DVD Label, or a Greeting Card, or a Photo Layout, or Album Pages). It doesn't matter whether you choose one of the optional Themes for your layout or not, because you'll be able to add one later (after all, this is what the tutorial is all about).

Step Two:
Once the layout is open in the Elements Editor, go to the Artwork and Effects palette (if for some reason this palette isn't visible, just go under the Window menu and choose Artwork and Effects and it will appear onscreen). At the top of the palette, click on the Themes button (the second icon from the left), to display the built-in themes (as shown here).

Continued

Step Three:

From the pop-up menu that appears directly below the word "Themes," choose which style of theme you'd like, and a listing of themes (displayed by thumbnail) will appear in the palette. In the example shown here, I chose Scrapbook from the pop-up menu, and the scrapbook themes are now displayed in the palette. If you scroll downward in the palette, you'll find some of the photographic themes (shown here), which I feel are some of the most usable, interesting themes.

Step Four:

You can replace your current theme (the theme includes both your background and frame, but not your photo, so don't worry), with any one of the themes shown in the palette by either: (a) dragging-and-dropping the theme onto your layout, (b) clicking on the theme in the palette and then clicking the Apply button at the bottom-right corner of the Artwork and Effects palette, or (c) double-clicking on the theme in the palette.

TIP: You can also add filters and layer styles the same way you add a new theme. Just click on the Special Effects button (the third icon from the left at the top of the palette), and choose Filters or Layer Styles from the pop-up menu.

Okay, let's say you have 12 really great shots. Now what do you do? That's right—it's calendar time—and using the built-in templates (and auto-dating), it's really so simple that you almost *have* to create your own calendars.

Creating Calendars

Step One:
Open the Organizer and Control-click on all the photos you want to appear in your calendar. (I probably don't have to say this, but open at least 13 so you have one for the cover and then one for every month.) Then, click once on the Create button in the task bar (above the Timeline) at the top of the Organizer and choose Photo Calendar from the pop-up menu (as shown here).

Step Two:
This brings up the Kodak/Adobe Photoshop Services window. If you don't already have an account, go ahead and create one (there's no charge for creating an account). Once you create your account (or log in if you already have an account), your photos are then automatically uploaded to Kodak. Don't worry—you haven't finalized anything yet, and you haven't spent a dime at this point, so you can always stop, change your mind, etc., at this point.

Continued

Step Three:

Once your photos are uploaded, press the Next button, and it launches your Web browser. A webpage will now appear where you can (1) choose the layout for your calendar from the list of calendar templates on the right side of the page, and (2) right above the list of templates you'll choose which month and year you want your calendar to start from. Once you've chosen your calendar template and starting month and year, click the Next button.

Step Four:

Once you click the Next button, a window will appear asking if you want to Autofill your calendar using the photos you uploaded earlier (in a random order), or do you want to do it manually, page by page. The choice is yours, but it's important to note that even if you choose Autofill, you still have the opportunity to change, reorder, and edit any photo used on any month of the calendar, so once again, at this point nothing is permanent or locked in yet. So, give Autofill a try (it will save you time, especially if you're not terribly picky about which photo goes in which month). Another window will appear asking you to confirm that you do indeed want to Autofill using the photos you uploaded earlier. When that page appears, once again, click the Next button.

Step Five:

The next window shows you a preview of the cover of your calendar, and you can view individual months by choosing them from the pop-up menu. You can also choose alternate layouts here. Perhaps most importantly, if you want to change a photo for a particular month, you can do that here as well. All your uploaded photos will appear in a filmstrip across the bottom of the window. To replace a particular month's photo (or the cover photo for that matter), you can just drag-and-drop the images from the film-strip right onto the calendar. Clicking on the photo brings up a toolbar that allows you to rotate, zoom, or move the image. Click in the boxes at the bottom of the calendar page to add text. Pretty easy stuff.

Step Six:

When everything looks like you want it to, click on the Order button. A window appears with pricing (including quantity pricing) and it gives you one more opportunity to see your final calendar, check for typos, etc., before your order is complete. Once you've double-checked everything, enter your desired quantity of calendars, then press the Add to Cart button, check-out, and wait for your calendar to arrive. All in all, it's a pretty darn painless way to have your own custom-made, pro-quality calendar without breaking a sweat, and at a price you can afford. Not too shabby.

Creating a CD or DVD Jacket, or a CD/DVD Label

I lumped these three together, because the process is pretty much identical for these three creations; the only thing that is really different is the size. Once again, you're going to follow the four-step process that you've done pretty much throughout this chapter, unless of course this is the first page you've read in this chapter, in which case...get ready for something completely new!

Step One:

Start by going to the Organizer and clicking on the photo you want to appear on your CD or DVD jacket, or your CD/DVD label. Then, click once on the Create button in the task bar at the top of the Organizer and choose which of these three designs you want to create from the pop-up menu. *Note:* You don't have to start by choosing a photo, you can have the Organizer create the layout first, then you can either drag-and-drop a photo onto your layout, or you can add your photo by clicking on the blank gray box that will appear on your jacket or label. It's totally up to you, but for this instance, go ahead and click on a photo in the Organizer before you make your choice from the Create menu.

Step Two:

When the creation's dialog appears, you're going to (1) choose the size you want for your CD or DVD jacket or CD/DVD label, then (2) choose how you want your photo(s) to appear on the page in the Select a Layout section. The first layouts are for one-photo jackets/labels, but if you want to have more than one photo on your jacket/label, you can choose one of the layouts that have up to three or four photos on it.

©ISTOCKPHOTO/ELIANET ORTIZ

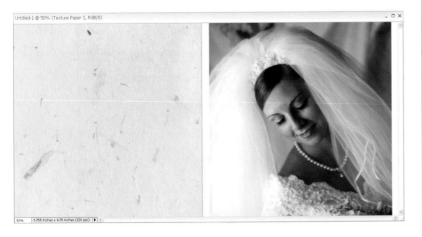

Step Three:

Now you have the option of adding a theme to your CD or DVD jacket or CD/DVD label from the list of built-in themes. These themes include different backgrounds that appear behind your photo and on the blank page on the facing side of the CD or DVD jacket, or around the circular face of the CD/DVD label, depending on which one you're building. Adding a theme is totally optional—you don't have to choose a theme if you don't want to, you can just ignore the Select a Theme section and move on to Step Four.

Step Four:

In the final section, you have a choice of two additional options: (1) if you selected photos in the Organizer before you started your creation, the checkbox for Auto-Fill with Selected Images from the Organizer will be turned on. Your only option is then to turn off that checkbox if you've changed your mind and want to add photos manually after the layouts are complete; otherwise, you'll just leave that checkbox turned on. And, (2) you can choose to include photo captions on your layout. By the way, if your photos already include captions (in other words, you added captions earlier when your photos were in the Organizer), and you turn on the Include Photo Captions checkbox, those captions will automatically appear as text with each photo. When you click OK, Elements 5 creates your document for you. Easy enough.

Creating a Video CD

If you've created some slide shows (using the Slide Show feature mentioned earlier in this chapter), you can take those slides shows and transfer them to a video CD, which will play on many DVD players (so you can play them directly on your TV), and you do the whole thing right from within Elements 5. Here's how it works:

Step One:
First, you need to create your slide shows, so go ahead and do that, because essentially what you'll create is a CD of slide shows with a default menu that's created by Elements. So if you don't have slide shows first, you can't create a CD, so start there (see the slide show tutorial earlier in this chapter). Once you have your slide show created, if you can see it in the Organizer, click on it first, then click once on the Create button (if you can't see it in the Organizer, don't sweat it for now, just continue on). When the menu appears, choose VCD with Menu (as shown here).

Step Two:
When the Create a VCD with Menu dialog appears, if you see your slide show there (meaning you found it in the Organizer and clicked on it before choosing Create's VCD with Menu), then you're set. If not, then you'll need to click on the Add Slide Shows button in the upper-left corner of the dialog. This brings up the Add Slide Shows dialog, and you can turn on the checkbox next to the slide show(s) you want to add.

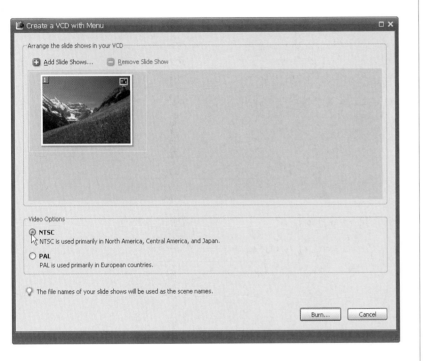

Step Three:
At the bottom of the Create a VCD with Menu dialog, there are two choices for your video format: NTSC (which is the video format used in North America, Central America, and Japan), or PAL (which is used in Europe). Since you're reading the English language version of this book, chances are you're going to leave these settings "as is" (set to NTSC), but it is nice to know that if you want to send a video disc to a friend who lives in Bath, England, you surely can. Hey, ya never know.

Step Four:
The final step is to press the Burn button at the bottom right-hand corner of the dialog (as shown here) and it burns your slide show to disc. That's it Bunky, you're done.

Creating Your Own Photo Website

If you want to expand the reach of your photos to a wider audience, there's no better way than to create a photo gallery online, and once again Elements 5 does all the hard work for you. All you have to do is basically choose which photos you want, which layout you want, and it does the rest. (I covered the HTML Photo Gallery in detail earlier in the book, but I wanted to cover it briefly here as well, since it's one of the Create functions, and you'll probably come looking for it in this chapter, too.) Here's how to go global with your photos:

Step One:

Open the Organizer and Control-click on the photos you want to appear on your Web gallery. Then, click once on the Create button in the task bar at the top of the Organizer, and when the menu pops up, choose Photo Galleries (as shown here).

Step Two:

This brings up the Photo Galleries Wizard (shown here). The photos you selected in the Organizer appear along the left side of the dialog, and in the center of the dialog is where you'll choose your gallery template and individual style. Let's look at your template choices first.

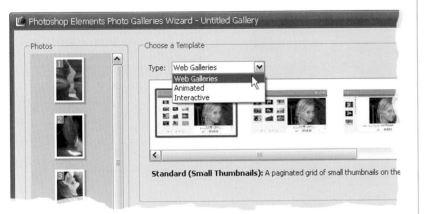

Step Three:
In the Choose a Template section, you pick which Type of Web gallery you want from the pop-up menu. These include a standard HTML Web gallery, an Animated Web gallery (which includes pre-designed animations behind your photos), or an Interactive Web gallery, where people viewing your photos actually get involved in the process, and move and reorder your photos (it's much cooler than it sounds). The last two are Flash-based templates and they are very nicely designed. Kudos to Adobe on adding such cool templates. Anyway, we'll start with the standard Web Galleries, so choose that from the pop-up menu.

Step Four:
When you choose Web Galleries from the pop-up menu, you'll first choose a template (from the top horizontal row). Each one has a different layout, and each gives you a small thumbnail preview, and a written description of the template below it. Click on the one that looks good to you, then choose the color combination (style) from the Style list in the lower horizontal row of thumbnails. Now, normally, you'd click the Next Step button at this point, but I'd like you to take a quick look at the Flash-based templates (Animated and Interactive) because they're just so darn cool. So, choose Animated from the template Type pop-up menu up top.

Continued

Step Five:

The first of the animations (the baby theme) is great if you've just had a baby. Otherwise…well, you get the idea. When you choose one, a large preview of your soon-to-be webpage appears in the bottom half of the dialog, so you can see what you're really getting. Click on the fourth choice, which is kinda cool for travel photos. Notice I said, "kinda," because compared to the interactive galleries, they're only kinda cool. The other two animations are well…barely cool. Hey, I calls 'em like I sees 'em.

Step Six:

Finally, the good stuff. Choose Interactive from the template Type pop-up menu. Now these are really cool. Very clever stuff here, and it makes things fun for your visitors. I like the first one (the dark photo slide mounts) the best, personally, but there's not one here I don't like. By the way, even the large preview you see is interactive, so you can grab those slides and drag them around. Try it (and some other interactive ones), I'll wait (I don't mind waiting while you have fun. I'll just wait over here). Okay, you done playing around? See, it's pretty cool, eh? So, just for example's sake, let's go with the first one (the black slide mounts), so click on it, then press the Next Step button on the bottom right of the dialog.

SCOTT KELBY

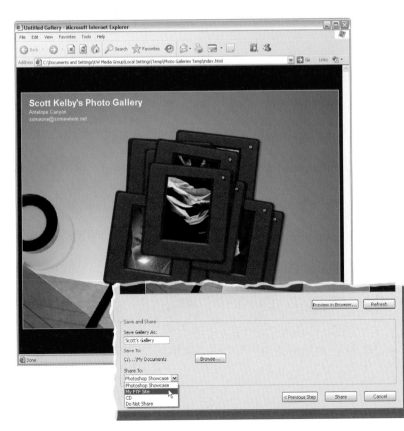

Step Seven:

This next screen is where you replace the dummy text with real text of your own. You start on the left side by giving your site a title. This will appear in the title bar of your webpage, and in large letters on your interactive webpage itself. You can add a smaller line of text below it, by entering in some text in the Subtitle field. Below that, enter the email address you'd like people to contact you at (if you want an email address included), and below that is a checkbox to have sound effects included on your webpage that happen when your visitors move your slide mounts, or zoom in on your photos. The sounds are kinda cute at first, but get old fast, so you might want to try it once with the sounds, and see if they don't get on your nerves in short order.

Step Eight:

Once you've entered your text, you can see a live preview of your gallery, with your selected photos and sound effects, in your Web browser just like the public will see it. Click the Preview in Browser button and it will launch your computer's default Web browser and show you your finished page. If you need to make changes, return to Elements 5, make your changes, then click the Refresh button. When the page looks the way you want it to, it's time to save it. In the Save and Share section at the bottom of the dialog, give your gallery a name, then choose where you want your gallery saved to on your hard disk, or choose to share your new webpage directly to the Web (via an FTP site) or to the online Photoshop Showcase (a free online place to share your images, courtesy of Adobe). You also can burn it to CD, or choose not to share it, and just save it. Lastly, click the Share button, and you're done.

Ordering Prints with Just One Click

This is more than just ordering prints with one click; this is setting up your friends and family so you can send them prints directly from Kodak's lab, straight to their house, and you do the whole thing from your computer. You can send yourself prints too, but you already figured that, right?

Step One:

Okay, first let's set up some friends and family members that you'll want to be able to send prints to (direct from Kodak's online service, which is built into Elements 5). You see that Order Prints palette (nested in the Organize Bin) in the bottom-right corner of the Organizer window? That's where it all happens. Start by clicking on the New button.

Step Two:

This brings up the New Order Prints Recipient dialog, which is basically where you're going to enter the contact info for the first family member or friend to whom you want to be able to send "one-click" prints. So, enter a name, mailing address, etc. (so Kodak will know where to ship the prints), then click OK, and that person will be added to your Order Prints palette. Keep clicking the New button and adding contacts until all the people you want to get prints (including yourself) are listed.

Step Three:
Once you've added some friends and family (and yourself as well), each of you will appear listed in the Order Prints palette. Now the hard part's over, and the fun can officially begin.

Step Four:
The next time you're looking at a photo and you think, "Ol' Jeff would like a print of this," just click on the photo, and drag-and-drop it right onto Jeff's name in the Order Prints palette. A Confirm Order button will appear next to his name, and once you've dragged over as many photos as you want to send to Jeff, click the Confirm Order button.

Step Five:
If this is the first time you've ordered prints from within Elements 5 (and I'm assuming it is, or you wouldn't be reading this tutorial, right?), then you'll have to create an account with Adobe Photoshop Services, which is partnering with Kodak to provide your prints. To set up your account (registration is free), when you click the Confirm Order button, the Adobe Photoshop Services window will appear where you can register for your online printing account. Once you've filled out the form on this screen, click the Next button, which takes you to the Review Order screen.

Continued

Step Six:

If you want to change your order, click the Change Quantities or Sizes button in the Order Details section at the top left of the Review Order screen. Here, you'll choose what style and size prints you want to send. In the example shown here, I'm going to send Jeff one 4x6" single print, which runs me 15 cents (not bad, eh?). If I want more copies or different sizes, I can choose them here as well (as long as my photo has enough resolution to create prints larger than 4x6", of course). Once you've made your choices, just click the Save Changes button, and it will ask you to review your order, add any coupons, and choose your delivery time. Once you proceed to checkout, it will ask you for some nasty things, like payment information and awful stuff like that.

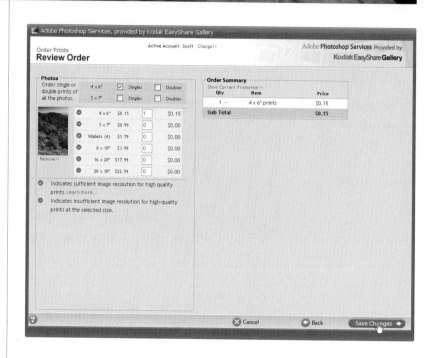

Step Seven:

After you place your order, you'll reach the Order Prints Confirmation screen, and your prints will be processed and sent directly to your friend's address. Although this takes a few steps the first time you register for this service, from now on you just drag-and-drop photos onto your friend's or family member's name in the Order Prints palette, and you can bypass almost all of this (of course, you'll still want to choose how many prints and what size), but besides that, it's almost a one-click process and prints are on the way. Try this service once, and you'll find it so easy and convenient, you'll use it again and again until you eventually file for bankruptcy.

Creating Real, Usable Postage Stamps

The reason I say "usable" is because what you're creating are real, honest-to-goodness, approved-by-the-U.S. Postal Service stamps you can use for mailing anything: from postcards you create in Elements 5 to your electric bill. I know, it's hard to imagine that you can just create real USPS-approved stamps, but maybe that's why this is so cool. Imagine using stamps with your child's photo, or your company's logo. Try this once, and it will make it hard to use the standard ones the post office sells ever again.

Step One:
Open the Organizer and click on all the photos you want to appear on your PhotoStamps®. Then click once on the Create button at the top of the Organizer, and from the pop-up menu choose PhotoStamps®. When you choose Photo-Stamps, the PhotoStamps window opens. Click on the Upload My Photos button and it automatically uploads your selected photo(s) to PhotoStamps.

Step Two:
Once your photo(s) is uploaded, it then takes you to the PhotoStamps Image Gallery, where you click on the image you want to use to make your first stamp. This takes you to the Image Details page, where you click on PhotoStamps on the right as the product you want to create. On the Customize Your PhotoStamps page, you can reposition your photo within the stamp layout, and choose to zoom in or out, rotate, or flip your photo, and even choose the color that will surround your photo, so you can choose a border that matches your image. You also choose what type of postage you want your PhotoStamps to be (postcard, regular envelope, etc.). Once your layout decisions are made, then you can choose how many stamps you want made, where to ship them, and how you're going to pay for them. When all that's done, you're done, and your stamps will be delivered directly to you.

Creating Your Own Custom Flipbook

Remember those little paper flipbook animations you used to make back when you were in school? You don't? Rats. Well, that would have made this explanation a lot easier, but in either case, a flipbook is a series of images that are displayed one right after another, like a stop-motion video (really, it's more like a really fast slide show with no transitions). If you have a camera that can shoot in burst mode (several shots in a row), then you could use this to simulate the effect of video, by rapidly animating that group of similar photos. Here's how:

Step One:
Start by going to the Organizer, then press-and-hold the Control key, and click on all the photos you want to include in your flipbook. Ideally, you'd click on photos taken at, or near, the same time (like a series of shots taken in rapid succession using your camera's burst mode), so when you create your flipbook it seems like stop-motion animation (in fact, you can use this feature to create a mini-stop-motion movie of something like a doll, or an action figure, doing a dance or one of a hundred clever things you might do when you have absolutely, positively nothing better to do with your time). Once you've selected your photos, click on the Create button at the top of the Organizer and choose Flipbook from the pop-up menu.

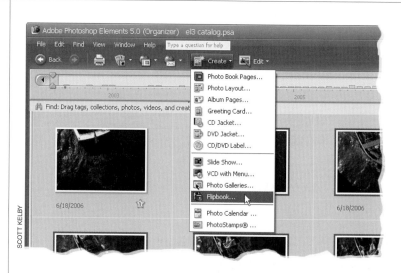

Step Two:
When the Flipbook dialog opens, you only have a few choices to make (things like "Why did I do this?" and perhaps, "Don't I have anything better to do with my time?" etc.). Actually, your main choice will be how fast your animation will appear, in frames per second. It will do up to 30 frames per second, which is as fast as regular video, but that also means that if you choose 30 photos in the Organizer, your flipbook will last only one second. So, you might try something a little slower (unless

you've got either a boatload of photos selected so your flipbook will last a few seconds, or you just have a very short attention span).

Step Three:
Once you've selected your Playback Speed, you can see a preview of your flipbook by clicking the Play button under the preview window. To stop the preview, click the Pause button. There's a checkbox to have your preview loop over and over again (it's on by default), and in the Playback section there's a checkbox to show your flipbook in reverse (as if creating a flipbook in the first place wasn't pleasure enough).

Step Four:
Once your flipbook is flipping you out (sorry, that was lame), you have but to choose which final size you'd like your flipbook movie saved to, by choosing it from the pop-up menu in the Output Settings section, and finally click the Output button at the bottom-right corner of the dialog to save your file to your computer. That's it. You've created your first (and hopefully only) flipbook. Now you can sit back, relax, and enjoy literally seconds of fascinating video-like entertainment. Can you tell this is getting near the end of the book? Can you tell it's late at night when I'm writing this? Can you tell I'm not a huge fan of the Flipbook feature? Okay, just wanted to make sure you're still with me.

Anger Management
color management and printing
step-by-step

Okay, there are entire books written on the subject of color management in Photoshop Elements, so how am I going to condense everything you need to know into one chapter? It's easy—I'm not. You see, color management is like quicksand—the more you try to understand it, the deeper it sucks you down into the muck. What we need (you, me, us, we, you again, then me) is less about color management. That's right. This chapter puts a new spin on color management by actually giving you "less." Less about all the different color spaces (in fact, I don't even mention them), less about color gamuts (same here), less about soft proofing (I don't cover that at all), less about profiles, less about warnings, less about theory (there is none), less graphs and charts (there are none), and less about all the stuff

you really don't care about. In fact, not only do we need a chapter that has less pages, we need one with less words, less ink, less spell checking, less editing, less royalties (less royalties?), less paper fiber, and less binding—and doggone it, I'm just the guy to do it. (For the record, I've never used the phrase "doggone it" in print before. This is the kind of groundbreaking stuff I'm talking about.) Anyway, here's my plan: If it's not a part of Element's color management (that you're not directly going to change, adjust, or otherwise mess with in some meaningful fashion), I'm just gonna ignore it. That way, we can focus on just one thing: setting Elements up so the prints that come out of your personal, color inkjet printer match exactly what you see onscreen. One thing. That's it. See, less is more. More or less. I think.

Configuring Your Camera for the Right Color Space

Although there are entire books written on the subject of color management, in this chapter we're going to focus on just one thing—getting what comes out of your color inkjet printer to match what you see onscreen. That's what it's all about, and if you follow the steps in this chapter, you'll get prints that pretty closely match your screen.

Setting your camera to the right color space:

One of the key themes of proper color management is consistency. If you want to get consistent color from your camera to Photoshop Elements to your printer, you'll want everybody speaking the same language, right? That's why I'm recommending, right from the start, that if your camera is set to shoot either JPEG or RAW+JPEG, you may be able to change your camera's color space from the default sRGB, which is an ideal space for images designed to be viewed on the Web, to Adobe RGB (1998), which is an ideal space for photographers whose final prints will come from a color inkjet printer. Now, if you only shoot in RAW, you can skip this because you'll assign the color space in the Photoshop Elements Camera Raw dialog, but if you shoot in JPEG, you'll need to do it now. As an example of what I mean, here's how to set up a Nikon D70 to tag your photos with the Adobe RGB (1998) color profile.

Nikon D70

Step One: On the back of the camera, on the left side, press the Menu button to bring up the user menu in the LCD window.

Step Two: Scroll down to the Shooting Menu and press the right arrow button on the back of the camera.

Step Three: When the Shooting Menu options appear, choose Optimize Image and press the right arrow button again.

Step Four: In the Optimize Image menu, scroll down to Custom and press the right arrow button yet again.

Setting up other cameras:
I'm showing the setup here for a Nikon D70. If you have a different digital camera, it's time to dig up your manual to find out how to "make the switch" to Adobe RGB (1998). If you cannot find your manual, try visiting the website for your camera's manufacturer. In the Support or Downloads area of the manufacturer's website, you should be able to choose your camera and download the User's or Instruction Manual. Once you have your manual, look under Image Settings or Image Adjustment for Color Space or Color Mode to learn how to switch to Adobe RGB (1998).

Step Five: When the Custom menu appears, scroll down to Color Mode and press the right arrow button again. (*Note:* The Ia symbol before the words "Color mode" tells you the current setting is sRGB.)

Step Six: When the Color Mode menu appears, scroll down to II (AdobeRGB), and then press the right arrow button again to choose OK.

Step Seven: When you press the right arrow button, it returns to the Custom screen, but now there's a "II" before Color Mode, indicating you're now using Adobe RGB (1998).

Configuring Photoshop Elements for Adobe RGB (1998)

Once you've got your camera set to the right color space (Adobe RGB [1998]), it's time to set up Photoshop Elements that way too, so the color space in your camera and the color space in Elements are consistent (don't worry, it's easier than setting up the camera, so if you got that down, this is a no-brainer).

Step One:

Before we do this, I just want to reiterate that you only want to make this change if your final print will be output to your own color inkjet printer. If you're sending your images out to an outside lab for prints, you should probably stay in sRGB—both in the camera and in Elements—because most labs are set up to handle sRGB files. Your best bet: ask your lab which color space they prefer. Okay, now on to Photoshop Elements. In the Editor, go under the Edit menu and choose Color Settings (or just press Control-Shift-K).

Step Two:

This brings up the Color Settings dialog. By default, Elements 5 is set to Always Optimize Colors for Computer Screens, which uses the sRGB color space. However, you want the Adobe RGB color space, so choose Always Optimize for Printing. Now just click OK, and you've done it—you've configured Elements' color space for the best results for printing, and it matches the color space for your camera, so now everything's consistent (well, at least at this point). But there's one more thing.

SCOTT KELBY

Step Three:

So, photos that you've taken since you switched your camera to Adobe RGB (1998) will now match your color space in Elements. But what happens when you open photos you took before you switched your camera, which are still in the sRGB color space? You have to throw these photos away immediately so they don't infect your computer. Okay, you knew I was kidding, right? Good. Here's what you really do: you convert them to the Adobe RGB (1998) color space (which is really simple—it's just a simple menu command), but how do you know which photos are still in sRGB? Just look in the title bar of your photo. After the photo's name, and viewing percentage, in parenthesis you'll see RGB/8*. That asterisk after the /8 is your cue that the photo is still in sRGB.

Step Four:

When you come across one of these sRGB asterisk-bearing photos, all you have to do in the Editor is go under the Image menu, under Convert Color Profile, and choose Apply Adobe RGB Profile (as shown here). That's it. The little asterisk goes away and your photo is now in the same color space as Elements. Okay, so what if a friend emails you a photo, you open it in Elements 5, and the photo doesn't have any color profile at all (the way to tell if it doesn't have any profile is that after the RGB/8 you'll see a # symbol)? You can convert that "untagged" photo to Adobe RGB (1998) by again going under the Image menu, under Convert Color Profile, and choosing Apply Adobe RGB Profile. Now you're set—your new photos from your camera will come in Adobe RGB (1998) and you know how to convert older (or emailed) photos to Adobe RGB (1998), as well. It's a consistency love fest.

Calibrating Your Monitor Using Adobe Gamma

If you have any hope of getting what comes out of your color inkjet printer to match what you see onscreen, you have to calibrate your monitor. It's the cornerstone of color management, and basically there are two ways to do this: (1) buy a hardware calibration sensor that calibrates your monitor precisely, or (2) use the free, built-in system software calibration, which is better than nothing, but not by much because you're literally just "eyeing" it. We'll start here with the built-in freebie calibration, but if you're really serious about this stuff, turn to the next tutorial and learn the hardware method.

Freebie Calibration:

First, we'll look at the worst-case scenario: you're broke (you spent all available funds on the upgrade to Elements 5 and Fergie's new CD), so you'll have to get a separate free utility from Adobe called Adobe Gamma that's used to calibrate monitors on Windows PCs. To get to Adobe Gamma on your Windows PC (if you're using Windows XP), go under the Start menu from the Taskbar, and then go to the Control Panel. Double-click on Adobe Gamma.

Step One:

This brings up the Adobe Gamma dialog. Choose Step By Step (Wizard), which will lead you through the steps for creating a pretty lame calibration profile. (Hey, I can't help it—that's what it does. Do you really want me to sugarcoat it? Okay, how's this? "It will lead you through the steps for proper calibration" [cringe].) *Note:* Results will vary depending on whether your monitor is a CRT, LCD, etc.

Step Two:
Click the Next button and you'll be asked to name the profile you're about to create. So, enter a name in the Description field. Now, it's possible that when you first hooked up your monitor a manufacturer's profile was installed at the same time. Although that canned factory profile won't do the trick, it can save you some time because it will automatically answer some of the questions in the dialog, so it's worth a look to see if you have one. Click on the Load button, and then navigate your way to the ICC profiles in your system (you should be directed to them by default). If you see a profile with your monitor's name, click on it and then click OK to load that profile.

Step Three:
From here on out, you'll be prompted with various directions (some with little square graphics with sliders beneath them). It asks you to move the sliders and then judge how the colors look. This is the very essence of the term "eyeing it," and it's why pros avoid this method. Everyone sees color and tone differently, and we're all viewing these "test squares" under different lighting conditions, etc., so it's highly subjective. But hey—it's free.

Step Four:
The questions will continue (along the lines of the Spanish Inquisition) until it completes the calibration process, and then it offers you a before and after. You can pretty much ignore the Carmen Miranda before/after photo—that's just for looks—your before and after will be nothing like that, but after you're prompted to save your profile, you're done.

Calibrating Your Monitor the Right Way

Hardware calibration is definitely the preferred method of monitor calibration. With hardware calibration, you're measuring your particular monitor and building a real profile for the real world, and it makes a huge difference. I use ColorVision's Spyder2PRO hardware calibration, which is popular with many pros because it's easy to use, works well, but it's not cheap (it lists for around $279), but if you don't want to spend that much, look at the Spyder2express, which lists for only $79, and is quick and easy to use. Another pro-quality hardware calibrator I would recommend is GretagMacbeth's Eye-One Display 2.

Step One:

After you install the Spyder2PRO software, plug the Spyder2PRO colorimeter sensor into your computer's USB port, and then launch the Spyder2PRO software. Like the freebie calibration software, it will ask you a series of boring questions (like do you have a tube CRT monitor or a flat-panel LCD monitor) similar to what the freebie software asks. What separates the two is the hardware—the Spyder2PRO colorimeter actually reads your monitor to create a custom profile for your real monitor (not a hypothetical monitor).

Step Two:

Once you've answered all their questions (including a series of probing personal questions about your arrest record, previous marriages, etc.), it then instructs you to position the Spyder2PRO sensor directly over the actual-size image of the Spyder2PRO that appears onscreen. Drape the sensor over the top of your monitor so it sits flat against your screen (there's a counterweight attached to the cable so you can set it to any length you want).

Step Three:
Once the colorimeter sensor is aligned with the one onscreen, click Continue, and it will conduct a series of tests, starting with reading your monitor's black point. It will continue by reading samples of red, green, and blue. The window onscreen (directly under the sensor) will start measuring each color while appearing nearly black, but then slowly each color will get brighter and more saturated until each reaches its full intensity. Once it reads the gray point, the process is done.

Step Four:
When all the measurements are done, you'll be asked to remove the hardware sensor and give your new profile a name (it suggests a name, but the name it suggests is too close to my existing canned profiles, so I usually rename it so it will be easier to find). Now click the Next button in the bottom right-hand corner of the screen.

Step Five:
The final screen is important in that you get to see how your monitor looked before calibration and how it looks now after being hardware calibrated. Click the Switch button at the bottom of the window to toggle between the before and after views. Chances are you'll gasp when you see how "off" your monitor was before calibration. You don't have to do anything else at this point—it will automatically tell Elements about your new monitor profile.

Downloading a Custom Profile for Your Printer

When you buy a color inkjet printer and install the printer driver that comes with it, you get what's known as a "standard" profile. It basically lets Photoshop Elements know what kind of printer is being used, and that's about it. But to get the best results, you need a profile that includes both the printer info and the exact paper you'll be printing on. Most inkjet paper manufacturers now create custom profiles for their papers, and you can download them free from their websites.

Step One:

Before you do any printing, you'll want to first go to the website of the company that makes the paper you're printing to and download their free custom profiles and install them on your computer. I use an Epson Stylus Photo R2400 color inkjet printer (which is one of the most popular 13x19" color inkjets for pros), and I usually use Epson papers with it. But, since I don't know which printer you have, we'll have to go with mine for our example. Go to Epson.com and select your country. Then from the Drivers & Support link at the top of the page, choose Printers. *Note:* Websites change their look and navigation fairly often, so if you go to Epson's site and it doesn't look just like this, don't be surprised.

Step Two:

When you get to the Drivers & Support page, choose Ink Jet from the Printers product category section. Then from the product list on the right, scroll down to find your particular printer (in my case, it's an Epson Stylus Photo R2400). Once you find yours in the list, click on it, and you'll arrive at the page for your printer. In the Drivers & Downloads section at the top of the page, click on Windows. Now scroll down to the ICC profiles for the type of paper you'll be using.

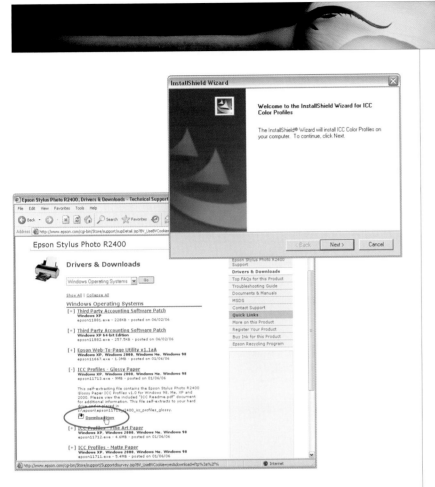

Step Three:
When you click on that link, you've finally reached the Holy Grail—the pot of gold at the end of the rainbow—and all you have to do now is click the "Download Now" link and your ICC profile will be downloaded to your computer. Now, is it really worth this treasure hunt? Well, here's what Epson says: "In most cases, these custom ICC profiles will provide more accurate color and black-and-white print quality than with the standard profiles already shipping with every printer." So, in short, if you want more accurate color and black-and-white prints, download these profiles. Download one for every paper you're using. (I've been using the Velvet Fine Art and Premium Luster, so I downloaded both the Glossy and Fine Art ICC profiles). When you download a profile from Epson's website, it comes with a built-in installer, so save the profile to your Desktop and then just double-click on it to unzip and install it automatically.

Step Four:
Once installed, quit Elements. Now go ahead and re-launch Elements knowing that your custom ICC profiles are installed, and you're ready to print (we'll get to the printing part on the next page). Now, here's the good news: you only have to do all this stuff (downloading and installing drivers, setting up your camera, setting up Elements 5, etc.) once. Once it's set up, you won't have to go through this every time. So if it feels like this is a lot of trouble to go through, just know you won't actually have to go through all this every time. Just once.

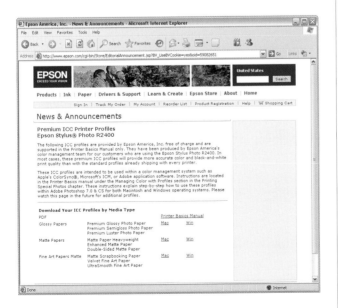

Printing (This Is Where It All Comes Together)

Okay, you've set your camera to Adobe RGB (1998); you've calibrated your monitor; you've set up Elements to use Adobe RGB (1998); and if you import any photos that are not in Adobe RGB (1998), you know how to convert them. You've even downloaded a printer profile for the exact printer model and style of paper you're printing on. In short—you're there. You're just a few clicks away from grabbing the brass ring, baby! Let's do it!

Step One:
Go under the Elements File menu and choose Print (as shown here).

Step Two:
In the resulting Print Preview dialog, click on the Page Setup button at the bottom. In the Page Setup dialog, choose your Paper Size (in this case, I chose Super B (13x19 in) and the Paper Source (where you're feeding the paper into your printer [from the manual feed in front, from a roll of paper, a single borderless sheet, etc.]). You can also choose your page Orientation here (either Portrait or Landscape), and click OK to return to the Print Preview dialog.

Step Three:

At the bottom left of the Print Preview dialog, turn on the Show More Options checkbox to reveal additional options, including the Color Management options. First, take a look at what's listed next to Source Space at the bottom center of the dialog. It should be Adobe RGB (1998) (meaning your photo is in the Adobe RGB [1998] color space). If it says sRGB IE61966-2.1 or Untagged RGB, that means this photo isn't in the right color space, and you'll need to convert it to the right space (Adobe RGB [1998]). To do that, press the Cancel button to close the Print Preview dialog, then go under the Image menu, under Convert Color Profile, and choose Apply Adobe RGB Profile. That's all you have to do—problem solved. Back to printing, so, go back under the File menu and choose Print.

Step Four:

Now we get to put that ICC color profile we downloaded earlier to use. Right under the Source Space, from the Printer Profile pop-up menu, choose the profile for the printer and paper you're printing to (in this case, we're printing to an Epson R2400 on Premium Luster paper, as shown here). Then, right below that, we have to choose our Rendering Intent. From the Rendering Intent pop-up menu, I recommend choosing Perceptual because it seems to give the most consistent results for printing photographic images to color inkjet printers.

Continued

Step Five:

Now you can click on the Print button, and when you do, another Print dialog will appear—your print driver's dialog. Your printer's name should appear in the name field at the top, but if for some reason it doesn't, choose it from the Printer Name pop-up menu (as shown here).

Step Six:

Now click on the Properties button (to the right of the Name pop-up menu), because we need to make a few changes in here to ensure the best-quality printing. In the Main tab, in the Quality Option section, choose Best Photo. Now, in the bottom-right corner of the dialog, click on the Advanced button (as shown here) to bring up the Advanced Settings dialog. (*Note:* You may receive a dialog letting you know that the Advanced settings are recommended for experienced users only. Just click Continue.)

Step Seven:

At the top right of the dialog, in the Color Management section, by default the Color Management option is set to Color Controls. This is bad. This is the printer's built-in color management, and you'll need to turn this off by clicking on the ICM radio button in that same section. The reason is, for this all to work, you can't use two different color management systems (one in the printer, and also the one in Elements using installed ICC profiles). They kind of cancel each other out. So, you'll need to turn off the printer's color management (by choosing ICM), so that way you only use the ICC color profiles in Elements to manage your color, and not the printer's built-in color management. Also, on the left side of the dialog, about three-quarters of the way down, in the Print Options section, turn off the checkbox for High Speed. That's really all you have to do in this Advanced dialog—those two things—and now you click OK.

Step Eight:

When you click OK, it takes you back to the regular Print dialog, and now you can just click OK there, too. That's it—you hit the OK button and as long as your printer is properly connected to your computer (and you have paper loaded into your printer), your prints (which should be spitting out of your printer shortly) will now pretty darn closely match your monitor, because you've color managed this photo from beginning to end.

My Suggested Elements 5 Workflow

One of the questions I get asked the most is: "What order are you supposed to do all this in?" Actually, when I hear that question, it's usually more like this: "What is your suggested digital workflow?" (Which actually means, "What order are you supposed to do all this in?") That's all "digital workflow" means. I wrote this book in kind of a digital workflow order, starting with importing your photos, correcting them, sharpening them, and then at the end creating presentations, and showing your work to friends and/or clients. But I thought that seeing it all laid out in one place (well, in these two pages), might really be helpful, so here ya go.

Step One:

You start your workflow by importing your photos into the Organizer, and I recommend adding your metadata (your name and copyright info) during this import process (you do this right in the Adobe Photo Downloader). Also, while you're in the Photo Downloader, go ahead and rename your photos now, so if you ever have to search for them, you have a hope of finding them (searching for photos from your trip to Hawaii is pretty tough if you leave the files named the way your camera named them, which is something along the lines of "DSC_1751.JPG"). So give them a descriptive name while you import them. You'll thank me later.

Step Two:

Once your photos are in the Organizer, then it's time to Tag them. If you take a few minutes to tag them now, it will save you literally hours down the road. Also, go ahead and sort your photos, deleting any that are hopelessly out of focus or beyond repair in Photoshop Elements, because there's no sense in having photos that should be in the trash taking up space on your hard disk.

SCOTT KELBY

Step Three:

Now it's time to start editing your best photos. What do you do first? Generally I try to deal with the biggest problem first (whatever you see as the biggest problem). If you feel like the photo is too dark, start with that. If it has a huge color cast, and you won't be able to concentrate on anything else, do that first. If you look in the "Digital Camera Image Problems" chapter (Chapter 5), that's usually the stuff I deal with first. Underexposure, overexposure, red eye, your subject is in the shadows, bad color problems, etc. Get that out of the way. Then work on things like general color correction using Adjust Levels, Adjust Color Curves, or even Quick Fix. After all your color correction is done, now you can add any special effects—if you want to add vignetting effects, or color tints, or basically any of the things in "Photographic Special Effects" (Chapter 9).

Step Four:

After all the effects you want have been added (*Tip:* Don't get carried away by using too many effects. When it comes to effects, less is more), then it's time to sharpen the photo using either the Unsharp Mask filter or the Adjust Sharpness control. We pretty much save this until the final editing stage (after fixing problems, after color correction, after special effects). Now, the photo is essentially done and you can add border effects, frame edges, and other presentation effects around or behind your photo (you normally don't have to sharpen them—just the photo, so you can add these after sharpening the photo). Lastly, now that you have a complete and final image, you can turn your final image into a Creation (Photo Book Pages, Calendars, Greeting Cards, a CD or DVD Jacket, Slide Show, etc.). There you have it, your Photoshop Elements 5 digital workflow. Hope that helps. :-)

Index

C

calendars, 439–441
calibrating monitors, 462–465
  Adobe Gamma utility for,
    462–463
  hardware used for, 464–465
Camera Raw, 55–73
  16-bit images, 71
  Auto corrections, 60, 63
  black-and-white conversions in,
    72–73
  bracketed images, 66–69
  Brightness slider, 62
  Color Noise Reduction slider, 64
  Contrast slider, 62, 73
  digital noise reduction, 64
  editing RAW images in, 56–63
  Exposure slider, 59, 60
  Luminance Smoothing slider, 64
  Saturation slider, 63, 72
  saving RAW files in, 70
  Shadows slider, 61, 73
  Sharpness slider, 65
  Temperature slider, 58
  Tint slider, 58
  tools used in, 57
  White Balance settings, 58–59
  See also RAW images
cameras
  color space configuration, 458–459
  image color correction, 122–129
  lens distortion problems,
    186–190
canvas area, 92–93
Canvas Extension Color pop-up
  menu, 388, 393
Canvas Options pop-up menu, 97
Canvas Size dialog, 320, 388,
  389, 393

captions
  entering for thumbnails, 18
  finding photos using, 38
  including in photo books, 434
CDs
  backing up photos to, 6–7
  contact sheets created for, 8–13
  jackets/labels created for,
    442–443
  slide shows transferred to,
    444–445
Channel pop-up menu, 147–148
circular selections, 197–198
classic vignette effect, 315–317
Clone Stamp tool
  photo restoration and, 342, 350,
    351, 352–354
  portrait retouching and, 222–223,
    229–230, 249–251, 253
  unwanted object removal and,
    268–272, 273–274, 282
clutter, reducing, 48–49
collaging techniques
  photo montages, 312–314
  photos inside photos, 308–309
  soft-edged vignette, 317
collections, 32–34
  creating, 32
  deleting, 34
  icons for, 33
color
  changing in objects, 298–300
  converting to black-and-white,
    72–73, 145–149, 330–331
  emphasizing objects with,
    294–295
  noise reduction methods, 64,
    160–161
  selecting areas by, 204–205
  slide, 426

color correction, 113–154
  Color Curves for, 150–154
  converting images to B&W,
    145–149
  cooling down photos, 140–141
  digital camera images and,
    122–129
  drag-and-drop technique for,
    134–136
  finding neutral midtones for,
    130–131
  flesh tone adjustments, 137–139
  Histogram palette and, 121, 128
  Levels dialog and, 122–125,
    127–128, 131, 133, 135
  multiple photos and, 134–136
  problem areas and, 142–144
  Quick Fix mode for, 116–120
  selection adjustments and, 195,
    198, 201, 205, 216
  settings for, 114–115
  studio portraits and, 132–133
  warming up photos, 140–141
Color Curves, 150–154
  Advanced Options, 151–153
  Reset button, 152
Color Dodge mode, 325
color management, 457, 458–465
  camera configuration, 458–459
  monitor calibration, 462–465
  Photoshop Elements
    configuration, 460–461
  printer configuration, 471
Color Management options, 407
color noise, 64, 160–161
Color Noise Reduction slider, 64
Color palette, 118
Color Picker, 123–124, 182,
  321, 426
Color Replacement tool, 298–300

Colophon

The book was produced by the author and design team using all Macintosh computers, including a Power Mac G4 733-MHz, a Power Mac G4 Dual Processor 1.25-GHz, a Power Mac G5 1.8-GHz, and a Power Mac G5 Dual Processor 2-GHz. We use Dell monitors.

Page layout was done using InDesign CS2. The headers for each technique are set in 20 point CronosMM700 Bold with the Horizontal Scaling set to 95%. Body copy is set using CronosMM408 Regular at 10 point on 13 leading, with the Horizontal Scaling set to 95%.

Screen captures were taken with TechSmith SnagIt 7.1.2 on a Dell Precision M60 and a Dell Precision Workstation 650 and were placed and sized within InDesign CS2. The book was output at 150-line screen, and all in-house proofing was done using a Tektronix Phaser 7700 by Xerox.

Additional Resources

Scott Kelby
For information about Scott's other books, visit www.scottkelbybooks.com. For background info on Scott, visit www.scottkelby.com.

http://www.scottkelbybooks.com

Adobe® Photoshop® Elements Techniques Newsletter
Adobe Photoshop Elements Techniques is a newsletter packed with practical, real-world tips and techniques from some of the leading Photoshop Elements gurus, including Matt Kloskowski, Dave Cross, Jan Kabili, Dave Huss, and Scott Kelby. Every issue of Elements is a valuable resource for digital photographers. Visit the website for subscription information.

http://www.photoshopelementsuser.com

Photoshop® Elements Techniques Website
The ultimate source for Photoshop Elements users features tutorials, downloads, forums, and much more! The site also contains up-to-date Elements news, tips and tricks, and contests.

http://www.photoshopelementsuser.com

Photoshoptraining.com
The online educational resource for Photoshop courses developed by the creative team at the National Association of Photoshop Professionals (NAPP).

http://www.photoshoptraining.com

KW Computer Training Videos
Scott Kelby, Dave Cross, and Matt Kloskowski are featured in a series of Adobe® Photoshop® and Adobe Photoshop Elements training DVDs, each on a particular Photoshop or Elements topic, available from KW Computer Training. Visit the website or call 800-201-7323 for orders or more information.

http://www.photoshopvideos.com

National Association of Photoshop Professionals (NAPP)
An accredited industry trade association for Adobe® Photoshop® users and the world's leading resource for Photoshop training, education, and news. NAPP is the largest graphics and digital imaging association with more than 50,000 members worldwide.

http://www.photoshopuser.com

Adobe® Photoshop® Seminar Tour
See Scott live on the Adobe Photoshop Seminar Tour, the nation's most popular Photoshop seminars. For upcoming tour dates and class schedules, visit the tour website.

http://www.photoshopseminars.com

Photoshop World Conference & Expo
The largest Adobe® Photoshop® event in the world and the bi-annual convention for NAPP members and Photosher users. Scott Kelby is technical chair and education director for the event, as well as one of the instructors.

http://www.photoshopworld.com

PlanetPhotoshop.com
"The Ultimate Photoshop® Site" features Photoshop news, tutorials, reviews, and articles. The site also contains the Web's most up-to-date resource on other Photoshop-related websites and information.

http://www.planetphotoshop.com

Layers magazine
Layers—The How-To Magazine for Everything Adobe—is the foremost authority on Adobe's design, digital video, digital photography, and education applications. Each issue features timely product news, plus quick tips, hidden shortcuts, and step-by-step tutorials for working in today's digital market. America's top-selling computer book author for 2004 and 2005, Scott Kelby is Editor and Publisher of *Layers*.

http://www.layersmagazine.com

onOne software

PhotoFrame 3 for Adobe® Photoshop® Elements is a plug-in that enables you to create extraordinary border and edge effects for your digital photos.

PhotoFrame 3
For PHOTOSHOP ELEMENTS

PhotoFrame 3
For **PHOTOSHOP ELEMENTS** 3

Unlimited border and edge effects

— **Enhance your photos with border and edge effects**

— **Includes hundreds of high-quality frames**

— **Includes realistic looking frames and mattes**

Visit www.onOneSoftware.com for more details and to download a fully-functional 30-day demo

BEFORE

AHOY MATE!

SMOOTH SAILING
Adobe® Photoshop® Elements Techniques makes it easy!

Chart a new course for your photos with *Adobe Photoshop Elements Techniques* newsletter and website. Learn how to:

• Enhance color and lighting
• Create mind-blowing effects
• Edit and retouch images
• Restore or repair heirloom photographs
• Organize and print your photos

Plus, get access to an exclusive subscriber-only website with a boatload of helpful tutorials; download free styles, brushes and shapes; or create and share your own image gallery. *Check it out!*

Limited Time Offer, Subscribe Today!

One-Year Subscription
$49* Plus get **50%** off the Portrait Retouching with Photoshop Elements DVD (pay just $19.99)
Use promotional code: ELEN-1UPCP

Two-Year Subscription
$79* And get the Portrait Retouching with Photoshop Elements DVD ($39.99 value) **FREE!**
Use promotional code: ELEN-2UPCP

To subscribe call 866-808-2793 or visit www.photoshopelementsuser.com

*Prices in U.S. funds. International and Canadian pricing is available online. Adobe and Photoshop are registered trademarks of Adobe Systems Incorporated.

SHADOW

MIDTONE

HIGHLIGHT

CAMERA RAW WHITE BALANCE